The Tanner Lectures on Human Values

THE TANNER LECTURES
ON HUMAN VALUES

VIII

1988

Michael Walzer, Stanley Cavell, Daniel C. Dennett,
T. M. Scanlon, Jr., Jürgen Habermas, Arnold S. Relman

Sterling M. McMurrin, *Editor*

UNIVERSITY OF UTAH PRESS — Salt Lake City
CAMBRIDGE UNIVERSITY PRESS — Cambridge, London, Melbourne, Sidney

Published in North and South America
and the Philippines
by the University of Utah Press,
Salt Lake City, Utah 84112, U.S.A.,
and in Great Britain and all other countries by
The Press Syndicate of the University of Cambridge
The Edinburgh Building, Shaftesbury Road,
Cambridge CB2 2RU, and
296 Beaconsfield Parade, Middle Park, Melbourne 3206
Australia.

The paper in this book meets the standards
for permanence and durability established by
the Committee on Production Guidelines for Book Longevity
of the Council on Library Resources.

THE TANNER LECTURES ON HUMAN VALUES

Appointment as a Tanner lecturer is a recognition of uncommon capabilities and outstanding scholarly or leadership achievement in the field of human values. The lecturers may be drawn from philosophy, religion, the humanities and sciences, the creative arts and learned professions, or from leadership in public or private affairs. The lectureships are international and intercultural and transcend ethnic, national, religious, or ideological distinctions.

The purpose of the Tanner Lectures is to advance and reflect upon the scholarly and scientific learning relating to human values and valuation. This purpose embraces the entire range of values pertinent to the human condition, interest, behavior, and aspiration.

The Tanner Lectures were formally founded on July 1, 1978, at Clare Hall, Cambridge University. They were established by the American scholar, industrialist, and philanthropist, Obert Clark Tanner. In creating the lectureships, Professor Tanner said, "I hope these lectures will contribute to the intellectual and moral life of mankind. I see them simply as a search for a better understanding of human behavior and human values. This understanding may be pursued for its own intrinsic worth, but it may also eventually have practical consequences for the quality of personal and social life."

Permanent Tanner lectureships, with lectures given annually, are established at eight institutions: Clare Hall, Cambridge University; Harvard University; Brasenose College, Oxford University; Stanford University; the University of California; the University of Michigan; the University of Utah; and Yale University. Each year lectureships may be granted to not more than four additional colleges or universities for one year only. The institutions are selected by the Trustees.

The sponsoring institutions have full autonomy in the appointment of their lecturers. A major purpose of the lecture program is the publication and wide distribution of the Lectures in an annual volume.

The Tanner Lectures on Human Values is a nonprofit corporation administered at the University of Utah under the direction of a self-perpetuating, international Board of Trustees. The Trustees meet annually to enact policies that will ensure the quality of the lectureships.

The entire lecture program, including the costs of administration, is fully and generously funded in perpetuity by an endowment of the University of Utah by Professor Tanner and Mrs. Grace Adams Tanner.

Obert C. Tanner was born in Farmington, Utah, in 1904. He was educated at the University of Utah, Harvard University, and Stanford University. He has served on the faculty of Stanford University and is presently Emeritus Professor of Philosophy at the University of Utah. He is the founder and chairman of the O. C. Tanner Company, manufacturing jewelers.

STERLING M. MCMURRIN
University of Utah

CONTENTS

PREFACE TO VOLUME VIII

The Tanner Lectures on Human Values were established at Clare Hall, Cambridge University, in 1978. Annual lectures have been delivered at the six institutions which were named permanent sponsors of the lectureships: Clare Hall, Cambridge University; Harvard University; Brasenose College, Oxford University; Stanford University; the University of Michigan; and the University of Utah. In addition, lectures have been delivered at Utah State University, the Hebrew University of Jerusalem, Australian National University, Jawaharlal Nehru University, and the University of Helsinki. Single lectures have been approved for the University of Warsaw, the University of Buenos Aires, and the Universidad de Complutense, Madrid.

The University of California and Yale University have been added to the institutions which are designated as permanent sponsors. Their lectures will begin during the academic year 1987–88.

The Tanner Lectures on Human Values are published in an annual volume. A general index to Volumes I through V is included in Volume V.

Volume VIII of the Lectures is comprised of lectures delivered during the academic year 1985–86, except for the lectures by Daniel C. Dennett and Jürgen Habermas, which were delivered early in the year 1986–87.

In addition to the Lectures on Human Values, Professor Tanner and the Trustees of the Tanner Lectures have funded special lectureships at selected colleges and universities which are administered and published independently of the series of lectures published in the annual volumes.

Because this is the last volume of the Tanner Lectures which I will edit, I would like to express my sincere appreciation to those who have contributed their superb talents to the design and production of Volumes I–VIII: Trudy McMurrin, who has been the press editor for the first seven volumes and most of Volume VIII; Donald M. Henriksen, who has created the typographical design and set the type for all volumes; and Rodger Reynolds, who has supervised the production and printing. The cover and jacket design of the Tanner volumes is by Bailey-Montague and Associates. I believe the Tanner volumes are a credit to the bookmakers' art.

STERLING M. MCMURRIN

Interpretation and Social Criticism

MICHAEL WALZER

THE TANNER LECTURES ON HUMAN VALUES

Delivered at
Harvard University

November 13 and 14, 1985

MICHAEL WALZER is many things — a political activist;
an editor, along with Irving Howe, of *Dissent* magazine;
a former professor at Harvard and Princeton universities,
and now a member of the permanent faculty at the Institute for Advanced Study, Princeton, New Jersey. Michael
Walzer was born in New York City, attended Brandeis,
Cambridge, and Harvard universities, and is the author
of many books including *Just and Unjust Wars*, *Radical
Principles*, *Spheres of Justice*, and *Exodus and Revolution*.

The first two of these lectures were given as the Tanner Lectures on Human Values at Harvard University on November 13 and 14, 1985. The third was given at Harvard Hillel on November 15. The three were written at roughly the same time, employ the same vocabulary, make the same arguments; they belong together, the last supplying what the first two largely lack: some degree of historical concreteness and specificity.

My aim is to provide a philosophical framework for the understanding of social criticism as a social practice. What do social critics do? How do they go about doing it? Where do the critic's principles come from? How does he establish his distance from the people and institutions he criticizes? The argument sustained through the three lectures, that social criticism is best understood as critical interpretation, runs parallel to arguments made in recent years by European philosophers. But I have tried to find my own way, in my own language, without direct reference to their work. I hope to publish in the near future a larger book dealing with the practice of criticism in the twentieth century — a more explicitly political book, for which these lectures constitute a theoretical preamble. There I will have occasion to address the question, as much political as it is philosophical, whether social criticism is possible without "critical theory."

I am grateful to the many members of the Harvard community, critics all, who attended these lectures and explained to me where I had gone wrong. My revisions certainly reflect their criticism — especially that of Martha Minow, Michael Sandel, Thomas Scanlon, Judith Shklar, and Lloyd Weinreb — though the reflection is probably, as often as not, obscure and incomplete. "The Prophet as Social Critic," in an earlier version, was discussed at a symposium on prophecy at Drew University and published in the Drew

Gateway *along with a helpful response by Henry French. A number of people here at the Institute for Advanced Study read the
lectures for me and commented on them in detail: Clifford Geertz,
Don Herzog, Michael Rustin, and Alan Wertheimer. They had
a lot to do with, though they are not responsible for, their final
form.*

I. THREE PATHS IN MORAL PHILOSOPHY

Despite my title, I shall not argue in this lecture that there are
three and only three ways of doing moral philosophy. It's not my
purpose to suggest an exhaustive list, only to look at three common and important approaches to the subject. I shall call these
the path of discovery, the path of invention, and the path of
interpretation. I mean to describe the last as the one (of the
three) that accords best with our everyday experience of morality.
Then, in my second lecture, I shall try to defend interpretation
against the charge that it binds us irrevocably to the status quo —
since we can only interpret what already exists — and so under-
cuts the very possibility of social criticism. Since criticism is a
feature of everyday morality, the charge has a twofold character:
it suggests not only that interpretation is a bad program for, but
also that it is a bad account of, moral experience. It is, as they say,
neither normatively nor descriptively correct. I shall argue against
both these aspects of the charge, proceeding in this first lecture by
way of theoretical contrast, in the second by way of practical example, focusing more on the account here, more on the program
there, but not tying myself to this simple and probably misleading
division. The third lecture will bring account and program together in an extended historical analysis of social criticism, in this
case biblical prophecy, in the interpretive mode.

1

We know the path of discovery first and best from the history
of religion. Here, to be sure, discovery waits upon revelation; but

someone must climb the mountain, go into the desert, seek out the God-who-reveals, and bring back his word. This man or woman is for the rest of us the discoverer of the moral law: if God reveals it to him, he reveals it to us. Like the physical world, like life itself, morality is a creation; but we are not its creators. God makes it, and we come, with his help and with the help of his servants, to know about it and then to admire and study it. Religious morality commonly takes the form of a written text, a sacred book, and so it requires interpretation. But we first experience it through the medium of discovery. The moral world is like a new continent, and the religious leader (God's servant) is like an explorer who brings us the good news of its existence and the first map of its shape.

I should note one significant feature of this map. The moral world is not only divinely created; it is constituted by divine commands. What is revealed to us is a set of decrees: do this! don't do that! And these decrees are critical in character, critical from the beginning, for it would hardly be a revelation if God commanded us to do and not do what we were already doing and not doing. A revealed morality will always stand in sharp contrast to old ideas and practices. That may well be its chief advantage. But it is, necessarily, a short-lived advantage, for once the revelation is accepted, once the new moral world is inhabited, the critical edge is lost. Now God's decrees, so at least we pretend to ourselves, regulate our everyday behavior; we are what he wants us to be. Any morality that has once been discovered, of course, can always be rediscovered. The claim to have found again some long-lost or corrupted doctrine is the basis of every religious and moral reformation. But God is not present now in the same way as he was in the beginning. *Re*discovery does not wait upon revelation; it is our own work, archaeological in form; and we have to interpret what we dig up. The moral law rediscovered lacks the blazing clarity of its first coming.

I mean this brief account of religious morality as a prelude to
a more secular story. There are natural as well as divine revela-
tions, and a philosopher who reports to us on the existence of
natural law, say, or natural rights, or any set of objective moral
truths has walked the path of discovery. Perhaps he has walked
it as a kind of moral anthropologist, searching for what is natural
in what is real. More likely, given the standard form of the philosophical enterprise, the search is internal, mental, a matter of
detachment and reflection. The moral world comes into view as
the philosopher steps back in his mind from his social position.
He wrenches himself loose from his parochial interests and loyalties; he abandons his own point of view and looks at the world,
as Thomas Nagel argued in his own Tanner Lectures, from "no
particular point of view." [1] The project is at least as heroic as
climbing the mountain or marching into the desert. "No particular point of view" is somewhere on the way to God's point of
view, and what the philosopher sees from there is something like
objective value. That is, if I understand the argument, he sees
himself and all the others, himself no different from the others,
and he recognizes the moral principles that necessarily govern the
relations of creatures like those.

The necessity, clearly, is moral, not practical, else we would
not have to step back to discover it. Hence the principles, once
again, are critical principles; they exist at some distance from our
parochial practices and opinions. And once we have discovered
them, or once they have been announced to us, we ought to incorporate them into our everyday moral life. But I confess to less
confidence in this secular discovery than in the earlier religious discovery. Most often, the moral principles here delivered to us are
already in our possession, incorporated, as it were, long ago, fami-

---

[1] "The Limits of Objectivity," in *The Tanner Lectures on Human Values*,
vol. I (Salt Lake City: University of Utah Press; Cambridge: Cambridge University
Press, 1980), p. 83. Cf. Nagel, *The View from Nowhere* (Oxford: Oxford University Press, 1986).

liar and well-thumbed by now. Philosophical discovery is likely to fall short of the radical newness and sharp specificity of divine revelation. Accounts of natural law or natural rights rarely ring true as descriptions of a new moral world. Consider Professor Nagel's discovery of an objective moral principle, the only one specified and defended in his lectures: that we should not be indifferent to the suffering of other people.[2] I acknowledge the principle but miss the excitement of revelation. I knew that already. What is involved in discoveries of this sort is something like a dis-incorporation of moral principles, so that we can see them, not for the first time but freshly, stripped of encrusted interests and prejudices. Seen in this way, the principles may well look objective; we "know" them in much the same way as religious men and women know the divine law. They are, so to speak, *there*, waiting to be enforced. But they are only there because they are really here, features of ordinary life.

I don't mean to deny the reality of the experience of stepping back, though I doubt that we can ever step back all the way to nowhere; even when we look at the world from *somewhere else*, however, we are still looking at the world. We are looking, in fact, at a particular world; we may see it with special clarity, but we will not discover anything that isn't already there. Since the particular world is also our own world, we will not discover anything that isn't already here. Perhaps this is a general truth about secular (moral) discoveries; if so, it suggests what we lose when we lose our belief in God.

But I have been assuming a philosopher who strains to see more clearly, if only in abstract outline, the moral reality in front of him. One can, by contrast, call that reality into question and set out in search of a deeper truth, like a physicist piercing the

---

2 "Limits of Objectivity," pp. 109–10. In his own social criticism, Professor Nagel relies on more substantive principles. To what extent these are "objective" principles, I am not sure. See Thomas Nagel, *Mortal Questions* (Cambridge: Cambridge University Press, 1979), chapters 5, 6, 7, and 8.

atom. Thus the moral philosophy called utilitarianism, founded
on a very small number of psychological axioms: godless in its
origins and radically unfamiliar in its outcomes, utilitarianism
suggests what we gain by the imitation of science. Bentham obviously believed that he had discovered objective truth, and the applications of this truth are, very often, not recognizable at all as
features of ordinary life.[3] Frightened by the strangeness of their
own arguments, most utilitarian philosophers fiddle with the felicific calculus so that it yields results closer to what we all think.
So they pull the exception back to the rule: without confidence in
revelation, we can only discover what we know. Philosophy is a
second coming (lower case) which brings us, not millennial
understanding, but the wisdom of the owl at dusk. There is,
though, this alternative, which I will later find more frightening
than attractive: the wisdom of the eagle at daybreak.

2

Many people, perhaps for good reasons, won't be satisfied with
the wisdom of the owl. Some will deny its objectivity, despite the
detachment of the philosophers who seek it out; but that is not a
denial I want to defend. I am inclined to agree with Professor
Nagel's sardonic view of the skeptic's question, What reason can
I possibly have for *not* being indifferent to my neighbor's pain?
What reason can I have for caring, even a little bit? Nagel writes:
"As an expression of puzzlement, [this] has that characteristic
philosophical craziness which indicates that something very fundamental has gone wrong." [4] Yes, but what is more worrisome than

---

[3] Bentham suggests that utilitarianism is the only plausible account of what
ordinary people think about morality, but his ambition goes far beyond providing
such an account. He claims to have discovered the foundation of morality: "Nature
has placed mankind under the governance of two sovereign masters, pain and pleasure. It is for them alone to point out what we ought to do. . . ." *The Principles
of Morals and Legislation*, ch. I. It is apparent in the rest of the *Principles* that
these two masters don't always point to what ordinary people think *they* ought to do.

[4] "Limits of Objectivity," p. 110.

this craziness is the sense I have already expressed, that the moral principles revealed in this or that undoubtedly sane philosophy lack the special edge, the critical force, of divine revelation. "Don't be indifferent . . ." is not at all the same thing as "Love thy neighbor as thyself." And the second of these is unlikely to figure in the list of philosophical discoveries — if only because the question, Why should I love him *that much*? isn't crazy. The principle of non-indifference — let's call it, more positively, the principle of minimal concern — is conceivably a critical principle, but its strength is uncertain. A great deal of work would have to be done, and it's not clear that it could be done by a man or woman standing nowhere in particular (or even by a man or woman standing somewhere else), to work out its relation to everyday social practice.

On the other hand, men and women standing nowhere in particular could construct an entirely new moral world — imitating God's creation rather than the discoveries of his servants. They might undertake to do this because they thought that there was no actually existing moral world (because God was dead, or mankind radically alienated from nature, or nature devoid of moral meaning) ; or they might undertake the construction because they thought that the actually existing moral world was inadequate or that our knowledge of it could never be, as knowledge, sufficiently critical in character. We might think of this undertaking in terms Descartes suggests when he describes his intellectual project (in the *Discourse on Method*): "to reform my own thoughts and to build on a foundation wholly my own." In fact, I suppose, Descartes was really launched on a journey of discovery, "like a man who walks alone, and in the dark," searching for objective truth.[5] But in the analogies that leap to his mind, there is no objective

---

[5] Descartes, *Discourse on Method*, trans. by F. E. Sutcliffe (Harmondsworth, Eng.: Penguin, 1968), pp. 38, 39.

truth to discover, and the project is explicitly constructive in character.

> So I thought to myself that the peoples who were formerly half savages, and who became civilized only gradually, making their laws only insofar as the harm done by crimes and quarrels forced them to do so, could not be so well organized as those who, from the moment at which they came together in association, observed the basic laws of some wise legislator; just as it is indeed certain that the state of the true religion, the laws of which God alone has made, must be incomparably better ordered than all the others. And, to speak of human things, I believe that, if Sparta greatly flourished in times past, it was not on account of the excellence of each of its laws taken individually, seeing that many were very strange and even contrary to good morals, but because, having been invented by one man only, they all tended towards the same end.[6]

This is the path of invention; the end is given by the morality we hope to invent. The end is a common life, where justice, or political virtue, or goodness, or some such basic value would be realized.

So we are to design the moral world under this condition: that there is no pre-existent design, no divine or natural blueprint to guide us. How should we proceed? We need a discourse on method for moral philosophy, and most philosophers who have walked the path of invention have begun with methodology: a design of a design procedure. (The existentialists, who don't begin that way, though they are clearly committed to an invented morality, are of little help in the business of invention.) The crucial requirement of a design procedure is that it eventuate in agreement. Hence the work of Descartes' legislator is very risky unless he is a representative figure, somehow embodying the range of opinions and interests that are in play around him. We can't adopt the simple expedient of making the legislator omnipotent, a

---

[6] *Discourse on Method*, p. 36.

rational and benevolent despot, for that would be to settle a basic feature of the design — the just distribution of power — before the design procedure had even gotten started. The legislator must somehow be authorized to speak for all of us or, alternatively, all of us must be present and accounted for from the beginning. It isn't easy to see how we might choose a representative, a proxy for humankind. But if we give up on representation and opt for the alternative, universal presence, we are more likely to produce cacophony than order, and the outcome will be "more the product of chance," as Descartes writes, "than . . . of a human will operating according to reason."[7]

There are a variety of solutions to this problem; the best known and most elegant is that of John Rawls, which I need hardly elaborate here.[8] The Rawlsian solution has the nice result that it ceases to matter whether the constructive or legislative work is undertaken by one, few, or many people. Deprived of all knowledge of their standing in the social world, of their interests, values, talents, and relationships, potential legislators are rendered, for the practical purposes at hand, identical. It makes no difference whether such people talk to one another or one among them talks only to himself: one person talking is enough. Other proposed solutions (that of Jürgen Habermas, for example) are more cumbersome, requiring that we imagine actual conversations, but only in circumstances carefully designed to lift the discourse above the level of ideological confrontation.[9] The participants

---

[7] *Discourse on Method*, p. 35.

[8] *A Theory of Justice* (Cambridge: Harvard University Press, 1971).

[9] *Communication and the Evolution of Society*, trans. by Thomas McCarthy (Boston: Beacon, 1979), especially chapter 1. But there is a dilemma here: if the circumstances of what Habermas calls ideal speech or undistorted communication are specified in detail, then only a limited number of things can be said, and these things could probably be said by the philosopher himself, representing all the rest of us. As Raymond Geuss has argued, it isn't as if we have a real choice about what opinions we will finally form. (See *The Idea of a Critical Theory: Habermas and the Frankfurt School* [Cambridge: Cambridge University Press, 1981], p. 72.) If, on the other hand, the circumstances are only roughly specified, so that ideal speech

must be liberated from the bonds of particularism, else they will never produce the rational outcome that they require, namely, a moral world so designed that all of them are prepared to live in it, and to think it just, whatever place they come to occupy, whatever projects they come to pursue.

Assume the death of God or the meaninglessness of nature — apparently painless assumptions in these latter days — and then we can say of these legislators that they invent the moral world that would have existed if a moral world had existed without their inventing it. They create what God would have created if there were a God. Now, this is not the only way of describing what happens on the path of invention. Descartes' Spartan analogy suggests a different view, which I think is also Rawls' view, a minimalist version of inventiveness. What Lycurgus creates is not the best city, the city that God would have created, but only the best city for the Spartans, the work, as it were, of a Spartan god. I will want to come back to this possibility later on. I need to consider first the stronger claim that the moral world that we invent behind the veil of ignorance or through an ideologically uncluttered conversation is the only world we could invent, universally inhabitable, a world for all persons.

The critical force of an invented morality is more like that of divine law than philosophical discovery (or, it is closer to the wisdom of the eagle than the owl). Rawls' difference principle, to take a much-discussed example, has something of the novelty and specificity of revelation. No one would think of saying that it was just plain crazy to call it into question. As divine law derives its force from its creator, so the difference principle derives its force from the process by which it was created. If we accept it, it is because we have participated, or can imagine ourselves having participated, in its invention. And if we invent one such principle,

---

resembles a democratic debate, then the participants can say almost anything, and there seems no reason why the results should not (sometimes) turn out to be "very strange and even contrary to good morals."

we can obviously invent others as we need them; or we can deduce from the one a whole system of rules and regulations. Bruce Ackerman, in his book on liberal justice, manages to cover a range of issues roughly equivalent to that covered by the Exodus and Deuteronomic codes — though his revelation is delivered not to one but to every actual and imaginable nation.[10] So we create a morality against which we can measure any person's life, any society's practices.

It is not the case, of course, that the lives and practices we measure are morally meaningless until we measure them. They embody their own values, which are distorted — so philosophers of invention must believe — by a radically imperfect design procedure. These values are created by conversation, argument, and political negotiation in circumstances we might best call social, over long periods of time. The point of an invented morality is to provide what God and nature don't provide, a universal corrective for all the different social moralities. But why should we bow to universal correction? What exactly is the critical force of the philosopher's invention — assuming, still, that it is the only possible invention? I will try to answer these questions by telling a story of my own, a story meant to parallel and heighten certain features of the Rawlsian account of what happens in the original position: a caricature, I'm afraid, for which I apologize in advance; but caricature has its uses.[11]

Imagine, then, that a group of travelers from different countries and different moral cultures, speaking different languages, meet in some neutral place (like outer space). They have to cooperate, at least temporarily, and if they are to cooperate, each of them must refrain from insisting upon his own values and practices. Hence we deny them knowledge of their own values and

---

[10] *Social Justice in the Liberal State* (New Haven: Yale University Press, 1980).

[11] The caricature is aimed at Rawls' epigones rather than at Rawls himself, who would not accept, I think, its first stipulation.

practices; and since that knowledge isn't only personal but also social knowledge, embodied in language itself, we obliterate their linguistic memories and require them to think and talk (temporarily) in some pidgin-language that is equally parasitic on all their natural languages — a more perfect Esperanto. Now, what principles of cooperation would they adopt? I shall assume that there is a single answer to this question and that the principles given in that answer properly govern their life together in the space they now occupy. That seems plausible enough; the design procedure is genuinely useful for the purposes at hand. What is less plausible is that the travelers should be required to carry those same principles with them when they go home. Why should newly-invented principles govern the lives of people who already share a moral culture and speak a natural language?

Men and women standing behind the veil of ignorance, deprived of all knowledge of their own way of life, forced to live with other men and women similarly deprived, will perhaps, with whatever difficulties, find a *modus vivendi* — not a way of life but a way of living. But even if this is the only possible *modus vivendi* for these people in these conditions, it doesn't follow that it is a universally valuable arrangement. (It might, of course, have a kind of heuristic value — many things have heuristic value — but I won't pursue that possibility now.) There seems to be a confusion here: it is as if we were to take a hotel room or an accommodation apartment or a safe house as the ideal model of a human home. Away from home, one is grateful for the shelter and convenience of a hotel room. Deprived of all knowledge of what my own home was like, talking with people similarly deprived, required to design rooms that any one of us might live in, we would probably come up with something like (but not quite so culturally specific as) the Hilton Hotel. With this difference: we would not allow luxury suites; all the rooms would be exactly the same; or, if there were luxury suites, their only purpose would be to bring more business to the hotel and enable us to improve all the other rooms, starting with those most in need of improvement. But even if the improvements went pretty far, we might still long for the homes we knew we once had but could no longer remember. We would not be morally bound to live in the hotel we had designed.

I have been assuming that my own view of hotels is widely shared, and so I should note one telling dissent — a line from Franz Kafka's journal that goes like this: "I like hotel rooms. I always feel immediately at home in hotel rooms, more than at home, really." [12] But note the irony: there is no other way to convey the sense of being in one's own place except to say "at home." It is a hard thing to suggest to men and women that they give up the moral comfort that those words evoke. But what if they don't share that comfort? What if their lives are like that of Kafka's K., or of any twentieth-century exile, outcast, refugee, or stateless person? For such people, hotels are very important. They need the protection of the rooms, decent (if bare) human accommodation. They need a universal (if minimal) morality or, at least, a morality worked out among strangers. What they commonly *want*, however, is not to be permanently registered in a hotel but to be established in a new home, a dense moral culture within which they can feel some sense of belonging.

Thus far my story. But there is another, and a more plausible, way of thinking about the process of moral invention. Let us assume now that the actually existing (social) moralities incorporate, as they claim to do, divine commands or natural laws or, at least, genuinely valuable moral principles however these are understood. Our purpose now is not invention *de novo*; rather, we need to construct an account or a model of some existing morality that gives us a clear and comprehensive view of the critical force of its own principles, without the intervening confusion of prejudice or self-interest. Hence we don't meet with travelers

[12] Quoted in Ernst Pawel, *The Nightmare of Reason: A Life of Franz Kafka* (New York: Farrar, Straus, and Giroux, 1984), p. 191.

in outer space but with fellow members in inner or social space. We consult our own moral understandings, our reflective awareness of principles, but we try to filter out, even to bar entirely, any sense of personal ambition or advantage. Our method, once again, is epistemic denial, which functions now, according to Rawls, as a "device of representation." [13] So we surrender all knowledge of our position in society and of our private connections and commitments — but not, this time, of the values (like liberty and equality) that we share. We want to describe the moral world in which we live from "no particular point of view" within that world. Although the description is carefully designed and its immediate conditions are highly artificial, it is nonetheless a description of something real. Hence it is more like philosophical discovery than divine revelation. The inventiveness of the philosopher consists only in turning moral reality into an ideal type.

The idealized morality is in origin a social morality; it is neither divine nor natural, except insofar as we believe that "the voice of the people is the voice of God" or that human nature requires us to live in society — and neither of these views commits us to approve of everything the people say or of every social arrangement. The project of modeling or idealizing an existing morality does depend, however, upon some prior acknowledgment of the value of that morality. Perhaps its value is simply this: that there is no other starting point for moral speculation. We have to start from where we are. I shall want to argue more than this later on, for where we are is always *someplace of value*, else we would never, so to speak, have settled there. Some such argument, it seems to me, is equally as important for invention in its second, minimalist version as it is for interpretation. Its importance is conceded by philosophers of invention who appeal to our intuitions, sometimes in constructing, sometimes in testing, their models and ideal types. Intuition is a pre-reflective, pre-

[13] "Justice as Fairness: Political not Metaphysical," *Philosophy and Public Affairs*, vol. 14, no. 3 (1985), p. 236.

philosophic knowledge of the moral world; it resembles the account a blind man might give of the furnishings of a familiar house. The familiarity is crucial. Moral philosophy is here understood as a reflection upon the familiar, a re-invention of our own homes.

This is, however, a critical reflection, re-invention with a purpose: we are to correct our intuitions by reference to the model we construct out of those same intuitions — or, we are to correct our more groping intuitions by reference to a model we construct out of our more confident intuitions. We move back and forth in either case between moral immediacy and moral abstraction, between an intuitive and a reflective understanding.[14] But what is it that we are trying to understand? And how does our understanding of it, whatever it is, acquire critical force? Clearly, at this point, we are not trying to understand divine law or to grasp an objective morality; nor are we trying to build an entirely new city. Our focus is on ourselves, our own principles and values — otherwise, intuition would be no help. Since this is also the focus of those committed to the path of interpretation, I want now to turn to them. They also face in an especially direct way the problem of critical force. Given that every interpretation is parasitic on its "text," how can it ever constitute an adequate criticism of the text?

3

The argument thus far is usefully summarized by way of an analogy. The three paths in moral philosophy can be compared, roughly, to the three branches of government. Discovery resembles the work of the executive: to find, proclaim, and then enforce the law. Enforcement is not, I admit, a common philosophical task, but those who believe that they have discovered the true moral law

---

[14] For a useful discussion of this process, which reaches for what Rawls has named "reflective equilibrium," see Norman Daniels, "Wide Reflective Equilibrium and Theory Acceptance in Ethics," *Journal of Philosophy*, vol. 76, no. 5 (1979), pp. 256–82.

are likely enough to want or, whatever their private preferences, to believe themselves duty bound to enforce it. Moses exemplifies this reluctant sense of duty. Irreligious writers like Machiavelli have called him a legislator, but if we attend to the biblical account, we see that he did not legislate at all; he received the law, taught it to the people, and strove to see that it was obeyed; he was an unwilling but at least occasionally energetic political leader. The obvious philosophical parallel is Plato's philosopher–king, who does not create the good, but finds it, and then sets himself, with similar reluctance, to enact it in the world. Utilitarianism provides more straightforward examples (as does Marxism, another example of scientific discovery).

Discovery is not itself execution; it simply points toward executive authority. But invention is legislative from the beginning, for the philosophical inventor means to invest his principles with the force of (moral) law. That's why invention is the work of representative men and women, who stand for us all because they could be any one of us. But invention is of two sorts, as I have already argued, and these two correspond to two different sorts of lawmaking and require two different sorts of representation. Invention *de novo* is like constitutional legislation. The lawmakers, since they are creating a new moral world, must represent every possible or potential member, that is, everybody, wherever he lives and whatever his current values and commitments. Minimalist invention is more like the work of legal codification. Now the lawmakers, since what they are codifying already exists, must represent the people for whom it exists, that is, a group of men and women who share intuitions, who are committed to a particular set of principles, however confused that set may be.

Codification is obviously an interpretive as well as an inventive or constructive enterprise: here the second path runs close to the third. Still, a code is a law or a system of laws, while an interpretation is a judgment, the proper work of the judicial branch. The claim of interpretation is simply this: that neither discovery nor invention is necessary because we already possess what they pretend to provide. Morality, unlike politics, does not require executive authority or systematic legislation. We don't have to discover the moral world because we have always lived there. We don't have to invent it because it has already been invented — though not in accordance with any philosophical method. No design procedure has governed its design, and the result no doubt is disorganized and uncertain. It is also very dense: the moral world has a lived-in quality, like a home occupied by a single family over many generations, with unplanned additions here and there, and all the available space filled with memory-laden objects and artifacts. The whole thing, taken as a whole, lends itself less to abstract modeling than to thick description. Moral argument in such a setting is interpretive in character, closely resembling the work of a lawyer or judge who struggles to find meaning in a morass of conflicting laws and precedents.

But lawyers and judges, it might be said, are bound to the legal morass; it is their business to find meaning there and they have no business looking elsewhere. The legal morass, or better, the meaning that can be found within it, is authoritative for them. But why should the moral morass be authoritative for philosophers? Why shouldn't they look elsewhere, in search of a better authority? The morality we discover is authoritative because God made it or because it is objectively true. The morality we invent is authoritative because anyone would invent it, could only invent it, so long as he adopted the proper design procedure and worked at the proper distance from his immediate, parochial self. But why is this existing morality authoritative — this morality that just *is*, the product of time, accident, external force, political compromise, fallible and particularist intentions? The easiest way to answer these questions would be to insist that the moralities we discover and invent always turn out, and always will turn out, remarkably similar to the morality we already have. Philosophical discovery and invention (I leave aside divine revelation) are disguised interpretations; there is really only one path in moral philosophy. I am and will continue to be tempted by this view, even though it does not do justice to the sincere ambition (or, sometimes, the dangerous presumption) of discoverers and inventors. But I don't want to deny that it is possible to walk the first two paths, nor to assert that people doing that are really doing something else. There are indeed discoveries and inventions — utilitarianism is one example — but the more novel these are the less likely they are to make for strong or even plausible arguments. The experience of moral argument is best understood in the interpretive mode. What we do when we argue is to give an account of the actually existing morality. That morality is authoritative for us because it is only by virtue of its existence that we exist as the moral beings we are. Our categories, relationships, commitments, aspirations are all shaped by, expressed in terms of, the existing morality. Discovery and invention are efforts at escape, in the hope of finding some external and universal standard with which to judge moral existence. The effort may well be commendable, but it is, I think, unnecessary. The critique of existence begins or can begin from principles internal to existence itself.

One might say that the moral world is authoritative for us because it provides us with everything we need to live a moral life — including the capacity for reflection and criticism. No doubt some moralities are more "critical" than others, but that does not mean they are better (or worse): it is more likely that they provide, roughly, what their protagonists need. At the same time, the capacity for criticism always extends beyond the "needs" of the social structure itself and its dominant groups. I don't want to defend a functionalist position. The moral world and the social world are more or less coherent, but they are never more than more or less coherent. Morality is always potentially subversive of class and power.

I will try in my second lecture to say why subversion is always possible and how it actually works. But I need now to elaborate on the claim that moral argument is (most often) interpretive in character. The claim seems more plausible with regard to the judicial analogy. For the question commonly posed to lawyers and judges takes a form that invites interpretation: what is the legal or the constitutional thing to do? The reference of the question is to a particular body of laws or to a particular constitutional text, and there is no way to answer the question except by giving an account of the laws or the text. Neither the one nor the other has the simplicity and precision of a yardstick against which we might measure the different actions urged by the contending parties. Deprived of a yardstick, we rely on exegesis, commentary, and historical precedent, a tradition of argument and interpretation. Any given interpretation will be contentious, of course, but there is little disagreement about what it is that we are interpreting or about the need for the interpretive effort.

But the question commonly posed to ordinary men and women arguing about morality has a different form: what is the right thing to do? And now it isn't clear at all what the reference of the question is or how we are to go about answering it. It doesn't appear that the question is about the interpretation of an existing and particular morality, for it is possible that the morality, however interpreted, doesn't tell us the right thing to do. Perhaps we should search for, or invent, a better morality. But if we follow the course of the argument, listen to it, study its phenomenology, we will see, I think, that it is the meaning of the particular moral life shared by the protagonists that is at issue. The general question about the right thing to do is quickly turned into some more specific question — about the career open to talents, let's say, and then about equal opportunity, affirmative action, quotas, and so on. These can be read as matters of constitutional law, requiring legal interpretation; but they are also moral matters. And then they require us to argue about what a career is, what sorts of talents we ought to recognize, whether equal opportunity is a "right," and what social policies it mandates if it is. These issues are pursued within a tradition of moral discourse — indeed, they only arise within that tradition — and they are pursued by interpreting the terms of that discourse.[15] The argument is about ourselves; it is the meaning of our way of life that is at issue. The question we actually answer is not quite the question we asked at first. It has a crucial addition: what is the right thing *for us* to do?

It is true nonetheless that the moral question is commonly put in more general terms than the legal question. The reason for this can only be that morality is in fact more general than law. Morality provides those basic prohibitions — of murder, deception, betrayal, gross cruelty — that the law specifies and the police sometimes enforce. We can, I suppose, step back, detach ourselves from our parochial concerns, and "discover" these prohibitions. But we can also step forward, as it were, into the thicket of moral experience where they are more intimately known. For they are themselves parochial concerns — concerns, that is, of every human parish. We can, again, adopt this or that design procedure and "invent" the prohibitions, much as we might invent the minimally decent accommodations of a hotel. But we can also study the actual historical processes by which they came to be recognized and accepted, for they have been accepted in virtually every human society.

These prohibitions constitute a kind of minimal and universal moral code. Because they are minimal and universal (I should say almost universal, just to protect myself against the odd anthropological example), they can be represented as philosophical discoveries or inventions. A single person, imagining himself a

---

15 The point seems obvious to me, but perhaps I should make it more specific. In a society where children inherited the employments and positions of their parents, and learned what they needed to know about their employments and positions largely from their parents, the "career open to talents" would not be a plausible, it might not even be a comprehensible, idea. Planning a career is not a universal human experience. Nor is there any reason to think that men and women who don't recognize that experience as their own, or who don't accord it the same centrality that it has for us, are morally benighted. Should we press it upon them? (How would we do that?) Increased social differentiation will make it available — and supply at the same time the moral language necessary to argue about its meaning.

stranger, detached, homeless, lost in the world, might well come up with them: they are conceivable as the products of one person talking. They are in fact, however, the products of many people talking, of real if always tentative, intermittent, and unfinished conversations. We might best think of them not as discovered or invented but rather as emergent prohibitions, the work of many years, of trial and error, of failed, partial, and insecure understandings — rather as David Hume suggests with regard to the ban on theft (for the sake of "stability of possession") which, he writes in the Treatise, "arises gradually, and acquires force by a slow progression and by our repeated experience of the inconvenience of violating it." [16]

By themselves, though, these universal or almost universal prohibitions barely begin to determine the shape of a fully developed or livable morality. They provide a framework for any possible (moral) life, but only a framework, with all the substantive details still to be filled in before anyone could actually live in one way rather than another. It's not until the conversations become continuous and the understandings thicken that we get anything like a moral culture, with judgment, value, the goodness of persons and things realized in detail. One can't simply deduce a moral culture, or for that matter a legal system, from the minimal code. Both of these are specifications and elaborations of the code, variations on it. And whereas deduction would generate a single understanding of morality and law, the specifications, elaborations, and variations are necessarily plural in character.

I see no way in which the pluralism might be avoided. But if it were avoided, it would be avoided equally in morality and law; in this sense there is no difference between the two. If we had, for example, a priori definitions of murder, deception, betrayal, and so on, then moral and legal specification could plausibly take shape as a series of deductive steps with a necessary end. But we

---

[16] *A Treatise of Human Nature*, bk. III, pt. II, ch. ii.

don't have such definitions, and so in both cases we are dependent on socially created meanings. The moral question is general in form because it refers to the minimal code as well as to the social meanings, while the legal question is more specific because it refers only to the social meanings established in the law. But in answering the first question as much as in answering the second, our method can only be interpretive. There is nothing else to do, for the minimal code, by itself, doesn't answer either question.

Nothing else to do: this is a stronger claim than that with which I began. We can always, I suppose, discover or invent a new and fully developed morality. It will indeed have to be fully developed if it is to reach all the way to the historically peculiar idea of human life as a career. Still, we may be tempted by discovery or invention when we see how the interpretive enterprise goes on and on, never moving toward definitive closure. Discovery and invention don't produce closure either, of course, and it is interesting to reflect for a moment on the ways in which they fail. They fail in part because there is an infinite number of possible discoveries and inventions and an endless succession of eager discoverers and inventors. But they also fail because the acceptance of a particular discovery or invention among some group of people gives rise immediately to arguments about the meaning of what has been accepted. A simple maxim: every discovery and invention (divine law is an obvious example) requires interpretation.

That is exactly right, someone might say, and it explains why interpretation is the familiar form of moral argument. It has its place and importance, but only during periods of "normal morality" — which are as workmanlike as the periods of normal science described by Thomas Kuhn — between the revolutionary, paradigm-shattering moments of discovery and invention.[17] With regard to morality, however, this view is more melodrama than

[17] *The Structure of Scientific Revolutions* (Chicago: University of Chicago Press, 1962).

realistic history. Certainly, there have been historically crucial discoveries and inventions: new worlds, the force of gravity, electro-
magnetic waves, the power of the atom; the printing press, the
steam engine, the computer, effective methods of contraception.
All these have transformed the way we live and think about the
way we live. Moreover, they have done so with the force and
abruptness of revelation — much as in the argument of the medieval Jewish philosopher Judah Halevi about religion: "A religion
of divine origin arises suddenly. It is bidden to arise, and it is
there. . . ." [18] Can we find anything like that in (secular) moral
experience? The principle of utility? The rights of man? Maybe;
but moral transformations seem to occur much more slowly, and
less decisively, than transformations in science and technology;
nor are they so clearly progressive in character, as greater factual
knowledge or expanded human capacities presumably are. Insofar as we can recognize moral progress, it has less to do with the
discovery or invention of new principles than with the inclusion
under the old principles of previously excluded men and women.
And that, as we will see, is more a matter of (workmanlike) social
criticism and political struggle, than it is of (paradigm-shattering)
philosophical speculation.

I will look closely at some "moments" of moral transformation in my second lecture. For now I only want to suggest that the
sorts of discoveries and inventions likely to be incorporated into
our moral arguments (I leave aside for now discoveries and inventions that are coercively imposed) are unlikely to have definitive effects upon those arguments. We can see this in a small way
in the body of literature that has grown up, already, around the
Rawlsian difference principle — focused most importantly on the
question of equality: how egalitarian would the principle actually
be in its effects? And then: how egalitarian was it meant to be?
how egalitarian should it be? Leave aside the deeper argument

[18] *The Kuzari*, trans. by Hartwig Hirschfeld (New York: Schocken, 1964),
p. 58.

about whether the difference principle is an invention in the strong or weak sense (or even itself an interpretation or misinterpretation of our existing morality) : whatever it is, it raises questions to which there are no definitive and final answers. The difference principle may have arisen "suddenly," but it's not just "there."

Still, there are better and worse answers to the questions I have just posed, and some of the better ones will be grafted onto the principle itself and become in their turn objects of interpretation. How can we recognize the better answers? It is sometimes said against interpretation as a method in moral philosophy that we will never agree on which ones are better without the help of a correct moral theory.[19] But in the case I am now imagining, the case of the difference principle, we are driven to interpretation because we already disagree about the meaning of what purports to be, or what some readers take to be, a correct moral theory. There is no definitive way of ending the disagreement. But the best account of the difference principle would be one that rendered it coherent with other American values — equal protection, equal opportunity, political liberty, individualism, and so on — and connected it to some plausible view of incentives and productivity. We would argue about the best account, but we would know roughly what we were looking for and would have little difficulty excluding a large number of inadequate or bad accounts.

It might be helpful at this point to contrast interpretation as I understand it with Michael Oakeshott's "pursuit of intimations." His is, no doubt, an interpretive enterprise, but it is significantly constrained by the fact that Oakeshott is prepared to pursue only the intimations of "traditions of behavior" and everyday social arrangements, without any reference to "general concepts" (like liberty or equality, or, for that matter, the difference principle).[20]

---

[19] This is Ronald Dworkin's objection to my own *Spheres of Justice* (New York: Basic Books, 1983): see "To Each His Own," in *The New York Review of Books*, April 14, 1983, pp. 4–6, and the subsequent exchange, *New York Review*, July 21, 1983, pp. 43–46.

[20] *Rationalism in Politics* (New York: Basic Books, 1962), pp. 123–25.

The shared understandings of a people, however, are often expressed in general concepts — in its historical ideals, its public rhetoric, its foundational texts, its ceremonies and rituals. It is not only what people do, but how they explain and justify what they do, the stories they tell, the principles they invoke, that constitute a moral culture. Because of this, cultures are open to the possibility of contradiction (between principles and practices) as well as to what Oakeshott calls "incoherence" (among everyday practices). And then it isn't always possible for interpretation to take the form that he prefers: "a conversation, not an argument." Oakeshott is right to insist that "there is no mistake-proof apparatus by means of which we can elicit the intimations most worthwhile pursuing. . . ." [21] Indeed, there isn't; but that is not to say that the pursuit might not be (has not been) considerably more adventurous than he allows. And in the course of the adventure, conversations turn naturally into arguments.

Interpretation does not commit us to a positivist reading of the actually existing morality, a description of moral facts as if they were immediately available to our understanding. There are moral facts of that sort, but the most interesting parts of the moral world are only in principle factual matters; in practice they have to be "read," rendered, construed, glossed, elucidated, and not merely described. All of us are involved in doing all these things; we are all interpreters of the morality we share. That doesn't mean that the best interpretation is the sum of all the others, the product of a complicated piece of survey research — no more than the best reading of a poem is a meta-reading, summing up the responses of all the actual readers. The best reading isn't different in kind, but in quality, from the other readings: it illuminates the poem in a more powerful and persuasive way. Perhaps the best reading is a new reading, seizing upon some previously misunderstood symbol or trope and re-explaining the entire poem. The case is the same with moral interpretation: it will sometimes confirm and

21 Ibid., p. 124.

sometimes challenge received opinion. And if we disagree with either the confirmation or the challenge, there is nothing to do but go back to the "text" — the values, principles, codes, and conventions that constitute the moral world — and to the "readers" of the text.

The readers, I suppose, are the effective authority: we hold up our interpretations for their approval.[22] But the matter isn't closed if they don't approve. For readers are also re-readers who change their minds, and the population of readers also changes; we can always renew the argument. I can best explain my own view of that argument, and conclude this lecture, with a Talmudic story (the Talmud is, after all, a collection of interpretations, simultaneously legal and moral in character). The background for this story is a text from Deuteronomy 30:11–14.

> For this commandment which I command thee this day, it is not hidden from thee, neither is it far off. It is not in heaven, that thou shouldest say, Who shall go up for us to heaven, and bring it unto us, that we may hear it, and do it? Neither is it beyond the sea, that thou shouldest say, Who shall go over the sea for us, and bring it unto us, that we may hear it, and do it? But the word is very nigh unto thee, in thy mouth and in thy heart, that thou mayest do it.

I won't quote the story itself but retell it, for stories of this sort are better told than recited.[23] We break in on a dispute among a group of sages; the subject doesn't matter. Rabbi Eliezer stood

---

[22] I mean readers in the widest sense: not only other interpreters, professionals, and adepts of one sort or another, members of what has been called the interpretive community. These people may be our most stringent readers, but they are nevertheless only an intermediate audience. The interpretation of a moral culture is aimed at all the men and women who participate in that culture — the members of what we might call a community of experience. It is a necessary, though not a sufficient, sign of a successful interpretation that such people be able to recognize themselves in it. For a similar view, see Geuss, *Idea of a Critical Theory*, pp. 64–65.

[23] The story is from the Talmudic tractate *Baba Metzia* 59b. See the discussion in Gershom Scholem, "Revelation and Tradition as Religious Categories in Judaism," in *The Messianic Idea in Judaism* (New York: Schocken, 1971), pp. 282–303.

alone, a minority of one, having brought forward every imaginable argument and failed to convince his colleagues. Exasperated, he called for divine help: "If the law is as I say, let this carob tree prove it." Whereupon the carob tree was lifted a hundred cubits in the air — some say it was lifted four hundred cubits. Rabbi Joshua spoke for the majority: "No proof can be brought from a carob tree." Then Rabbi Eliezer said, "If the law is as I say, let this stream of water prove it." And the stream immediately began to flow backwards. But Rabbi Joshua said, "No proof can be brought from a stream of water." Again, Rabbi Eliezer: "If the law is as I say, let the walls of this schoolhouse prove it." And the walls began to fall. But Rabbi Joshua rebuked them, saying that they had no business interfering in a dispute among scholars over the moral law; and they stopped falling and to this day still stand, although at a sharp angle. And then, Rabbi Eliezer called on God Himself: "If the law is as I say, let it be proved from heaven." Whereupon a voice cried out, "Why do you dispute with Rabbi Eliezer? In all matters the law is as he says." But Rabbi Joshua stood up and exclaimed, "It is not in heaven!"

Morality, in other words, is something we have to argue about. The argument implies common possession, but common possession does not imply agreement. There is a tradition, a body of moral knowledge; and there is this group of sages, arguing. There isn't anything else. No discovery or invention can end the argument; no "proof" takes precedence over the (temporary) majority of sages.[24] That is the meaning of "It is not in heaven." We have to

---

[24] Compare a midrashic commentary on Psalm 12:7: "The words of the Lord are . . . silver tried in the open before all men, refined seven times seven." "Rabbi Yannai said: The words of the Torah were not given as clear-cut decisions. For with every word which the Holy One, blessed be He, spoke to Moses, He offered him forty-nine arguments by which a thing may be proved clean, and forty-nine other arguments by which it may be proved unclean. When Moses asked: Master of the universe, in what way shall we know the true sense of a law? God replied: The majority is to be followed. . . ." The majority does not, of course, make an arbitrary decision; its members search for the best of the ninety-eight arguments. *The Midrash on Psalms*, trans. by William G. Braude, vol. I (New Haven: Yale University Press, 1959), p. 173.

continue the argument: perhaps for that reason, the story doesn't tell us whether, on the substantive issue, Rabbi Eliezer or Rabbi Joshua was right.

On the procedural issue, however, Rabbi Joshua was exactly right. That at least is the central claim of this lecture. The question now is whether Rabbi Joshua, who gave up revelation, and his contemporary descendants who have given up discovery and invention, can still say something useful, that is, something critical, about the real world.

II. THE PRACTICE OF SOCIAL CRITICISM

1

Social criticism is such a common activity — so many people, in one way or another, participate in it — that we must suspect from the beginning that it doesn't wait upon philosophical discovery or invention. Consider the phrase itself: "social criticism" is not like "literary criticism," where the adjective tells us only the object of the enterprise named by the noun. The adjective "social" also tells us something about the subject of the enterprise. Social criticism is a social activity. "Social" has a pronominal and reflexive function, rather like "self" in "self-criticism," which names subject and object at the same time. No doubt, societies do not criticize themselves; social critics are individuals, but they are also, most of the time, members, speaking in public to other members who join in the speaking and whose speech constitutes a collective reflection upon the conditions of collective life.

This is a stipulative definition of social criticism; I want now to defend and elaborate it. I don't mean to argue that it is the single possible or correct definition, only that if we imagine the dictionary's usual list, this one should come first. The argument that I shall oppose denies that reflection-from-within belongs on the list at all. For how can it ever be a satisfactory form of reflection? Don't the conditions of collective life — immediacy, closeness, emotional attachment, parochial vision — militate against a critical self-understanding? When someone says "our country," emphasizing the possessive pronoun, isn't he likely to go on to say "right or wrong"? Stephen Decatur's famous toast is often taken as an example of the sort of commitment that precludes criticism. It isn't, of course, since one can still say "wrong" — as Carl Schurz did in the U.S. Senate in 1872: "Our country, right or wrong! When right to be kept right; when wrong to be put right!" When our country behaves badly, it is still ours, and we are, perhaps, especially obligated to criticize its policies. And yet the possessive pronoun is a problem. The more closely we identify with the country, so we are commonly told, the harder it is for us to recognize or acknowledge its wrongs. Criticism requires critical distance.

It's not clear, though, how much distance critical distance is. Where do we have to stand to be social critics? The conventional view, I think, is that we have to stand outside the common circumstances of collective life. Criticism is an external activity; what makes it possible is radical detachment — and this in two senses. First, critics must be emotionally detached, wrenched loose from the intimacy and warmth of membership: disinterested and dispassionate. Second, critics must be intellectually detached, wrenched loose from the parochial understandings of their own society (standardly taken to be self-congratulatory): open-minded and objective. This view of the critic gains strength from the fact that it matches closely the conditions of philosophical discovery and invention and so seems to suggest that only discoverers or inventors, or men and women armed by discoverers or inventors, can be properly critical.

Radical detachment has the additional and not insignificant merit of turning the critic into a hero. For it is a hard business (though harder in some societies than in others) to wrench oneself loose, either emotionally or intellectually. To walk "alone . . .

and in the dark" is bound to be frightening, even if one is on the road to enlightenment. Critical distance is an achievement, and the critic pays a price in comfort and solidarity. It has to be said, however, that the difficulty of finding a properly detached position is compensated for by the ease of criticism once one is there.

Not surprisingly, radical detachment doesn't seem to me a prerequisite of social criticism, not even of radical social criticism. It's only necessary to put together a list of critics, from the prophets of ancient Israel onward, to see how few people it actually fits. The description has become conventional in part because of a confusion between detachment and marginality. The prophets, as I will suggest in the last of these lectures, were not even marginal men, but many of their successors were. Marginality has often been a condition that motivates criticism and determines the critic's characteristic tone and appearance. It is not, however, a condition that makes for disinterest, dispassion, open-mindedness, or objectivity. Nor is it an external condition. Marginal men and women are like Simmel's stranger, in but not wholly of their society.[1] The difficulties they experience are not the difficulties of detachment but of ambiguous connection. Free them from those difficulties and they may well lose the reasons they have for joining the critical enterprise. Or, criticism will look very different than it looks when it is worked up on the margins by "alienated intellectuals," or members of subject classes or oppressed minorities, or even outcasts and pariahs. Now we have to imagine not a marginal critic but a critic detached from his own marginality. He might still be critical of any society in which groups of men and women were pushed to the margins (or he might not, seeing that the margins are so often a setting for creative activity). But his own marginality, if he remembered it, would only be a distorting factor, undercutting his capacity for objective judgment. So would his centrality, his close involvement, if he were involved, with the

[1] George Simmel, "The Stranger," in *The Sociology of George Simmel*, trans. and ed. by Kurt H. Wolff (New York: Free Press, 1950), pp. 402–8.

rulers of society. Detachment stands to the marginal and the central in exactly the same way: free of the tensions that bind the two together.

On the conventional view, the critic is not really a marginal figure; he is — he has made himself into — an outsider, a spectator, a "total stranger," a man from Mars. He derives a kind of critical authority from the distance he establishes. We might compare him (I shall suggest other comparisons later on) to an imperial judge in a backward colony. He stands outside, in some privileged place, where he has access to "advanced" or universal principles; and he applies these principles with an impersonal (intellectual) rigor. He has no other interest in the colony except to bring it to the bar of justice. We must grant him benevolence, I suppose; he wishes the natives well. Indeed, let's make the analogy tighter and say that he is a native himself, one of the Queen's Chinese, for example, or a westernized and Anglophile Indian, or a Parisian Marxist who happens to be Algerian. He has gone to school at the imperial center, at Paris or Oxford, say, and broken radically with his own parochialism. He would have preferred to stay at Paris or Oxford, but he has dutifully returned to his homeland so that he can criticize the local arrangements. A useful person, possibly, but not the only or the best model of a social critic.

I want to suggest an alternative model — though I don't mean to banish the dispassionate stranger or the estranged native. They have their place in the critical story but only alongside, and in the shadow of, someone quite different and more familiar: the local judge, the connected critic, who earns his authority, or fails to do so, by arguing with his fellows — who, angrily and insistently, sometimes at considerable personal risk (he can be a hero too), objects, protests, and remonstrates. This critic is one of us. Perhaps he has traveled and studied abroad, but his appeal is to local or localized principles; if he has picked up new ideas on his travels, he tries to connect them to the local culture, building on his own intimate knowledge; he is not intellectually detached. Nor is he emotionally detached; he doesn't wish the natives well, he seeks the success of their common enterprise. This is the style of Alexander Herzen among nineteenth-century Russians (despite Herzen's long exile from Russia), of Ahad Ha-am among East European Jews, of Gandhi in India, of Tawney and Orwell in Britain. Social criticism, for such people, is an internal argument. The outsider can become a *social* critic only if he manages to get himself inside, enters imaginatively into local practices and arrangements. But these critics are already inside. They see no advantage in radical detachment. If it suits their purposes, they can play at detachment, pretend to see their own society through the eyes of a stranger — like Montesquieu through the eyes of Usbek. But it is Montesquieu, the well-connected Frenchman, not Usbek, who is the social critic. Persian naivete is a mask for French sophistication.

Now this alternative description fits the great majority of men and women who are plausibly called social critics. But it isn't philosophically respectable. I shall try to defend its respectability by responding, as best I can, to two legitimate worries about the connected critic. Does his connection leave room enough for critical distance? And are standards available to him that are internal to the practices and understandings of his own society, and at the same time properly critical?

2

I will take the second question first. Social criticism must be understood as one of the more important byproducts of a larger activity — let's call it the activity of cultural elaboration and affirmation. This is the work of priests and prophets; teachers and sages; storytellers, poets, historians, and writers generally. As soon as these sorts of people exist, the possibility of criticism exists. It's not that they constitute a permanently subversive "new class," or that they are the carriers of an "adversary culture." They carry the common culture; as Marx argued, they do (among other things) the intellectual work of the ruling class. But so long as they do *intellectual* work, they open the way for the adversary proceeding of social criticism.

The argument that Marx first worked out in *The German Ideology* is helpful here. Marxist social criticism is based on a grand discovery — a "scientific" vision of the end of history. But this vision is only possible because the end is close at hand, its principles already apparent within bourgeois society. Criticism in other societies has been based on other visions, other principles, and Marxism is intended to provide a general account, not only of itself but of all other critical doctrines. What makes criticism a permanent possibility, according to this account, is the fact that every ruling class is compelled to present itself as a universal class.[2] There is no legitimacy in mere self-assertion. Trapped in the class struggle, seeking whatever victories are available, the rulers nevertheless claim to stand above the struggle, guardians of the common interest, their goal not victory but transcendence. This presentation of the rulers is elaborated by the intellectuals. Their work is apologetic, but the apology is of a sort that gives hostages to future social critics. It sets standards that the rulers will not live up to, cannot live up to, given their particularist ambitions. One might say that these standards themselves embody ruling class interests, but they do so only within a universalist disguise. And they also embody lower class interests, else the disguise would not be convincing. Ideology strains toward universality as a condition of its success.

The Italian Marxist Antonio Gramsci provides a useful if somewhat sketchy analysis of this double embodiment. Every hegemonic culture, he argues, is a complex political construction.

---

[2] Marx and Engels, *The German Ideology*, R. Pascal, ed. (New York: International Publishers, 1947), pp. 40–41: "For each new class which puts itself in the place of the one ruling before it, is compelled, merely in order to carry through its aim, to represent its interest as the common interest of all the members of society, put in an ideal form; it will give its ideas the form of universality. . . ."

The intellectuals who put it together are armed with pens, not swords; they have to make a case for the ideas they are defending among men and women who have ideas of their own. "The fact of hegemony," Gramsci writes in his *Prison Notebooks*, "presupposes that one takes into account the interests and tendencies of the groups over which hegemony will be exercised, and it also presupposes a certain equilibrium, that is to say that the hegemonic groups will make some sacrifices of a corporate nature." [3] Because of these sacrifices, ruling ideas internalize contradictions, and so criticism always has a starting point inside the dominant culture. Upper class ideology carries within itself dangerous possibilities. Gramsci's comrade in the Italian Communist Party, Ignazio Silone, describes the origins of radical criticism and revolutionary politics in exactly these terms: we begin, he writes,

> by taking seriously the principles taught us by our own educators and teachers. These principles are proclaimed to be the foundations of present-day society, but if one takes them seriously and uses them as a standard to test society as it is organized . . . today, it becomes evident that there is a radical contradiction between the two. Our society in practice ignores these principles altogether . . . . But for us they are a serious and sacred thing . . . the foundation of our inner life. The way society butchers them, using them as a mask and a tool to cheat and fool the people, fills us with anger and indignation. That is how one becomes a revolutionary. [4]

Gramsci himself describes a somewhat more complex process, and one seemingly without the motivating force of indignation; it begins, however, at the same place. Radical critics initiate, he

---

[3] Quoted in Chantal Mouffe, "Hegemony and Ideology in Gramsci," in Mouffe, ed., *Gramsci and Marxist Theory* (London: Routledge and Kegan Paul, 1979), p. 181.

[4] *Bread and Wine*, trans. by Gwenda David and Eric Mosbacher (New York: Harper and Brothers, 1937), pp. 157–58. Silone's example suggests that one ceases to be a revolutionary in the same way: by comparing the creed of the revolutionary party to its actual practice.

says, "a process of differentiation and change in the relative weight that the elements of the old ideologies used to possess. What was previously secondary and subordinate . . . is now taken to be primary and becomes the nucleus of a new ideological and theoretical complex." [5] So new ideologies emerge from old ones by way of interpretation and revision. Let's look at a concrete example.

Consider the place of equality in bourgeois and then in later critical thought. Conceived in Marxist terms as the credo of the triumphant middle classes, equality has a distinctly limited meaning. Its reference, among French revolutionaries, say, is to equality before the law, the career open to talents, and so on. It describes (and also conceals) the conditions of the competitive race for wealth and office. Radical critics delight in "exposing" its limits: it guarantees to all men and women, as Anatole France wrote, an equal right to sleep under the bridges of Paris. But the word has larger meanings — it wouldn't be so useful if it didn't — subordinated within but never eliminated from the ruling ideology. These larger meanings are, to use a Gramscian term, "concessionary" in character; with them or through them the middle classes gesture toward lower class aspiration. We are all citizens here, they claim, no one is better than anyone else. I don't mean to underestimate the sincerity of the gesture on the part, at least, of some of the people who make it. If it weren't sincere, social criticism would have less bite than it does have. The critic exploits the larger meanings of equality, which are more mocked than mirrored in everyday experience. He condemns capitalist practice by elaborating one of the key concepts with which capitalism had originally been defended. He shows the rulers the idealized pictures their

---

[5] The same argument can be made with regard to the bourgeois creed itself. Thus Tocqueville on the radicals of 1789: ". . . though they had no inkling of this, they took over from the old regime not only most of its customs, conventions, and modes of thought, but even those very ideas which prompted [them] to destroy it . . . ." Alexis de Tocqueville, *The Old Regime and the French Revolution*, trans. by Stuart Gilbert (Garden City, N.Y.: Doubleday Anchor Books, 1955), p. vii (Foreword).

artists have painted and then the lived reality of power and oppression. Or, better, he interprets the pictures and the reality, for
neither one is straightforwardly revealed. Equality is the rallying
cry of the bourgeoisie; equality reinterpreted is (in the Gramscian
story) the rallying cry of the proletariat.[6]

It is entirely possible, of course, that the critic's reinterpretation won't be accepted. Perhaps the greater number of workers
believe that the equality realized in capitalist society is genuine
equality or that it is equality enough. Marxists call such beliefs
"false consciousness" — on the assumption that equality has a
single true meaning, if not for all of us then at least for the
workers, namely, the meaning that corresponds to their "objective" interests. I doubt that this view can be satisfactorily defended. The workers can indeed be wrong about the facts of their
case, the actual extent of income differentials, say, or the real
chances of upward mobility. But how can they be wrong about
the value and significance of equality in their own lives? Here
criticism depends less on true (or false) statements about the
world than on evocative (or unevocative) renderings of a common
idea. The argument is about meaning and experience; its terms
are set by its cultural as well as its socioeconomic setting.

But not all arguments are similarly internal. Imagine the social
critic as a Marxist militant or a Christian preacher who comes
(like my imperial judge) to a foreign country. There he finds
natives whose conception of the world or of their own place in
the world, so the newcomer believes, is radically mistaken. He
measures the mistake by a wholly external standard, carried, as it
were, in his luggage. If he challenges local practices, he does so
in terms likely to be, at least at first, incomprehensible to the natives. Understanding waits upon conversion, and the primary task
of the newcomer is a missionary task: to offer a persuasive account

---

[6] Gramsci, *Selections from the Prison Notebooks*, trans. and ed. by Quinton
Hoare and Geoffrey Nowell Smith (New York: International Publishers, 1971),
p. 195.

of a new moral or physical world. He must appear to the natives like an eagle at daybreak; they have their own owls. It is only after the new ideas have been naturalized in their new setting, woven into the fabric of the already existing culture, that native critics (or the missionary himself, if he has been naturalized too) can put them to use. Conversion and criticism are different activities — rather like conquest and revolution. What marks off the latter terms in each of these pairs is their partly reflexive character. In the language of the police, they are both of them, at their best, "inside jobs."

The newcomers might also criticize local practices in terms of what I called, in the first of these lectures, the minimal code — and this sort of criticism, though it might require explanation, would presumably not require conversion. Consider the example of the Spaniards in Central America, who claimed sometimes to speak for Catholicism, sometimes only for natural law: they had, to be sure, a Catholic understanding of natural law, but they may still have been right to oppose human sacrifice, for example, not because it was contrary to orthodox doctrine but because it was "against nature." The Aztecs probably did not understand, and yet the argument didn't have the same degree of externality as did arguments about the blood and body of Christ, Christian communion, and so on (and it may well have connected with the feelings, at least, of the sacrificial victims).[7] In the event, however, the naturalistic critique of human sacrifice by Spanish missionaries seems to have been largely ideological in character, a justification for external conquest, not internal reform or revolution. I will consider a purer example of minimalist criticism in my last lecture.

---

[7] See Bernice Hamilton, *Political Thought in Sixteenth-Century Spain: A study of the political ideas of Vitoria, De Soto, Suarez, and Molina* (Oxford: Oxford University Press, 1963), pp. 125ff. Vitoria argues that Spain has no right to enforce natural law in Central America since the Indians do not "acknowledge" any such law, but it does have a right under natural law to defend the innocent: "No one can give another man the right to kill him either for food or sacrifice. Besides, it is unquestionable that in most cases these people are killed against their wills — children for example — so it is lawful to protect them." Quoted p. 128.

If missionary work and conversion are morally necessary, if Marxism or Catholicism or any other developed creed is the only correct standard of social criticism, then correct social criticism has been impossible in most actually existing moral worlds. Nevertheless, the resources necessary for criticism of some sort, and more than a minimalist sort, are always available — available because of what a moral world is, because of what we do when we construct it. The Marxist account of ideology is only one version of this construction. Another version, more familiar to contemporary philosophers, might go like this. Men and women are driven to build and inhabit moral worlds by a moral motive: a passion for justification. Sometimes only God can justify us, and then morality is likely to take shape as a conversation with God or a speculation on the standards that he might, reasonably or unreasonably, apply to our behavior. These will, in any case, be high standards, hence highly critical standards; the feeling of sin arises in part from the sense that we will never manage to live up to them.

In a secular age God is replaced by other people. Now we are driven, as Thomas Scanlon has written, by a "desire to be able to justify [our] actions to others on grounds they could not reasonably reject." [8] (We won't tolerate unreason in our peers.) It's not only rulers who want to be justified in the eyes of their subjects; each of us wants to be justified in the eyes of all the others. Scanlon suggests that this desire is triggered by the moral beliefs we already have. So it is, but it is also itself the trigger of moral belief — and then of moral argument and creativity. We try to justify ourselves, but we can't justify ourselves by ourselves, and so morality takes shape as a conversation with particular other people, our relatives, friends, and neighbors; or it takes shape as a speculation on what arguments might, or should, persuade such

---

[8] "Contractualism and Utilitarianism," in *Utilitarianism and Beyond*, Amartya Sen and Bernard Williams, eds. (Cambridge: Cambridge University Press, 1982), p. 116.

people of our righteousness. Because we know the people, we can, we have to, give these arguments some specificity: they are more like "love thy neighbor" (with a suitable gloss on all three words) than "don't be indifferent to the suffering of others." They are worked out with reference to an actual, not merely a speculative, moral discourse: not one person but many people talking.

We experience morality as an external standard because it is always, necessarily, the standard of God or of other people. That's also why it is a critical standard. I suggest in my first lecture that discovered and invented moralities were critical "from the beginning" — else there would be no cachet in discovery or invention. But our everyday morality is also critical from the beginning: it only justifies what God or other people can recognize as just. We want that recognition, even if we also want, sometimes, to do things that we know can't be justified. Morality doesn't fit these other wants, though it is always possible to interpret it in a way that makes it fit. We might think of such an interpretation as the private version of an ideology. But we live anxiously with our ideologies; they are strained and awkward; they don't ring true, and we wait for some angry or indignant neighbor or friend or former friend, the private version of a social critic, to tell us so.

This account of private morality can be recapitulated at the level of collective life. Every human society provides for its members — they provide for themselves through the medium of justification — standards of virtuous character, worthy performance, just social arrangements. The standards are social artifacts; they are embodied in many different forms: legal and religious texts, moral tales, epic poems, codes of behavior, ritual practices, and so on. In all their forms, they are subject to interpretation, and they are interpreted in both apologetic and critical ways. It is not the case that the apologetic interpretations are the "natural" ones, that moral standards readily fit social practices and make for smoothness and comfort, as in some functionalist utopia. The standards have to be interpreted to fit. A sustained apologetic interpretation

is, again, an ideology. Since social practices, like individual practices, are morally recalcitrant, ideologies are always problematic.
We know that we don't live up to the standards that might justify
us. And if we ever forget that knowledge, the social critic appears
to remind us. It's his critical interpretation that is the "natural"
one, given what morality is. Like Shaw's Englishman, the social
critic "does everything on principle." But he is a serious, not a
comic, figure because his principles are ones we share. They are
only apparently external; they are really aspects of the same collective life that is perceived to require criticism. The same men
and women who act badly create and sustain the standards by
which (at least sometimes) they know themselves to act badly.

3

But how can we recognize better and worse interpretations of
moral standards? The critic can, of course, get things wrong;
good social criticism is as rare as good poetry or good philosophy.
The critic is often passionate, obsessive, self-righteous; his hatred
for the hypocrisy of his fellows may well outmeasure hypocrisy
itself — "the only evil that walks/Invisible, except to God alone."
How can we judge the proper measure? Or again, some critical
interpretations of the existing morality look backward, like Cato's;
some forward, like Marx's. Is the one way of looking better than
the other? I have already suggested my own answer, or non-
answer, to such questions: they set the terms of moral argument,
and the argument has no end. It has only temporary stopping
points, moments of judgment. In a passive and decadent society,
looking back may well be the best thing to do; in an activist and
progressive society, looking forward may be best. But then we
will argue about the meaning of decadence and progress. Can't
the critic step back from such endless arguments? Can't he detach
himself from the conditions that make for obsession and self-
righteousness? Can't he provide some objective reading of moral
experience? And if he can't do these things, mightn't it be better

to say of him that he is angry or resentful rather than to credit him with the qualification — since it is an honorable qualification — of *critical*?

Criticism requires critical distance. But what does that mean? On the conventional view, critical distance divides the self; when we step back (mentally), we create a double. Self$_1$ is still involved, committed, parochial, angry, and so on; self$_2$ is detached, dispassionate, impartial, quietly watching self$_1$. The claim is that self$_2$ is superior to self$_1$, at least in this sense, that his criticism is more reliable and objective, more likely to tell us the moral truth about the world in which the critic and all the rest of us live. Self$_3$ would be better still. This view is plausible, at least for self$_2$, because we have all had the experience of remembering with embarrassment, chagrin, or regret occasions on which we behaved badly. We form a certain picture of ourselves (from a distance), and the picture is painful. But this is most often a picture of ourselves as we are seen or think we are seen by people whose opinion we value. We don't look at ourselves from nowhere in particular but through the eyes of particular other people — a morally but not an epistemologically privileged position. We apply standards that we share with the others to ourselves. Social criticism works differently: we apply standards that we share with the others *to the others*, our fellow citizens, friends and enemies. We don't remember with embarrassment, we look around with anger. It may be that a critic from the ruling classes learns to see society through the eyes of the oppressed, but one of the oppressed who sees through his own eyes is no less a social critic. He will, of course, find himself caught up in arguments about what he claims to see and what he says the standards are. But he can't win these arguments by stepping back; he can only speak again, more fully and more clearly.

The hope implicit in the conventional view is that the argument can be won once and for all. Hence that heroic figure, the perfectly disinterested spectator, imagined as a kind of all-purpose, general service social critic. We might ask, though, why such a person would be a critic at all, rather than a radical skeptic or a mere spectator or a playful interventionist, like the Greek gods. Perhaps self$_1$ and self$_2$ don't represent different degrees of moral authority but only different orientations toward the world. Arthur Koestler makes an argument of this sort in his autobiography. There are "two parallel planes in our minds," he writes, "which should be kept separate: the plane of detached contemplation in the sign of infinity, and the plane of action in the name of certain ethical imperatives." Koestler believes that the two coexist in contradiction. He bravely announces, for example, that European civilization is doomed: "This is, so to speak, my contemplative truth. Looking at the world with detachment . . . I find it not even disturbing. But I also happen to believe in the ethical imperative of fighting evil. . . ." [9] Social criticism, a matter of ethical imperatives, clearly belongs to "the plane of action." It is curious that the plane of contemplation is so much more melodramatic. Still, contemplative men and women, on Koestler's reading, are not critics.

In his defense of detachment, Thomas Nagel has insisted that the detached observer, self$_2$, need not be undisturbed by the doom of civilization or by anything else happening in the real world because he need not abandon the moral beliefs and motivations of self$_1$. But I don't see how he can experience those beliefs and motivations in the same way once he has evacuated the moral world within which they have their immediate reality and distanced himself from the person for whom they are real. "When we take up the objective standpoint," writes Nagel, as if to confirm this skepticism, "the problem is not that values seem to disappear, but that there seem to be too many of them, coming from every life and drowning out those that arise from our own." [10]

---

[9] *Arrow in the Blue* (New York: Stein and Day, 1984), p. 133.

[10] "Limits of Objectivity," p. 115.

I will concede that this is still an experiencing of values, though not quite in the common mode, and that self$_2$ is somehow motivated to choose out of the flood of conflicting values those that now seem to him best — which may or may not be the values of self$_1$. But would he establish any very passionate commitment to defend those values in a particular time and place? Surely one of the standard motives for detaching oneself is to escape passionate commitment (for the sake, as with Koestler, of contemplation in the sign of infinity). And if that is so, then a critic looking at society is bound to be more critical than a critic looking at himself looking at society.[11]

But there is an alternative possibility. If the effect of detachment is literally the "drowning out" of the values that arise from the critic's own life in his own time and place, then the way may be opened for an enterprise far more radical than social criticism as I have been describing it — an enterprise more like conversion and conquest: the total replacement of the society from which the critic has detached himself with some (imagined or actual) other. Replacement obviously depends upon the criticism of what is to be replaced; I won't attempt a definitional exclusion: this is social criticism. I shall want to argue later on, however, that it is most often a morally unattractive form of social criticism and not one whose "objectivity" we should admire.

It will be useful at this point to consider, if only briefly, some historical examples. (My third lecture is an extended historical argument.) I have chosen to begin with John Locke and his well-known and rightly admired *Letter Concerning Toleration*. This is obviously a critical text even though it was published in 1689, the year of the Toleration Act, whose principles it vindicates. The *Letter* was written some years earlier, while Locke was living in exile in Holland, and it was aimed at what were still the conven-

---

[11] This suggests that self$_2$ would be the preferred author of a history or sociology of criticism, perhaps even of a philosophy of criticism (it is my own self$_2$ who is writing these words). But self$_1$ is the preferred critic.

tional views of England's political elite. Moreover, it defends a
revolutionary idea; it marks a significant turning point — for
Europe after the long centuries of religious persecution is a different place from Europe before. How does criticism work at
moments like this?

Locke's exile might be taken as a kind of detachment from
English politics, at least from established and conventional politics. Exile, we might say, is a literal enacting of critical distance.
On the other hand, Holland was hardly a realm of objectivity, and
Locke's presence there did not represent anything like a philosophical "stepping back." Holland must have appeared to Locke
as a (slightly) more advanced England, securely Protestant and
committed to toleration. Political refugees don't escape to nowhere in particular; if they can, they choose their refuge, applying
standards they already know, looking for friends and allies. So
Locke's exile tied him more closely than ever before to the political forces fighting against Stuart "tyranny." It committed him to
a cause. And when he defended religious toleration he did so in
terms familiar to his political associates. The *Letter* is a partisan
tract, a whiggish manifesto.

But it's not only that. Locke's arguments are said to have set
the terms of political discourse for the next century or more, and
yet at the most crucial point in the *Letter*, he looks resolutely backward and invokes an idea that doesn't figure much in Whig politics or in the philosophies of the Enlightenment — the idea of personal salvation. Locke appeals to the meaning of salvation in
Protestant thought and practice. "It is in vain," he writes, "for an
unbeliever to take up the outward show of another man's profession. Faith only and inward sincerity are the things that procure
acceptance with God." [12] The *Letter* provides a particular reading, but not an idiosyncratic or outlandish reading, of Lutheran
and Calvinist theology. In no sense does it call for a replacement

---

[12] *A Letter Concerning Toleration*, intro. by Patrick Romanell (Indianapolis:
Bobbs-Merrill, 1950), p. 34.

of that theology or of the moral world of English Protestantism. Locke moves on to a powerful conclusion (which Rousseau seems to have copied and misunderstood) : "Men cannot be forced to be saved whether they will or no . . . . [T]hey must be left to their own consciences." [13] He doesn't speak here in the new language of natural rights; this is very much the old language of "salvation by faith alone." But Locke's lines suggest how one might move from old to new — not so much by discovering rights as by interpreting faith, "inward sincerity," and conscience. (Hence Locke's use of rights language was never a surprise sprung on his contemporaries.) Given what salvation is, he says, or, better, given what we mean by salvation (where the pronoun doesn't refer only to Locke's fellow exiles), persecution cannot serve the purposes claimed by its defenders. It is an injury to the moral self, also to the physical self, and nothing more.

Arguing for toleration is likely to seem to us today the ideal type of a dispassionate enterprise. Religious belief, so we believe, makes for passion, fanaticism, and then for persecution; toleration is the product of skepticism and disinterest. In practice, toleration is more often the product of exhaustion: all passion spent, there is nothing left but co-existence. But one can readily imagine a philosophical defense, starting from a detached observation of the folly of religious war. The theological zeal for persecution seems somehow diminished once we recognize, from a distance, the value of each and every human life. For many seventeenth-century Englishmen, however, Locke probably among them, the value of each and every human life was closely tied to the idea of conscience, the divine spark within each of us. Toleration was itself a theological matter, a position defended with as much zeal as any other in the ongoing wars. Detachment might provide a (distanced) reason for endorsing that position; it doesn't provide a reason — at any rate, it doesn't provide Locke's reason — for taking it up. Indeed, an emphasis on critical distance may be a mis-

[13] Ibid., p. 12.

take here, if it leads us to miss the substantive character of Locke's argument and to disregard its intellectual location: within and not outside a tradition of theological discourse; within and not above the political fray.

It is opposition, far more than detachment, that determines the shape of social criticism. The critic takes sides in actual or latent conflicts; he sets himself against the prevailing political forces. As a result he is sometimes driven into exile in foreign lands or into that internal exile that we call "alienation." It isn't easy, I admit, to imagine John Locke as an alienated intellectual; he is so central to our own political tradition. Although he wrote anonymously on politics and religion, and thus carved out room for his own radicalism, he nevertheless cultivated centrality, referring himself in the *Second Treatise*, for example, to that "judicious" conservative, Richard Hooker, and always inviting readers to admire his own judiciousness. A matter of prudence, no doubt, and of temperament, and of luck: Locke's political associates were powerful men, and he may have sensed that his exile would be, as it was, short. Judiciousness was a wise choice. When his *Letter* was published, his friends were in power. So we need to look at less lucky critics, whose opposition was more prolonged and embittered. It's not the case that such people achieve detachment, far from it, but their connection to common values and traditions of discourse is far more problematic than Locke's was. They are tempted by a kind of leave-taking very different from that suggested by the philosophical idea of stepping back and different too from Lockeian exile. They are tempted to declare a state of war — and then to join the other side.

The easiest examples come from the history of war itself, especially from interventionist and colonial war. But before considering an example of that sort, I want to return briefly to the Marxist account of ideology and class struggle. It is one of the major failures of Marxism that neither Marx himself nor any of his chief intellectual followers ever worked out a moral and political theory of socialism. Their arguments assumed a socialist future — without oppression or exploitation — but the precise shape of that future was rarely discussed. When Marxists wrote social criticism (rather than learned analyses of the laws of capitalist development), this assumption provided a reassuring background. The force of their criticism derived, however, from the exposure of bourgeois hypocrisy — as in Marx's caustic comment on English apologists for the twelve-hour working day and the seven-day week: "and that in a country of Sabbatarians!" [14] Marxists never undertook the sort of reinterpretation of bourgeois ideas that might have produced Gramsci's "new ideological and theoretical complex." The reason for this failure lies, I think, in their view of the class struggle as an actual war in which their task, as intellectuals, was simply to support the workers. Implicitly, sometimes explicitly, they rejected the idea of social criticism as a collective reflection on collective life — because they denied the reality of collective life, of common values and a shared tradition. Even Marx's brief appeal to the idea of Sabbath rest is enough to suggest the foolishness of this denial, but the denial is nonetheless a major force within Marxism. It accounts for the essentially polemical and agitational character of the Marxist critique and the ever-present readiness to abandon "the arm of criticism" for the "criticism of arms."

In a sense, Marxists are not properly called critics of bourgeois society, for the point of their politics is not to criticize but to overthrow the bourgeoisie. They are critics of the workers instead, insofar as the workers are ideological prisoners and so prevented from fulfilling their historical role as the agents of overthrow. Hence the theory of false consciousness, which we might think of as a Marxist gesture toward common values. The theory acknowledges the commonality but treats it as a kind of collective mistake—and so misses a critical opportunity to describe socialism

[14] *Capital*, ed. by F. Engels, trans. by Samuel Moore and Edward Aveling (New York: International Publishers, 1967), vol. I, p. 264.

in socially validated and comprehensible terms. The only alternative is not to describe it at all. To discover or invent a set of socialist values doesn't seem to have been a practical possibility. Why should the workers stake their lives for *that*? Marx would have done better to take seriously his own metaphorical account of the new society growing in the womb of the old.

But at least Marxist writers have, fairly consistently, been critics of working class ideology and then of the organization and strategy of working class movements. There is another way of going over to the other side that abandons criticism altogether. Consider the case of Jean-Paul Sartre and the Algerian war. Sartre professed to believe that the intellectual is a permanent critic. Set loose from his own class by his search for universality, he joins the movement of the oppressed. But even here he is unassimilable: "he can never renounce his critical faculties if he is to preserve the fundamental meaning of the ends pursued by the movement." He is the "guardian of fundamental ends," which is to say, of universal values. The intellectual achieves this guardianship by a Sartrean version of "stepping back," that is, "by constantly criticizing and radicalizing [himself]." [15] But this path to universality is a dangerous one. Having "refused" what Sartre calls his "petty bourgeois conditioning," the intellectual is likely to find himself with no concrete and substantive values at all. Universality turns out to be an empty category for de-conditioned men and women — and so their commitment to the movement of the oppressed is (as Sartre at one point says it should be) "unconditional." Once committed, they are supposed to rediscover tension and contradiction: theirs is "a divided consciousness, that can never be healed." In practice, however, unconditional commitment can feel like healing; at least, it can produce the symptoms of wholeness. We can see this clearly in Sartre's own life, for after he committed himself to the Algerian FLN he seemed incapable of a critical word about

[15] "A Plea for Intellectuals," in *Between Existentialism and Marxism*, trans. by John Mathews (New York: Pantheon, 1983), p. 261.

its principles or policies. Henceforth he aimed his ideas, as a soldier with more justification might aim his gun, in only one direction.

Of course, Sartre was a critic, and a consistent and brave critic, of French society — of the Algerian war and then of the conduct of the war, both of these viewed as necessary consequences of French colonialism. But since he described himself as an enemy and even a "traitor," as if, with characteristic hauteur, to accept the charge of his right-wing foes, he cut the ground from under his own enterprise.[16] An enemy is not recognizable as a social critic; he lacks standing. We accept and simultaneously discount criticism from our enemies. And the discount is especially easy if the criticism is made in the name of "universal" principles that are applied only to us. But perhaps we should think of Sartre's self-description, and of his elaborate account of the critic's "role," as a kind of theoretical smokescreen behind which he and his friends engaged in a familiar politics, a politics of internal opposition. Certainly the principles he applied were well-known in France; that, indeed, is where the leaders of the FLN had learned them. French intellectuals hardly had to step back or subject themselves to all that much self-criticism in order to discover, say, the idea of self-determination. The idea was already theirs; they had only to apply it, that is, to extend its application to the Algerians. What prevented Sartre from adopting this view of his own activity was his conception of criticism as war. The war was real enough, but the critique of the war was a distinct and separate enterprise. Join the two, and the critique is, as it was in Sartre's case, corrupted.

----

[16] Compare the following passage from an even more hard-pressed critic of his own society, the Afrikaner writer Andre Brink: "If the Afrikaner dissident today encounters such a vicious reaction from the Establishment, it is because he is re-garded as a traitor to everything Afrikanerdom stands for (since apartheid has usurped for itself that definition) — whereas, in fact, the dissident is fighting to assert the most positive and creative aspects of his heritage. . . ." Brink, *Writing in a State of Siege: Essays on Politics and Literature* (New York: Summit Books, 1983), p. 19. Brink is a connected critic, but that is not to deny that he might one day be driven into physical exile or even into a kind of moral exile, as it were, beyond his brave "whereas."

There are then two extremes (the description is convenient if inexact): philosophical detachment and a "treasonous" engagement, stepping back and going over. The first is a precondition of the second; under-commitment to one's own society makes, or can make, for over-commitment to some theoretical or practical other. The proper ground of social criticism is the ground that the detached philosopher and the Sartrean "traitor" have alike abandoned. But does this ground allow for critical distance? It is obvious that it does, else we would have far fewer critics than we do. Criticism does not require us to step back from society as a whole but only to step away from certain sorts of power relationships within society. It's not connection but authority and domination from which we must distance ourselves. Marginality is one way of establishing (or experiencing) this distance; certain sorts of internal withdrawal provide other ways. I am inclined to think that something like this is a requirement of intellectual life generally — as in the following piece of advice given by a Talmudic sage to would-be sages: "Love work, do not domineer over others, and never seek the intimacy of public officials." [17] The actual wielding of power and the Machiavellian ambition to whisper in the ear of the prince: these are real obstacles to the practice of criticism because they make it difficult to look with open eyes at those features of society most in need of critical scrutiny. But opposition is not a similar obstacle, though we are no more objective in opposition than in power.

Think for a moment of critical distance in the caricatured and slightly comic categories of age. The old are critics rather as Cato was, who believe that things have gone steadily downhill since their youth. The young are critics rather as Marx was, who believe that the best is yet to be. Age and youth both make for critical distance; the uncritical years presumably come in between. But note that the principles of the old and the young are not distant, and they are certainly not objective, principles. The old remember

[17] *Pirke Avot* (Sayings of the Fathers) I:10.

a time that is not so long ago. The young are newly socialized: if they are also (sometimes) radical and idealistic, that says something about the intellectual content of socialization. What makes criticism possible, or what makes it relatively easy, for both these groups is a certain quality of not being involved, or not fully involved, in the local forms of getting and spending, not being responsible for what happens, not being politically in control. The old may have relinquished control reluctantly; the young may be eager to win it. But, willingly or not, they stand a little to the side. They are, or they can be, kibitzers.

A little to the side, not outside: critical distance is measured in inches. Though old and young are not in control of the major economic or political enterprises of their society, they are also not without some commitment to the success of those enterprises, at least to their eventual success. They want things to go well. This is also, I think, the common stance of the social critic. He is not a detached observer, even when he looks at the society he inhabits with a fresh and skeptical eye. He is not an enemy, even when he is fiercely opposed to this or that prevailing practice or institutional arrangement. His criticism doesn't require either detachment or enmity because he finds a warrant for critical engagement in the idealism, even if it is a hypocritical idealism, of the actually existing moral world.

4

But this, it might be said, is a picture of the social critic as he commonly is; it's not a picture of the ideal social critic. I confess immediately that I can't imagine such a person — not, at least, if we have to imagine him as a single type of person, with a single (objective) standpoint and a single set of critical principles. Nevertheless, I have managed to smuggle into my picture a certain idealism of my own, which is different from the local and various idealisms of actual social critics. I have, not at all surreptitiously, attached value to the critic's connection to his own society. But why should connection be generally valuable, given that societies are so different? Of course, criticism works best if the critic is able to invoke local values, but it's not the case that it doesn't work at all if he isn't able or doesn't want to do that. Consider the case of the Bolshevik intellectuals in Russia, which Gramsci has summed up in a nice couple of sentences:

> An elite consisting of some of the most active, energetic, enterprising and disciplined members of the society emigrates abroad and assimilates the cultural and historical experiences of the most advanced countries of the West, without however losing the most essential characteristics of its own nationality, that is to say without breaking its sentimental and historical ties with its own people. Having thus performed its intellectual apprenticeship it returns to its own country and compels the people to an enforced awakening, skipping historical stages in the process.[18]

The reference to "sentimental ties" is necessary to explain why these enterprising intellectuals, having assimilated Western culture, don't just remain in the West. They see the sun but nevertheless go back to the cave. Once back, however, they don't seem to have been animated much by sentiment. They brought with them a great discovery—more scientific than moral in character—for the sake of which they had traveled a great distance, not only in space: they had also gone forward in time (far more so than Locke in Holland). Theoretical advancement was the form of their detachment from Old Russia. Now they confronted Russia with a true doctrine that had no Russian roots. Bolshevik social criticism draws heavily, to be sure, on Russian circumstances and arguments. It was necessary, Lenin wrote, "to collect and utilize every grain of every rudimentary protest," and rudimentary protest, unlike doctrinal discovery, is always a local phenomenon.[19] But this kind of criticism was crudely instrumental in character.

---

[18] Gramsci, *Prison Notebooks*, pp. 19–20.

[19] Lenin, *What Is To Be Done?* (Moscow: Foreign Languages Publishing House, 1947), p. 101.

The Bolshevik leaders made no serious effort to connect themselves to the common values of Russian culture. And that is why,
once they had seized power, they were compelled to "compel the
people to an enforced awakening."

I am tempted to say of Lenin and his friends that they were
not social critics at all — since what they wrote was narrowly
analytical in character or narrowly agitational. But it is probably
better to say that they were bad social critics, looking at Russia
from a great distance and merely disliking what they saw. Similarly, they were bad revolutionaries, for they seized power through
a coup d'état and ruled the country as if they had conquered it.
The group of Russian radicals who called themselves Social Revolutionaries makes for a useful comparison. The SR's labored hard
to recover the communal values of the Russian village and so to
construct a Russian argument against the new rural capitalism.
They told a story about the *mir*. I suspect that this story, like most
such stories, was largely fanciful. The values, though, were real —
that is, recognized and accepted by many Russians, even if they
were not, even if they had never been, institutionally embodied.
And so the SR's developed a critique of social relations in the Russian countryside that had some (I don't want to exaggerate) rich-
ness, detail, and nuance — and that was comprehensible to the
people whose relations those were. The Bolsheviks, by contrast,
were either incomprehensible or insincere, moving erratically back
and forth between Marxist theory and an opportunistic politics.

The problem with disconnected criticism, which is also to say,
with criticism that derives from newly discovered or invented
moral standards, is that it presses its practitioners toward manipulation and compulsion. Many, of course, resist the pressure; detachment and dispassion are built-in defenses against it. But insofar as the critic wants to be effective, wants to drive his criticism
home (though the home is, in a sense, no longer his own), he will
find himself driven to one or another version of an unattractive
politics. It is for this reason that I have tried to distinguish his

enterprise from collective reflection, criticism from within, or as it is sometimes called, "immanent critique." His is a kind of asocial criticism, an external intervention, a coercive act, intellectual in form but pointing toward its physical counterpart. Perhaps there are some societies so closed in upon themselves, so rigidly confined even in their ideological justifications, that they require asocial criticism; no other kind is possible. Perhaps; but it is my own belief that such societies are more likely to be found in social science fiction than in the real world.[20]

Sometimes though, even in the real world, the critic will be driven into a kind of asociability, not because he has discovered new moral standards but because he has discovered a new theology or cosmology or psychology, unknown, even outrageous, to his fellows, from which moral arguments seem to follow. Freud is the best modern example—and for now my last example. His critique of sexual morality might have been based, as similar critiques were later based, on liberal ideas of freedom and individuality. Freud argued instead from his newly discovered psychological theory. He was indeed a great discoverer, an eagle among discoverers, and then a heroic critic of repressive laws and practices. And yet a Freudian or therapeutic politics would be as unattractive, as manipulative, as any other politics founded on discovery and disconnected from local understandings. It is a good thing, then, that neither criticism nor oppositional politics depends upon discoveries of this sort. Social criticism is less the practical offspring of scientific knowledge than the educated cousin of common complaint. We become critics naturally, as it were, by elabo-

---

[20] It is easier to think of sub-groups within larger societies that might meet this description: tightly-knit orthodox religious communities, for example, like the Amish or like Hasidic Jews in the United States today. Orthodoxy itself is no bar to internal criticism, as the endless heresies of medieval Christendom or the dissidence of dissent among Protestants clearly suggest. But the smaller and more beleaguered the community, the less likely it is to offer resources to the connected critic. He will have to appeal to some wider political or religious tradition within which his own is (uneasily) located — as a critic of Amish or Hasidic society might appeal to Protestantism or Judaism more generally or to American liberalism.

rating on existing moralities and telling stories about a society more just than, though never entirely different from, our own.

It is better to tell stories, better even though there is no definitive and best story — better even though there is no last story that, once told, would leave all future storytellers without employment. I understand that this indeterminacy prompts, not without reason, a certain philosophical apprehension. And from this there follows the whole elaborate apparatus of detachment and objectivity, whose purpose is not to facilitate criticism but to guarantee its correctness. The truth is that there isn't any guarantee, any more than there is a guarantor. Nor is there a society, waiting to be discovered or invented, that would not require our critical stories.

III. BACK TO THE BEGINNING: THE PROPHET AS SOCIAL CRITIC

1

The contrasts and contradictions that I have been discussing — discovered or invented morality, on the one hand, and interpreted morality, on the other; external and internal criticism; shared values and everyday practices; social connection and critical distance — all these are very old. They aren't the property of the modern age; although I have described them in what is undoubtedly a modern idiom, they have in other times and places been described in other idioms. They are fully visible in the very earliest examples of social criticism, and I want in this last lecture to see how they look in what may well have been their first appearance, at least in Western history. I have had occasion up until now only for quick references and briefly elaborated illustrations. But with my argument laid out, I can now attempt a more careful and detailed demonstration of its reality, add historical flesh, as it were, to the theoretical bones. And how better to prove that the connected critic is flesh of our flesh than to give him the name of

Amos, the first and possibly the most radical of Israel's literary prophets?

I shall try to understand and explain the practice of prophecy in ancient Israel. I don't mean the personality of the prophet; I am not interested in the psychology of inspiration or of ecstasy. Nor do I mean the prophetic texts; these are painfully obscure at many points, and I don't possess the historical or philological knowledge necessary to decipher them (or even to offer speculative readings of disputed passages). I want to understand prophecy as a social practice: not the men or the texts but the message — and also the reception of the message. Of course, there were prophets before the ones we know, seers and soothsayers, oracles, diviners, and clairvoyants; and there is nothing very puzzling about their messages or about their audiences. Foretellings of doom and glory will always find listeners, especially when the doom is for enemies, the glory for ourselves. The people say, says Isaiah, "Speak unto us smooth things" (30:10), and that's what the professional prophets of courts and temples commonly do.[1] It's only when these foretellings are set, as Amos first sets them, within a moral frame, when they are an occasion for indignation, when prophecies are also provocations, verbal assaults on the institutions and activities of everyday life, that they become interesting. Then it's a puzzle why people listen — and not only listen but copy down, preserve, and repeat the prophetic message. It's not a smooth message; it can't be happily heard or readily followed; the people, most of them, don't do what the prophet urges them to do. But they choose to remember his urging: why?

It is here, writes Max Weber, "that the demagogue appears for the first time in the records of history."[2] But that's not quite

---

[1] On the professional prophets, see the opening chapters of Johannes Lindblom, *Prophecy in Ancient Israel* (Oxford: Basil Blackwell, 1962), and Joseph Blenkensopp, *A History of Prophecy in Israel* (London: SPCK, 1984).

[2] *Ancient Judaism*, trans. by H. H. Gerth and Don Martindale (Glencoe, Ill.: Free Press, 1952), pp. 268–69.

right (as Weber himself suggests later on in his *Ancient Judaism*),
for though the prophets spoke to the people and, arguably, on
their behalf, and though they spoke with the fierceness and anger
we conventionally attribute to demagogues, they do not seem to
have sought a popular following, nor ever to have aspired to
political office. Weber is closer to the truth when he argues that
the prophecies, written down and circulated in the cities of Israel
and Judah, represent the earliest known example of the political
pamphlet.[3] But that suggestion is too narrow. Prophetic religion
embraced not only politics but every aspect of social life. The
prophets were (the term is only mildly anachronistic) social
critics. Indeed, they were the inventors of the practice of social
criticism — though not of their own critical messages. And so we
can learn from reading them and studying their society something
about the conditions that make criticism possible and give it force,
and something too about the place and standing of the critic
among the people he criticizes.

2

The first thing to notice is that the prophetic message depends
upon previous messages. It isn't something radically new; the
prophet is not the first to find, nor does he make, the morality he
expounds. We can detect a certain theological revisionism in
some of the later prophets, but none of them presents an entirely
original doctrine. For the most part, they disclaim originality —
and not only in the obvious sense that they attribute their message
to God. It is more important that they continually refer themselves to the epic history and the moral teaching of the Torah:
"He hath showed thee, O man, what is good . . ." (Micah 6:8).
The past tense is significant. The prophets assume the previous
messages, the divine "showings," the immediacy of history and
law in the minds of their listeners. They have no esoteric teach-

[3] Ibid., p. 272.

ing, not even for their closest disciples. They speak to a large audience and, for all their anger, they seem to take that audience for granted; they assume, writes Johannes Lindblom, "that their words could be [not, however, that they would be — M. W.] immediately understood and accepted . . . ." [4]

This assumption finds its sociological correlate in the political and communal structure of ancient Israel: a loose, localized, and conflict-ridden set of arrangements that stood at some distance from the unified hierarchies of Egypt to the west and Assyria to the east. In Israel, religion was not the exclusive possession of priests, and law was not the exclusive possession of royal bureaucrats. Prophecy in the form we know it, in critical form, would not have been possible except for the relative weakness of priesthood and bureaucracy in the everyday life of the country. The necessary background conditions are indicated in the prophetic texts: justice is done (or not done) in the "gates" of the city, and religion is discussed in the streets.[5] The Bible clearly suggests the existence among the Israelites of a strong lay and popular religiosity. This had two aspects, individual piety and a more or less common, though fiercely disputed, covenantal creed; taken together, the two made for a culture of prayer and argument that was independent of the more formal religious culture of pilgrimage and sacrifice. Sustained no doubt, as Weber says, by "circles of urban intellectuals," this informal religiosity also reached beyond such circles.[6] Had it not done so, the prophet would never have found his audience.

Or, prophecy would have taken a wholly different form. I will try to illustrate one alternative possibility out of the book of Jonah, a tale about a prophet sent by God to the city of Nineveh, where the appeal to Israel's history and law would obviously make

[4] *Prophecy in Ancient Israel*, p. 313.

[5] On the importance of "the court in the gates," see James Luther May, *Amos: A Commentary* (Philadelphia: Westminster, 1969), pp. 11, 93.

[6] *Ancient Judaism*, p. 279.

no sense. But first I need to say something more about the conditions under which the appeal does make sense — most crucially,
about the strength and legitimacy of lay religion. In part, this is a
matter of popular practices, like the practice of spontaneous prayer
that Moshe Greenberg has recently revealed to us.[7] But there is
also what we might call an idea or even a doctrine of lay religiosity. The doctrine is entirely appropriate to a covenantal
creed, and it is most clearly set forth in Deuteronomy, the crucial
exposition of Israel's covenant theology. The precise relation of
Deuteronomy to the prophetic movement is a subject of ongoing
scholarly debate. Did the prophets influence the Deuteronomic
writers, or the writers the prophets? It seems likely that influence
worked in both directions and in ways that we shall never wholly
understand. In any case, a large number of passages in the prophetic books echo (or anticipate?) the Deuteronomic text as we
now have it, and the covenantal tradition that Deuteronomy
elaborates is surely older than Amos, though the "discovery" of
the text did not take place until a century and a half after Amos'
prophecies.[8] So I shall take the book to suggest the doctrinal background of prophecy: a normative account of the informal and
unpriestly culture of prayer and argument.

I want to look briefly at two passages, the first from the end of
the book, the second from the beginning. Whether either of these
was part of the manuscript that turned up in Jerusalem in the year
621, I can't say; nor can anyone else. But they share the spirit of
the original as a covenantal document. The first passage is already
familiar to you since it formed the basis of the Talmudic story
with which I concluded my first lecture.

> For this commandment which I command thee this day, it is not
> hidden from thee [Hebrew: *felah*, alternatively translated, it is

---

[7] *Biblical Prose Prayer as a Window to the Popular Religion of Ancient Israel*
(Berkeley: University of California Press, 1983).

[8] See Anthony Phillips, "Prophecy and Law," in R. Coggins, A. Phillips, and
M. Knibb, eds., *Israel's Prophetic Tradition* (Cambridge: Cambridge University
Press, 1982), p. 218.

not too hard for thee]; neither is it far off. It is not in heaven,
that thou shouldest say, Who shall go up for us to heaven, and
bring it unto us, that we may hear it, and do it? Neither is it
beyond the sea .... But the word is very nigh unto thee, in thy
mouth, and in thy heart, that thou mayest do it.

[Deut. 30:11–14]

Moses, indeed, climbed the mountain, but no one need do that
again. There is no longer any special role for mediators between
the people and God. The law is not in heaven; it is a social possession. The prophet need only show the people their own hearts.
If his is a "voice in the wilderness" (Isaiah 40:3), it is not because
he has embarked on a heroic quest for God's commandments.
The image recalls the history of the people themselves, their own
wilderness time, when God's voice was the voice in the wilderness,
and reminds them that they already know the commandments.
And though they may need to be reminded, the knowledge is
readily renewed — for the Torah is not an esoteric teaching. It
isn't hidden, obscure, difficult (the Hebrew word has all these
meanings; also, marvelous and "set aside," as a sacred text might
be set aside for a body of specially trained priests). The teaching
is available, common, popular, so much so that everyone is commanded to speak about it:

> And these words which I command thee this day shall be in
> thine heart: And thou shalt teach them diligently unto thy chil-
> dren, and shalt talk of them when thou sittest in thine house,
> and when thou walkest by the way, and when thou liest down
> and when thou risest up.
>
> [Deut. 6:6–7]

Prophecy is a special kind of talking, not so much an educated
as an inspired and poetic version of what must have been at least
sometimes, among some significant part of the prophet's audience,
ordinary discourse. Not only ritual repetition of key texts, but
heartfelt prayer, storytelling, doctrinal debate: the Bible provides

evidence for all of this, and prophecy is continuous with it, dependent upon it. Although there is conflict between the prophets and the established priesthood, prophecy does not in any sense constitute an underground or, as we shall see, a sectarian movement. In the dispute between Amos and the priest Amaziah, it is the prophet who appeals to religious tradition, the priest only to reason of state (7:10–17). Prophecy aims to arouse remembrance, recognition, indignation, repentance. In Hebrew, the last of these words derives from a root meaning to turn, to turn back, to return, and so it implies that repentance is parasitic upon a previously accepted and commonly understood morality. The same implication is apparent in prophecy itself. The prophet foretells doom, but it isn't only fear of coming disasters but also knowledge of the law, a sense of their own history, and a feeling for the religious tradition that motivate his listeners. Prophetic admonition, writes Moshe Greenberg,

> presupposes common ground on which prophet and audience stand, not only regarding historical traditions but religious demands as well. The prophets seem to appeal to their audience's better nature, confronting them with demands of God that they know (or knew) but wish to ignore or forget. . . . There is more than a little optimism underlying the generations-long succession of reforming prophets; it reflects the prophets' confidence that, in the final analysis, they had advocates in the hearts of their audience.[9]

3

Contrast this view, now, with the example provided by the book of Jonah. This is a late (post-exilic) tale commonly taken to argue for the universalism of divine law and divine concern — though universalism is, as we will see, an ancient argument. Perhaps Jonah is an ancient tale, retold sometime after the return from Babylonia as an attack upon the parochialism of the Judean

---

[9] *Prose Prayer*, p. 56.

restoration. The immediate issue of the story is the reversibility of divine decree, an issue raised, at least implicitly, in the earliest prophets.[10] That God Himself is capable of "repentance" is suggested by Amos (7:3), and there is a striking example even earlier, in the Exodus story. But I want to stress another feature of the book of Jonah, and contrast the content of Jonah's message with that of the prophets in Israel. The contrast would be sharper if the Jonah of the tale could be identified with the prophet Jonah son of Amitai mentioned in II Kings 14:25, a contemporary of Amos, but it does not depend upon the identification. For my immediate purposes the provenance of the tale and its author's intentions matter less than the tale itself. I shall take the "plot" literally and pass over its obvious ironies (the fact, for example, that the Ninevans actually repented, while none of Israel's own prophets could report a similar success). When he prophesies doom in Nineveh, Jonah is necessarily a different sort of prophet than Amos in Beth-El or Micah in Jerusalem — for doom is the entire content of his prophecy. He can't refer to a religious tradition or a moral law embodied in covenantal form. Whatever the religion of the inhabitants of Nineveh, Jonah appears to know nothing about it and to take no interest in it. He is a detached critic of Ninevan society, and his prophecy is a single sentence: "Yet forty days and Nineveh shall be overthrown" (3:4).

Now, "overthrown" is the verb used in Genesis to describe the fate of Sodom and Gomorrah, and it serves to assimilate Nineveh to these two cities. All three are condemned because of the "wickedness" of their inhabitants. Nahum Sarna suggests a further comparison, based on another repeated word. Nineveh is charged with the crime of "violence," echoing the charge that explains the flood: "and the earth was filled with violence" (Genesis 6:11).

---

[10] Yehezkel Kaufmann, *The Religion of Israel*, trans. by Moshe Greenberg (Chicago: University of Chicago Press, 1960), pp. 282–84, argues that the book of Jonah as we have it dates from the eighth century, but few scholars agree with him.

In neither case is anything more specific said.[11] Sodom's wickedness is at least minimally specified: its immediate form is the sexual mistreatment of guests and strangers. But we actually know very little about the internal life of Sodom or the moral history or commitments of its citizens. And we know even less about the world before the flood or about the faraway city of Nineveh. Jonah tells us nothing at all: this is prophecy without poetry, without resonance, allusion, or concrete detail. The prophet comes and goes, an alien voice, a mere messenger, unconnected to the people of the city. Even the regard for the people that God teaches him at the end is only a rather abstract "pity" for the "six score thousand persons that cannot discern between their right hand and their left hand . . ." (4:11).

This last phrase probably refers to the children of Nineveh; the adults, it appears, have some discernment, for they do repent. Though Jonah does not say anything about it, there is some moral knowledge to which they can return, some basic understanding that God and his prophet alike presuppose. Of course, Nineveh has its own moral and religious history, its own creed, its own code, its own shrines and priests — its own gods. But it's not Jonah's purpose to remind the people of what is their own; only a local prophet (a connected critic) could do that. Try to imagine Jonah in conversation with the Ninevans: what could he have said? Conversation is parasitic on commonality, and since commonality is minimal here, we can imagine only a minimal conversation. It's not that there is nothing to say, but the talk would be thin, centered on those moral understandings that don't depend upon communal life; there would be little room for nuance or subtlety. Thus Jonah's prophecy, and his achievement: the people recognize and turn away "from the violence that is in their hands" (3:8). Now, what is this "violence" whose recognition does not depend upon a particular moral or religious history?

[11] Nahum Sarna, *Understanding Genesis: The Heritage of Biblical Israel* (New York: Schocken, 1970), p. 145.

The first two chapters of the book of Amos provide an answer to this question. Here the prophet "judges" a group of nations with which Israel has recently been at war, and he provides a brief, though sometimes obscure, account of their crimes. Damascus "threshed Gilead with sledges of iron" — a reference, apparently, to extreme cruelty in warfare; Gaza "carried away captive a whole captivity"; Tyre violated a treaty; Edom pursued "his brother with the sword, and did cast off all pity"; Ammon "ripped up the women with child of Gilead"; Moab burned the bones of the king of Edom — denying him honorable burial. All these are crimes of "violence," and in all of them the victims are enemies and strangers, not fellow citizens. These are the only crimes for which the "nations" (in contrast to Israel and Judah) are punished. The prophet judges Israel's neighbors only for violations of a minimal code, "a form of international religious law," Weber suggests, "presupposed as valid among the Palestine peoples." [12] Of the substantive social morality of these peoples, their domestic practices and institutions, Amos, like Jonah in Nineveh, has nothing to say.

Amos' judgment of the nations suggests not a late and innovative but an early and familiar universalism. The existence of a kind of international law, fixing the treatment of enemies and strangers, seems to be presupposed in the story of Sodom and Gomorrah, to which Amos refers casually (4:11) as if his audience knows it well, and some such minimal code may also underlie the story of the flood. The author of the book of Jonah, centuries later, adds nothing to the argument. God will punish "violence" wherever it occurs. But alongside this universalism there is a more particularist message, delivered only (at least by Israelite prophets) to the children of Israel:

> You only have I known of all the
>   families of the earth;
> Therefore I will visit upon you all
>   your iniquities [3:2].

[12] *Ancient Judaism*, p. 302.

All your iniquities, domestic as well as international: the elaboration of this phrase constitutes the particular morality, the substantive argument of the prophets.

4

The concern of the prophets is for *this* people, their own people, the "family" that came up out of Egypt (2:10). (I will ignore for my present purposes the political division between the rival kingdoms of Israel and Judah; the two share a history and a law, and prophets like Amos go back and forth between them.) Jonah has no personal interest in Nineveh and no knowledge, as I have already argued, of its moral history. Hence Martin Buber is wrong to call the Jonah story a "paradigm of the prophetic nature and task." [13] The paradigmatic task of the prophets is to judge the people's relations with one another (and with "their" God), to judge the internal character of their society, which is exactly what Jonah does not do. Prophetic teaching, writes Lindblom more accurately, "is characterized by the principle of solidarity. Behind the demand for charity and justice . . . lies the idea of the *people*, the people as an organic whole, united by election and covenant" — singled out, we might say, by a peculiar history.[14] Committed to this solidarity, the prophets avoid sectarianism just as they avoid any larger universalism. They attempt no further singling out; they make no effort to gather around themselves a band of "brethren." When they address their audience they always use inclusive proper names — Israel, Joseph, Jacob; their focus is always on the fate of the covenanted community as a whole.

For the same reason, the message of the prophets is resolutely this-worldly. Theirs is a social and workaday ethic. Two points are crucial here, both of which I take from Weber, whose com-

---

[13] Martin Buber, *The Prophetic Faith* (New York: Harper and Brothers, 1960), p. 104.

[14] *Prophecy in Ancient Israel*, p. 344 (emphasis in the original).

parative perspective is especially illuminating.[15] First, there is no prophetic utopia, no account (in the style of Plato, say) of the "best" political or religious regime, a regime free from history, located anywhere or nowhere. The prophets don't have philosophical imaginations. They are rooted, for all their anger, in their own societies. The house of Israel is here, and it needs only to be ordered in accordance with its own laws. Second, the prophets take no interest in individual salvation or in the perfection of their own souls. They are not religious adepts or mystics; they never advocate asceticism or world-rejection. Wrong-doing and right-doing are alike social experiences, and the prophet and his listeners are involved in these experiences in accordance with the principle of solidarity, whether or not any given right or wrong act is their own. Utopian speculation and world-rejection are two forms of escape from particularism. The two always take culturally specific forms, of course, but they are in principle available without regard to cultural identity: anyone can leave the world behind, anyone can come to "nowhere." The prophetic argument, by contrast, is that this people must live in this way.

The prophets invoke a particular religious tradition and a particular moral law, both of which they assume their audience to know. The references are constant, and while some of them are mysterious to us, they were presumably not mysterious to the men and women who gathered at Beth-El or Jerusalem to listen. We need footnotes, but prophecy is not, like some modern poetry, meant to be read with footnotes. Consider, for example, these lines from Amos, which follow close upon the famous passage about selling the righteous for silver and the needy for a pair of shoes:

> And they lay themselves down beside
>   every altar
> Upon clothes taken in pledge [2:8].

---

[15] *Ancient Judaism*, pp. 275, 285, 313–14.

The reference here is to the law of Exodus 22:26–27 (part of the Book of the Covenant): "If thou at all take thy neighbor's raiment to pledge, thou shalt deliver it unto him by the time the sun goeth down: For that is his covering only, it is his raiment for his skin: wherein shall he sleep?" The prophet's complaint makes no sense without the law. Whether the law was already written down (as seems likely in this case) or known only through an oral tradition, the point is that it was known — and, judging from the form of the reference, commonly known. It's also worth saying that it isn't universally known, not the law and not the morality behind the law. We have different ideas about the pledge (the pawn), and it's not obvious that our ideas are unjust.

But the prophets don't only recall and repeat the tradition, they also interpret and revise it. I have sometimes encountered efforts to deny the value of the prophetic example for a general understanding of social criticism by arguing that Israel possessed an unusually coherent moral tradition — whereas we, by contrast, have only competing traditions and endless disagreements.[16] But the coherence of Israelite religion is more a consequence than a precondition of the work of the prophets. Their prophecies, together with the writings of the Deuteronomic school, begin the creation of something we might call normative Judaism. It is important to stress, as I have done, the pre-existing moral and legal codes, the sense of a common past, the depth of popular religiosity. But all this was still theologically inchoate, highly contentious, radically pluralistic in form. In fact, the prophets pick and choose among the available materials. What priests like

---

[16] Or, alternatively, it is pointed out that Amos can speak in the name of God, while we can claim no such authority. This makes a difference, of course, but not of a relevant kind. Criticism is an adversarial proceeding, and the relevant comparison is between the critic and his adversary, not between critics from one culture and critics from another. And Amos' adversaries also spoke in God's name, while the adversaries of contemporary social critics make no such claim. What is similar across cultures is the similarity within cultures: the same resources — authoritative texts, memories, values, practices, and conventions — are (always) available to social critics and to defenders of the status quo.

Amaziah take to be "secondary and subordinate" in Israelite religion, the prophets take "to be primary . . . the nucleus of a new . . . theoretical complex." Or, to put the same point differently, the prophets try to work up a picture of the tradition that will make sense to, and connect with the experience of, their own contemporaries. They are parasitic upon the past, but they also give shape to the past upon which they are parasitic.[17]

Even here, they probably don't act alone. Just as we need to resist the portrayal of ancient Israel as a special case of moral coherence, so we need to resist the portrayal of the prophets as peculiar, eccentric, and lonely individuals. They are no more alone when they interpret the Israelite creed than they are when they repeat the creed. Interpretation as I have been describing it, as the prophets practiced it, is a common activity. The new emphasis upon the social code of Exodus, for example, is almost certainly rooted in discussions and arguments that went on — they are easy to imagine — in the cities of Israel and Judah. Amos can hardly have been the first person to realize that the law of the pledge was being violated. He speaks against a background of urban growth and class differentiation that gave that law, and all the Exodus laws, a new relevance. Similarly, the prophetic de-emphasis of ritual sacrifice is rooted in popular piety, in the rejection or avoidance of priestly mediation, in a spontaneous acting out, through individual prayer, of the ancient dream that all Israel would be "a kingdom of priests and a holy nation." [18] Still, it is the proph-

---

[17] Some commentators have argued that the prophets break more radically with the past than this last paragraph suggests. Walther Zimmerli, for example, writes that the prophetic "proclamation" overwhelms, even as it exploits, traditional material and therefore cannot be captured under the rubric of "interpretation." Tradition, he writes, "in the salutary sense of the term, shatters and becomes an empty shell of mere historical recollection. . . ." But this ignores the content of the prophetic proclamation, the terms or standards to which Israel is held. Judgment would be entirely arbitrary if it did not refer to standards with which the people were, or were supposed to be, familiar. Amos makes that reference systematically. See "Prophetic Proclamation and Reinterpretation," in *Tradition and Theology in the Old Testament*, Douglas Knight, ed. (Philadelphia: Fortress Press, n.d.), p. 99.

[18] Greenberg, *Prose Prayer*, p. 52.

ets who most clearly establish the link between piety and conduct and who most explicitly use the Exodus laws as a weapon of social criticism.

As I have already been doing, I shall follow here the argument of Amos, in whose work both the new emphasis and the new de-emphasis are dramatically displayed. We must assume the social changes that precede and motivate his prophecy: the introduction of greater and greater inequalities into what had been, and still was ideally, an association of freemen. No doubt, inequality of some sort was already ancient, else there would have been no ancient social code aimed at ameliorating its effects. But by the eighth century, the years of monarchic rule had produced in and around the court and in the growing cities a new upper class feeding on a new lower class. Archaeological finds, more explicit in this case than they usually are, confirm the development: "the simple, uniform houses of the earlier centuries had been replaced by luxurious dwellings of the rich on the one hand, by hovels on the other." [19] Amos is, above all, a critic of this new upper class, whose members were increasingly capable of and committed to what we now call a high standard of living, with winter houses and summer houses (3:15), couches of ivory (6:4), sumptuous feasts, and costly perfumes:

> That drink wine in bowls
> And anoint themselves with the chief
> ointments ... [6:6].

The prophet's caustic description of all this is often characterized as a kind of rural puritanism, the dislike of a countryman for city fanciness.[20] Perhaps there is something to this view,

---

[19] Martin Smith, *Palestinian Parties and Politics that Shaped the Old Testament* (New York: Columbia University Press, 1971), p. 139.

[20] For example, Blenkensopp, *History of Prophecy*, p. 95, and Henry McKeating, *The Cambridge Bible Commentary: Amos, Hosea, Micah* (Cambridge: Cambridge University Press, 1971), p. 5.

though I have already suggested that prophecy draws upon urban experience and argument. If the prophet sometimes looks at the city from a distance, he more often looks only at the city's rich and powerful citizens from a distance, that is, from the perspective of the men and women they oppressed. And he then invokes values that even the oppressors pretend to share. Amos' main charge, his critical message, is not that the rich live well but that they live well at the expense of the poor. They have forgotten not only the laws of the covenant but the bond itself, the principle of solidarity: "They are not grieved for the hurt of Joseph" (6:6). More than this: they are themselves responsible for the hurt of Joseph; they are guilty of the Egyptian crime of oppression.

Amos' word for "oppress" is *'ashok*; he uses the Exodus word *lahatz* only once (6:14), when he is describing what will happen to Israel at the hands of an unnamed foreign power. The shift in terminology suggests nicely how Amos (or unknown speakers or writers before him) responds, within the tradition, to a new social experience. *Lahatz* means to press down, to squeeze, to crush, to constrain, to coerce. The range of meanings evoked by *'ashok* is quite different: to maltreat, to exploit, to wrong, to injure, to extort, to defraud. *Lahatz* has political, *'ashok* economic connotations. Of course, Egyptian oppression was also economic in character, and in eighth-century Israel and Judah the oppression of the poor was upheld by the monarchic regimes. Amos condemns both the "great houses" and the "palaces." But the primary experience was of tyranny in the first case, extortion and exploitation in the second. The new bondage had its origin in commerce — usury, indebtedness, default, and confiscation; its setting was more significantly the market than the state. Amos addresses himself specifically to avaricious merchants:

> Hear this, O ye that would swallow
>   the needy
> And destroy the poor of the land,
> Saying, When will the new moon be
>   gone, that we may sell grain?

> And the Sabbath, that we may set
>   forth corn?
> Making the ephah small and the
>   shekel great?
> And falsifying the balances of
>   deceit;
> That we may buy the poor for silver,
> And the needy for a pair of shoes,
> And sell the refuse of the corn [8:4–6].

The address, indeed, is doubly specific: avaricious *Israelite* merchants, who can hardly wait for the end of Israel's holy days, when business dealings were forbidden, so that they could return to the business of extortion and fraud. Amos suggests a hard question: what kind of religion is it that provides only temporary and intermittent restraints on avarice and oppression? What is the quality of worship if it does not direct the heart toward goodness? As the prophet describes them, the oppressors of the poor and needy are scrupulously "orthodox." They observe the festival of the new moon, they keep the Sabbath, they attend the religious assemblies, offer the required sacrifices, join in the hymns that accompany the priestly rites. But all this is mere hypocrisy if it doesn't translate into everyday conduct in accordance with the covenantal code. Ritual observance alone is not what God requires of Israel. Pointing toward the real requirement, Amos evokes the memory of the Exodus: "Did ye bring unto Me sacrifices and offerings in the wilderness forty years, O house of Israel?" (5:25). In the Exodus story as we have it, they did; perhaps Amos had access to an alternative tradition.[21] But the practice of sacrifice is not, in any case, what was to be learned from the experience of liberation. Indeed, if oppression continues, nothing has been learned, however many animals are sacrificed.

This is the standard form of social criticism, and though later critics rarely achieve the angry poetry of the prophets, we can

---

[21] McKeating, *Amos, Hosea, Micah*, p. 47.

recognize in their work the same intellectual structure: the identification of public pronouncements and respectable opinion as
hypocritical, the attack upon actual behavior and institutional arrangements, the search for core values (to which hypocrisy is
always a clue), the demand for an everyday life in accordance
with the core. The critic begins with revulsion and ends with
affirmation:

> I hate, I despise your feasts,
> And I will take no delight in your
>   solemn assemblies.
> Yea, though ye offer me burnt-
>   offerings and your meal-
>   offerings,
> I will not accept them. . . .
> Take thou away from me the noise of
>   thy songs;
> And let me not hear the melody of
>   thy psalteries.
> But let justice well up as waters,
> And righteousness as a mighty
>   stream [5:21–24].

The only purpose of the ceremonies is to remind the people of
their moral commitments: God's law and the wilderness covenant.
If that purpose is not served, then the ceremonies are of no use.
Less than no use: for they generate among rich and avaricious
Israelites a false sense of security — as if they were safe from
divine wrath. The prophecies of doom, which make up so much
of Amos' message, are designed to dispel that sense, to shatter the
confidence of the conventionally pious: "Woe to them that are at
ease in Zion" (6:1). Neither "woe" nor "hate" constitutes the
substance of Amos' argument, however; the substance is "justice"
and "righteousness."

But how does the prophet know that justice and righteousness
are the core values of the Israelite tradition? Why not pilgrimage

and sacrifice, song and solemnity? Why not ritual decorum and deference to God's priests? Presumably if Amaziah had offered a positive defense of his own activities at Beth-El, he would have given us a different picture of Israelite values. How then would the argument between Amaziah and Amos move toward closure? Both priest and prophet could cite texts — there is never a lack of texts — and both would find supporters in the crowd that gathered at the shrine. I have been arguing that disagreements of this sort don't in fact move toward closure, not, at least, definitive closure. Nor would they even if God Himself were to intervene: for all He can provide is another text, subject to interpretation exactly like the earlier ones. "It is not in heaven." Still, we can recognize good and bad arguments, strong and weak interpretations along the way. In this case, it is significant that Amaziah makes no positive claims at all. His silence is a kind of admission that Amos has provided a convincing account of Israelite religion — also, perhaps, that he has found, as Greenberg says, advocates in the hearts of the people. That doesn't end the disagreement, and not only because the prophet is apparently forced to leave Beth-El, while Amaziah continues his priestly routines. The claim that God is better served by scrupulous worship of Himself than by just dealings with one's fellows, even if it is only made implicitly, has an enduring appeal: worship is easier than justice. But Amos has won a kind of victory, the only kind that is available: he has evoked the core values of his audience in a powerful and plausible way. He suggests an identification of the poor in Israel with the Israelite slaves in Egypt, and so makes justice the primary religious demand. Why else did God deliver the people, *this people*, from the house of bondage?

5

Amos' prophecy is social criticism because it challenges the leaders, the conventions, the ritual practices of a particular society and because it does so in the name of values recognized and shared in that same society.[22] I have already distinguished this sort of prophecy from the sort represented by Jonah in Nineveh: Jonah is a mere messenger who makes no appeal to social values, though he may appeal, without saying so, to a minimal code, a kind of international law. He isn't a missionary, carrying with him an alternative doctrine; he doesn't try to convert the people of Nineveh to Israel's religion, to bring them into the Sinai covenant. He just represents the minimal code (and God, its minimal author, who can have for the Ninevans none of the historical specificity that he has for the Israelites). We can think of Jonah as a minimalist critic; we don't really know what sorts of changes he required in the life of Nineveh, but they were presumably nowhere near so extensive as those required by Amos in Israel.

What makes the difference is Amos' membership. His criticism goes deeper than Jonah's because he knows the fundamental values of the men and women he criticizes (or because he tells them a plausible story about which of their values ought to be fundamental). And since he in turn is recognized as one of them, he can call them back to their "true" path. He suggests reforms that they can undertake while still remaining fellow members of the same society. Amos can, of course, be read differently: the prophecies of doom are so powerful and unrelenting that, on some interpretations, they overwhelm any possible argument for repentance and reform. And then the pleas for justice and the promises of divine comfort at the end seem unconvincing — as if they come (as many commentators believe, at least of the promises) from another hand.[23] The animating passion of the book as a whole, however, is surely a deep concern for "the hurt of

---

[22] It is useful to compare this account of prophecy with Raymond Geuss's preferred version (it isn't the only version) of critical theory: "A critical theory is addressed to members of *this* particular social group . . . it describes *their* epistemic principles and *their* ideal of the 'good life' and demonstrates that some belief they hold is reflectively unacceptable for agents who hold their epistemic principles and a source of frustration for agents who are trying to realize this particular kind of 'good life.'" *Idea of a Critical Theory,* p. 63 (emphasis in the original).

[23] May, *Amos,* pp. 164–65, but see McKeating, *Amos, Hosea, Micah,* pp. 69–70.

Joseph," a powerful sense of solidarity, a commitment to the covenant that makes Israel . . . Israel. It isn't only his anger but also his concern and commitment that make Amos a critic. He aims at an internal reformation that will bring the new oppression of Israel, or of poor and needy Israelites, to an end. That is the social meaning he has in mind when he repeats (or anticipates) the Deuteronomic injunction, "Seek good, and not evil, that ye may live" (5:15; cf. Deut. 30:15–20).

Amos also prophesies, as we have seen, against nations other than Israel. Here he is a critic from the outside, like Jonah, and he limits himself to external behavior, violations of some sort of international law. I don't mean to suggest, however, that the provisions of Israel's covenant have no general validity. No doubt, one could abstract universal rules from them — above all, one universal rule: *don't oppress the poor* (for oppression is, as Weber writes, "the pre-eminent vice" in the eyes of the Israelite prophets).[24] And then one could judge and condemn the oppression of Syrians, or Philistines, or Moabites by their avaricious fellows in the same way that the prophets judge and condemn the oppression of Israelites. But not, in fact, in the same way; not with the same words, images, references; not with regard to the same practices and religious principles. For the power of a prophet like Amos derives from his ability to say what oppression means, how it is experienced, in this time and place, and to explain how it is connected with other features of a shared social life. Amos has an argument to make about oppression and religious observance, for example, and it is one of his chief arguments: that it is entirely possible to trample upon the poor and to observe the Sabbath. And from this he concludes that the laws against oppression take precedence over the Sabbath laws. The hierarchy is specific; it invites the prophet's listeners to remember that one of the purposes of the Sabbath was "that thy manservant and thy maid-

[24] *Ancient Judaism*, p. 281.

servant may rest as well as thou" (Deut. 5:14). Prophecy would
have little life, and little effect, if it could not evoke memories of
this sort. We might think of it then as an academic exercise. In a
strange country, Amos would resemble Samson in Gaza. Not eye-
less, but tongueless: he might indeed see the oppression, but he
would not be able to give it a name or speak about it to the hearts
of the people.

Of course, other nations can read and admire the Israelite
prophets, translate the prophecies into their own language (foot-
noting the references), and find analogies in their own society for
the practices the prophets condemn. Just how wide the actual
range of reading and admiration is, I am not sure. It obviously
doesn't coincide with the possible range, and it may well be
limited to those nations whose history is in some significant sense
continuous with the history of Israel. In principle, though, it could
extend further than that. What would it mean if it did? It's unlikely, I think, that what distant readers would learn from the
prophets would be a set of abstract rules — or, again, a single
rule: *don't oppress the poor.* If they knew what oppression was
(if they could translate the Hebrew word *'ashok*), they would
already know that much. The rule, though it might have different
references and applications, would be familiar. More likely, distant readers would be moved to imitate the practice of prophecy
(or, perhaps, to listen in a new way to their own prophets). It is
the practice, not the message, that would be repeated. Readers
might learn to be social critics; the criticism, however, would be
their own. Indeed, the message would have to be different if the
practice was to be the same — else it would lack the historical
reference and moral specificity that prophecy (and social criticism) requires.

The case is different with regard to Amos' prophecies against
the nations. Here it is precisely the message, the minimal code,
that gets repeated: don't violate treaties, don't kill innocent
women and children, don't transport whole nations into involun-

tary exile. Confirmed from many sides, these rules are incorporated into a law of nations that isn't all that more extensive than the "international" law of Amos' time. But their prophetic utterance is quickly forgotten. For the utterance is a mere assertion and not an interpretation or elaboration of the law; reference and specificity, though Amos provides a brief version of both, are in fact unnecessary. Can a useful distinction be drawn between these two sorts of rules — those against violence and those against oppression? The two have the same linguistic form; each of them extends toward the other and there will always be considerable overlap between them. The minimal code is relevant to and presumably plays a part in the development of more substantive social values; and then the code itself takes on some particular form depending on how those values develop. And yet the two are not the same. The rules against violence arise from the experience of international as well as internal relations, the rules against oppression from internal relations alone. The first regulate our contacts with all humanity, strangers as well as citizens; the second regulate only our common life. The first are stereotyped in form and application; they are set against a background of standard expectations, based on a narrow range of standard experiences (war the most prominent among them). The second are complex in form and various in application; they are set against a background of multiple and conflicting expectations, rooted in a long and dense social history. The first tend toward universality, the second toward particularity.

It is a mistake, then, to praise the prophets for their universalist message. For what is most admirable about them is their particularist quarrel, which is also, they tell us, God's quarrel, with the children of Israel. Here they invested their anger and their poetic genius. The line that Amos attributes to God, "You only have I known of all the families of the earth," could have come from his own heart. He knows one nation, one history, and it's that knowledge that makes his criticism so rich, so radical, so concrete. We can, again, abstract the rules and apply them to other nations, but that's not the "use" that Amos invites. What he invites is not application but reiteration. Each nation can have its own prophecy, just as it has its own history, its own deliverance, its own quarrel with God.

> Have I not brought up Israel out of
>   the land of Egypt,
> And the Philistines from Caphtor,
> And Aram from Kir? [9:7]

The Uncanniness of the Ordinary

STANLEY CAVELL

The Tanner Lectures on Human Values

Delivered at
Stanford University

April 3 and 8, 1986

STANLEY CAVELL was born in Atlanta, Georgia, in 1926. He is currently Walter M. Cabot Professor of Aesthetics and the General Theory of Value at Harvard University. He is author of many books including *Must We Mean What We Say?* and *Disowning Knowledge: In Six Plays of Shakespeare*. In 1985 he received the Morton Dauwen Zabel Award in Criticism and was selected for the Frederick Ives Carpenter Lectures at the University of Chicago. In 1987 he received an honorary Doctor of Humane Letters, also from the University of Chicago. His latest work, *In Quest of the Ordinary: Lines in Skepticism and Romanticism*, will be published in 1988.

The prospect of delivering the Tanner Lecture inclined me and encouraged me to attempt to fit together into some reasonable, or say convivial, circle a collection of the main beasts in my jungle or wilderness of interests. An obvious opening or pilot beast is that of the concept of the ordinary, since the first essay I published that I still use (the title essay of the collection *Must We Mean What We Say?*) was begun as a defense of the work of my teacher J. L. Austin, the purest representative of so-called ordinary language philosophy. In anticipation of this attempt I scheduled last year at Harvard a set of courses designed to bring myself before myself. In that fall I offered a course entitled The Philosophy of the Ordinary in which I lectured for the first time in six or seven years on certain texts of Austin's and on Wittgenstein's *Philosophical Investigations*, with an increasing sense at once of my continuing indebtedness to this body of thought and practice, and at the same time with a sense of its relative neglect in contemporary intellectual life — a neglect at any rate of the aspect of this thought and practice that engages me most, namely the devotion to the so-called ordinariness or everydayness of language. In the spring semester I turned to one seminar on recent psychoanalytic literary criticism and to another on some late essays of Heidegger's, in both of which bodies of work desperate fresh antagonisms seem to be set up against the ideas of ordinary language philosophy. What I propose to do here is mostly to sketch a topography of certain texts and concepts from that year of courses in which these fresh antagonisms may serve to test the resources of the views in question.

Before entering the topography I must say something about the title I have given this material — the uncanniness of the ordinary. When I hit on this phrase I remembered it as occurring in

Freud's essay "The Uncanny," [1] but when I checked the text I learned that it does not. I had at the same time forgotten that the phrase more or less does occur in Heidegger, in "The Origin of the Work of Art." [2] Its occurrence in Heidegger is pertinent, but my intuition of the ordinariness of human life, and of its avoidance of the ordinary, is not Heidegger's. For him the extraordinariness of the ordinary has to do with forces in play, beyond the grasp and the reach of ordinary awareness, that constitute our habitual world; it is a constitution he describes as part of his account of the technological, of which what we accept as the ordinary is as it were one consequence; it is thus to be seen as a symptom of what Nietzsche prophesied, or diagnosed, in declaring that for us "the wasteland grows." [3] Whereas for me the uncanniness of the ordinary is epitomized by the possibility or threat of what philosophy has called skepticism, understood (as in my studies of Austin and of the later Wittgenstein I have come to understand it) as the capacity, even desire, of ordinary language to repudiate itself, specifically to repudiate its power to word the world, to apply to the things we have in common, or to pass them by. (By "the desire of ordinary language to repudiate itself" I mean — doesn't it go without saying? — a desire on the part of speakers of a native or mastered tongue who desire to assert themselves, and despair of it.) (An affinity between these views of the ordinary, suggesting the possibility of mutual derivation, is that both Heidegger's and mine respond to the fantastic in what human beings will accustom themselves to, call this the surrealism of the habitual — as if to be human is forever to be prey to turning your corner of the human race, hence perhaps all of it, into some new species of the genus of humanity, for the better or for the worse.

[1] Sigmund Freud, "The Uncanny," Standard Edition, vol. 17, pp. 219–52.

[2] In *Poetry, Language, Thought*, trans. Albert Hofstadter (New York: Harper and Row, 1971), p. 54.

[3] Martin Heidegger, *What Is Called Thinking?*, trans. J. Glenn Gray and Fred D. Wieck (New York: Harper and Row, 1968), pp. 38, 49, 60, 64, and elsewhere.

I might describe my philosophical task as one of outlining the necessity, and the lack of necessity, in the sense of the human as inherently strange, say unstable, its quotidian as forever fantastic. In what follows I am rather at pains to record variations of this sense in certain writers not customarily or habitually, say institutionally, called philosophers.) What all of this comes from and leads to is largely what the five hundred pages of *The Claim of Reason* is about. I hope enough of it will get through in this lecture to capture a sense of what I take to be at stake.

One general caution. I am not here going to make a move toward deriving the skeptical threat philosophically. My idea is that what in philosophy is known as skepticism (for example as in Descartes and Hume and Kant) is a relation to the world, and to others, and to myself, and to language, that is known to what you might call literature, or anyway responded to in literature, in uncounted other guises — in Shakespeare's tragic heroes, in Emerson's and Thoreau's "silent melancholy" and "quiet desperation," in Wordsworth's perception of us as without "interest," in Poe's "perverseness." Why philosophy and literature do not know this about one another — and to that extent remain unknown to themselves — has been my theme it seems to me forever.

It may help give a feel for what is at stake for me if I spell out a little my response to discovering that the phrase "the uncanniness of the ordinary" is not in Freud's text. My response was, a little oddly and roughly, to think: "That's not my fault, but Freud's; he hadn't grasped his own subject." A cause of my response has to do with a pair of denials, or rather with one denial and one error, in Freud's reading of the E. T. A. Hoffmann story called "The Sandman" with which the essay on the uncanny occupies itself.[4] Freud introduces the Hoffmann story by citing its treatment in the only discussion in German in the "medico-

---

[4] I use the translation of the Hoffmann story in *Selected Writings of E. T. A. Hoffmann*, ed. and trans. by Elizabeth C. Knight and Leonard J. Kent (Chicago: University of Chicago Press, 1969), vol. 1, pp. 137–67.

psychological" literature Freud had found on the subject of the uncanny, an article from 1906 by a certain Jentsch. Jentsch attributes the sense of the uncanny to the recognition of an uncertainty in our ability to distinguish the animate from the inanimate: Hoffmann's story features the beautiful automaton Olympia whom its hero falls in love with (precipitated by his viewing her through a magic spyglass constructed by one of her constructors). At first this love serves for the amusement of others who are certain they see right through the inanimateness of the machine; but then the memory of the love serves to feed their anxiety that they may be making the same error with their own beloveds — quite as though this anxiety about other minds, or other bodies, is a datable event in human history. (As in Hoffmann's story: "A horrible distrust of human figures in general arose.") The hero Nathaniel goes mad when he sees the automaton pulled apart by its two fathers, or makers. He is, before the final catastrophe, nursed back to health by his childhood sweetheart Clara, whom he had forgotten in favor of Olympia.

Now Freud denies, no fewer than four times, that the inability to distinguish the animate from the inanimate is what causes the sense of the uncanny, insisting instead that the cause of the undoubted feeling of the uncanny in Hoffmann's tale is the threat of castration. I find Freud's denial in this context to be itself uncanny, I mean to bear a taint of the mechanical or the compulsive and of the return of the repressed familiar, since there is no intellectual incompatibility between Freud's explanation and Jentsch's. One would have expected Sigmund Freud, otherwise claiming his inheritance of the poets and creative writers of his culture, to invoke the castration complex precisely as a new explanation or interpretation of the particular uncertainty in question, that is, to suggest it as Hoffmann's insight that one does not resolve the uncertainty, or achieve the clear distinction, between the animate and the inanimate, until the Oedipal drama is resolved under the threat of castration. Put otherwise: until that resolution one does not see others as other, know and acknowledge their (separate, animate, opposed) human existence. So put, this issue of the other's automatonity shows itself as a form of the skeptical problem concerning the existence of (what Anglo-American philosophy calls) other minds. And this opening of philosophy in the Hoffmann story suggests a way to understand Freud's as it were instinctive denial of the problem of animatedness as key to it. It is a striking and useful instance of Freud's repeated dissociation of psychoanalysis from philosophy, a dissociation, as I have argued elsewhere, in which Freud seems to me to be protesting too much, as though he knows his own uncertainty about how, even whether, psychoanalysis and philosophy *can* be distinguished, without fatal damage to each of them.[5]

Freud's insistent denial that the uncanny is unsurmountable (that is, his denial that it is a standing philosophical threat) is perhaps what causes (or is caused by) the straightforward error he makes in reading (or remembering) the closing moments of Hoffmann's tale.[6] Freud recounts as follows:

> From the top [of the tower] Clara's attention is drawn to a curious object moving along the street. Nathaniel looks at this thing through Coppola's spy-glass, which he finds in his pocket, and falls into a new attack of madness. . . . Among the people who begin to gather below there comes forward the figure of the lawyer Coppelius, who has suddenly returned. We may suppose that it was his approach, seen through the spy-glass, which threw Nathaniel into his fit of madness.

It is true that one *expects* Nathaniel — and doubtless so does he — as he takes out the glass, to direct it to whatever had caught

---

[5] Freud's repeated attempts to dissociate psychoanalysis from philosophy is one of the guiding topics of my essay "Psychoanalysis and Cinema: The Melodrama of the Unknown Woman," to appear in a volume entitled *The Images in Our Souls: Cavell, Psychoanalysis, Cinema*, constituting Volume X of the series sponsored by the Forum on Psychiatry and the Humanities, edited by Joseph Smith, M.D., to be published by the Johns Hopkins University Press in 1987.

[6] Samuel Weber, "The Sideshow, or: Remarks on a Canny Moment," *MLN* 88 (1973), 1102–33, notes the error but interprets it differently.

Clara's attention, and the ending suggests that this would have
been his father. But in fact (that is to say, in Hoffmann's tale)
what happens is something else: "Nathaniel . . . found Coppola's
spy-glass and looked to one side. Clara was standing in front of
the glass. There was convulsive throbbing in his pulse . . . ."
What we are, accordingly, climactically asked to think about is
not why a close spotting of Coppelius (whom Nathaniel never
finds in the glass), but rather a chance vision of Clara, causes
Nathaniel's reentry into madness. (We are asked to think indeed
of the significance that the woman has come between Nathaniel
and the object he sought, call this his father; rather than, as Freud
claims, of the father coming between the man and his desire. The
divided pairs of fathers would then signify not the father's power
but his impotence, or resignation.) Then the leap from the tower
is to the father, in accusation and appeal. Freud is awfully casual
about the power of the father's gift (or curse) of vision: what we
know about the father's glass until the climax on the tower is that,
in the glass, inanimate, constructed Olympia achieves animation
for Nathaniel. So let us continue at the end to grant the glass
that power. But how? Since Clara is — is she not? — animate,
shall we reverse the direction of the power of the glass and say
that it transforms Clara into an automaton? This is not unimag-
inable, but the irony of reversal seems too pat, too tame, to call
upon the complexity of issues released in Hoffmann's text.

I recall that Nathaniel had, in outrage at Clara's rejection of
his poetry, called her a "damned lifeless automaton," and from
the opening of the tale he expresses impatience with her refusal
to credit lower and hence higher realms of being — impatience
with, let me say, her ordinariness. (He has something of Heidegger's sense of the ordinary, the sense of it in one form of Romanticism.) Then when Nathaniel glimpses Clara in his glass we might
glimpse that again something has come to life for him — Clara as
she is, as it were, in her ordinariness, together with the knowledge
that he could not bear this ordinariness, her flesh-and-bloodness,

since it means bearing her separateness, her existence as other to him, exactly what his craving for the automaton permitted him to escape, one way or the other (either by demanding no response to the human or by making him an automaton). The concluding paragraph of the tale passes on a report that many years later Clara "had been seen in a remote district sitting hand in hand with a pleasant-looking man in front of the door of a splendid country house, two merry boys playing around her . . . that quiet, domestic happiness . . . which Nathaniel, with his lacerated soul, could never have provided her." My reading in effect takes this description as of the image Nathaniel came upon in the spyglass on the tower.

The glass is a death-dealing rhetoric machine, producing or expressing the consciousness of life in one case (Olympia's) by figuration, in the other (Clara's) by literalization, or say defiguration. One might also think of it as a machine of incessant animation, the parody of a certain romantic writing; and surely not unconnectedly as an uncanny anticipation of a movie camera. The moral of the machine I would draw provisionally this way: There is a repetition necessary to what we call life, or the animate, necessary for example to the human; and a repetition necessary to what we call death, or the inanimate, necessary for example to the mechanical; and there are no marks or features or criteria or rhetoric by means of which to tell the difference between them. From which, let me simply claim, it does not follow that the difference is unknowable or undecidable. On the contrary, the difference is the basis of everything there is for human beings to know, or say decide (like deciding to live), and to decide on no basis beyond or beside or beneath ourselves. Within the philosophical procedure of radical skepticism, the feature specifically allegorized by the machine of the spyglass is skepticism's happening all at once, the world's vanishing at the touch, perhaps, of the thought that you may be asleep dreaming that you are awake, the feature Descartes expresses in his "astonishment."

The essay of mine I cited a moment ago (note 5) in which I press the case of Freud's inheritance of philosophy, against his fervent dissociation of his work from it, is framed by a reading of Max Ophuls' film *Letter from an Unknown Woman* focused on the melodramatic gesture of horror elicited from the man who is sent the depicted letter, as he completes its reading. My reading of his death-dealing vision is very much along the lines of the one I have just given of Nathaniel's horror on looking through (or reading the images offered by) the spyglass — a horrified vision of ordinariness, of the unremarkable other seen as just that unremarkable other. You may feel, accordingly, that I wish to force every romantic melodrama to yield the same result. Or you may, I hope, feel that I have honestly come upon a matter that romantic tales of horror, and certain films that incorporate them, have in fact and in genre taken as among their fundamental subjects for investigation, say the acknowledgment of otherness, specifically as a spiritual task, one demanding a willingness for the experience of horror, and as a datable event in the unfolding of philosophical skepticism in the West.

Now let us turn to those courses I mentioned and their topography, associated with ideas of the ordinary, with the name of Heidegger, and with psychoanalytic literary criticism.

Wittgenstein says in the *Investigations*, "When I talk about language (words, sentences, etc.) I must speak the language of every day. Is this language somehow too coarse and material for what we want to say? *Then how is another one to be constructed?* — And how strange [merkwürdig] that we should be able to do anything at all with the one we have!" (§ 120). Strange, I expect Wittgenstein means immediately to imply, that we can formulate so precise and sophisticated a charge within and against our language as to find it "coarse" and "material." Are these terms of criticism themselves coarse and material? Now listen to words from two texts of Heidegger's, from the essay "Das Ding"

("The Thing")[7] and from his set of lectures *Was Heisst Denken?* (translated as *What Is Called Thinking?*), both published within three years before the publication of the *Investigations* in 1953. From "The Thing": "Today everything present is equally near and far. The distanceless prevails." And again: "Is not this merging [or lumping] of everything into [uniform distancelessness] more unearthly than everything bursting apart? Man stares at what the atom bomb could bring with it. He does not see that the atom bomb and its explosion are the mere final emission of what the atom bomb could bring with it. He does not see that the atom bomb and its explosion are the mere final emission of what has long since taken place, has already happened." What has already happened according to Heidegger is the shrinking or disintegration of the human in the growing dominion of a particular brand of thinking, a growing violence in our demand to grasp or explain the world. (I put aside for the moment my distrust, almost contempt, at the tone of Heidegger's observation, its attitude of seeming to exempt itself from the common need to behave under a threat whose absoluteness makes it [appear to us] unlike any earlier.) A connection with ordinary language of the fate of violent thinking and of distancelessness comes out in *What Is Called Thinking?*, where Heidegger says:

> A symptom, at first sight quite superficial, of the growing power of one-track thinking is the increase everywhere of designations consisting of abbreviations of words, or combinations of their initials. Presumably no one here has ever given serious thought to what has already come to pass when you, instead of University, simply say "Uni." "Uni" — that is like "Kino" ["Movie"]. True, the moving picture theater continues to be different from the academy of the sciences. [Does this suggest that one day they will not be different? How would this matter? How to Heidegger?] Still, the designation "Uni" is not accidental, let alone harmless. [P. 34]

---

[7] In *Poetry, Language, Thought*.

Reading this I ask myself: When I use the word "movies" (instead of "motion pictures"?, "cinema"?) am I really exemplifying, even helping along, the annihilation of the human? And then I think: The writer Heidegger cannot hear the difference between the useful non-speak or moon-talk of acronyms (UNESCO, NATO, MIRV, AIDS) and the intimacy (call it nearness) of passing colloquialisms and cult abbreviations (Kino, flick, shrink, Poli Sci, Phil). But then I think: No, it must be just that the force of Heidegger's thought here is not manifest in his choice of examples any more than it is in his poor efforts to describe the present state of industrial society (as if our awareness of the surface of these matters is to be taken for granted, as either sophisticated or as irredeemably naïve). In descriptions of the present state of Western society, the passion and accuracy of, say, John Stuart Mill's prose quite eclipses Heidegger's. And as to his invoking of popular language and culture, Heidegger simply hasn't the touch for it, the ear for it. These matters are more deeply perceived in, say, a movie of Alfred Hitchcock's.

To dispel for myself Heidegger's condescension in this region I glance at a line from Hitchcock's *North by Northwest* (the one in which Cary Grant is attacked by a crop-dusting plane in a Midwestern cornfield and in which he rescues a woman from the Mount Rushmore monument of the heads of four American presidents). The line is said by a man in response to Grant's asking him whether he is from the F.B.I.: "F.B.I., C.I.A., we're all in the same alphabet soup"; after which their conversation is drowned out by the roar of an airplane, toward which they are walking. At first glance, that line says that it doesn't matter what you say; but at second glance, or listening to the growl of the invisible motor, what the line says is that it matters that this does not matter. That line invokes (1) the name of a child's food, something to begin from; and (2) a colloquialism meaning that we are in a common peril; and (3) is a sentence whose six opening letters (initials) signal that we have forgotten, to our peril, the

ABC's of communication, namely the ability to speak together out of common interest. But have we forgotten it because we lack long or ancient words? It seems more worthwhile to ask why "F.B.I." abbreviates a name that has in it the same word as Wittgenstein's *Philosophical Investigations*, and to ask what the concept of intelligence is that the military have agencies and communities of it whereas universities do not. But if I am willing to excuse Heidegger provisionally for his lack of ear in such regions, then I must wait for my approach to them until I can invoke the writing of Ralph Waldo Emerson and of his disciple Henry David Thoreau, for both of whom the idea of nearness, or as Thoreau puts it, of nextness (by which he explicitly says he means *the nearest*), is also decisive, and whose concepts I feel I can follow on.

For the moment I turn to the other material I mentioned that is apparently antagonistic to ordinary language and its philosophy, that represented in my seminar on recent psychoanalytically shaped literary criticism, which began — in my effort to begin studying recent French thought in some systematic way — by reading moments in Jacques Lacan's controversial and perhaps too famous study of Edgar Allan Poe's tale "The Purloined Letter." [8] Lacan's professed reason for taking up the Poe story is its serviceability as an illustration of Freud's speculations concerning the repetition compulsion in *Beyond the Pleasure Principle*, an illustration suggested by the narrative feature of Poe's tale that a compromising letter, stolen by one person who leaves a substitute in its place, is restolen and returned to its original position by another person who leaves another substitute (or construction), in turn, in its place. Fastening on the shifts of identification established by this repeated structure of thefts or displacements of a letter, Lacan in effect treats Poe's tale as an allegory of what he understands psychoanalytic understanding to require — the tracing and return

---

[8] Jacques Lacan, "Seminar on the Purloined Letter," *Yale French Studies* 48 (*French Freud*) (1973).

of displaced signifiers. This understanding, together with the special art by which the letter is concealed, also constitutes the tale as an allegory of writing. I ask those of you for whom this, and the aftermath it has inspired, has all become too familiar to bear with me while I go over the tale again just far enough to indicate (something that has surprised me, even alarmed me) that it also forms at least as exact and developed an allegory of ordinary language philosophy. The sense of this application is given in Poe's tale's all but identifying itself as a study — and hence perhaps as an act — of mind-reading.

I believe that a certain offense taken toward ordinary language philosophy (from its inception in Austin and Wittgenstein until the present) is a function of some feeling that it claims mind-reading powers for itself: what else in fact could be the source of the ferocious knowledge the ordinary language philosophers will claim to divine by going over stupidly familiar words that we are every bit as much the master of as they? For example, Austin claims[9] that when I say "I know" I am not claiming to penetrate more deeply or certainly into reality than when I say "I believe"; I am, rather, taking a different stance toward what I communicate, I give my word, stake my mind, differently — the greater penetration is perhaps into my trustworthiness. And it seems to me that an immediate philosophical yield Austin wants from this observation (and perhaps similar yields from a thousand similar observations) is its questioning, perhaps repudiation, of Plato's ancient image of one set of ascending degrees of knowledge, an image Plato specifies in his allegory of the "divided line" of knowledge, an idea, if not an image, philosophers are still likely to hold without being able to question. From Austin's questioning or repudiation here a further consequence would be to question whether there is, or ought to be, or what the fantasy is that there is, a special class of persons to be called philosophers, who possess and

[9] In his great essay "Other Minds," in *Philosophical Papers* (Oxford: Oxford University Press, 1961).

are elevated by a special class or degree of knowledge. Austin's idea would seem to be that the decisive philosophical difference between minds lies not in their possession of facts and their agility of manipulation — these differences are reasonably obvious — but in, let us say, their intellectual scrupulousness, their sense of what one is or could be in a position to say, to claim authority for imparting, in our common finitude, to a fellow human being.

Does my elaboration of Austin's implication from the difference he has discovered between saying "I believe" and "I know" (that is, the difference between belief and knowledge) convey the kind of offense he may give, may indeed cultivate? I guess I was just now cultivating, or inviting, offense in my parenthetical, casual use of "that is" to move from our use of the words "belief" and "knowledge" to, perhaps I can say, the nature of belief and of knowledge. This casual move (or, as Emerson would put it, this casualty) is worded in Wittgenstein's motto "Grammar says what kind of object something is" (§ 373). This is, I think, not just one more offense, because without this sense of discovery (of the nature of things) the examples of ordinary language philosophy would altogether, to my mind, fail in their imagination; but if this is right, its persistent obscurity is a reason that the production of such examples is so hard, perhaps impossible, to teach. When in the opening essays of *Must We Mean What We Say?* I sought to characterize and defend this move by aligning the motivation of the *Investigations* with that of the *Critique of Pure Reason* as the exploration of transcendental logic, not only was I not given credit but my work was accused of being a discredit to empirically sound philosophy.[10] While as an initial reaction this is understandable enough, and while I am not now attempting to add to *this* defense, but rather to take up what I called at the beginning of this essay "fresh antagonisms" to the ordinary, I yet wish to derive a practical consequence from the move I described as

[10] See "The Availability of Wittgenstein's Later Philosophy," in *Must We Mean What We Say?* (Cambridge: Cambridge University Press, 1976), p. 65.

from language to nature (a move that cries out for further description, in particular descriptions that account for the sense of there being so much as a "move" in question) — the practical consequence, namely, that one cannot know in advance when or whether an example from the appeal to ordinary language will *strike* the philosophical imagination, motivate conversation philosophically. As if ordinary language procedure *at each point* requires the experience of conversion, of being turned around. Talk about offense.

　　Take one further example, this time from Wittgenstein: "Other people cannot be said to learn of my sensations *only* from my behavior — for I cannot be said to *learn* of them. I *have* them" (*Investigations*, § 246). But first of all, virtually every philosopher who has been gripped by the skeptical question whether and how we can know of the existence of so-called other minds has found himself or herself saying something of this sort, that others know of me at best from my behavior (as if facing themselves with the queries: How else? Through mind-reading, or some other telepathy?). And one might imagine the fun an advanced Parisian sensibility might wish to make out of such a prim appeal to what "cannot" be said, as though Wittgenstein were appealing to our sense of propriety or of, say, linguistic cleanliness — why should we, especially we serious philosophers, stoop to such considerations, or propriety, mere manners? (Would this be a fresh criticism? It seems to resemble the criticism Bertrand Russell and others in the English-speaking world of philosophy initially leveled against the *Investigations* upon its first appearance and to Austin's work published in the preceding years, that such work amounted to exhortations about how we ought to speak, that it sought to correct our, as it were, rough deportment. This is surely not entirely, or on every understanding, wrong. It is a piece of what Wittgenstein would mean in comparing the present philosophically advanced human race with "primitives.")

Yet it may at any time come over us, the truth of the matter, that
we cannot, so to speak, speak of someone learning of our sensations only from our behavior, without *insisting* that the words
make sense; and on no apparent ground for this insistence than
philosophical need: and *should* this need be satisfied? But why
should philosophy insist on the significance of "only" here?
"Only" here suggests some disappointment with my behavior as a
route to the knowledge of what is going on in me, our route
faute de mieux — not a disappointment with this or that piece
of my behavior, but with behavior as such, as if my body stands in
the way of your knowledge of my mind.

This now begins to show its madness, as though philosophy is
insisting on, driven to, some form of emptiness. And some such
diagnosis is indeed Wittgenstein's philosophical conclusion, or
his conviction about philosophy. His idea, I might say, is that this
philosophical use of "only" — that all but unnoticeable word in
his apparently trivial claim about what cannot be said (one trivi-
ality among a thousand others) — is not merely a sign that we,
say, underestimate the role of the body and its behavior, but that
we falsify it, I might even say, falsify the body: in philosophizing
we turn the body into as it were an integument. It is as though I,
in philosophizing, *want* this metamorphosis, want to place the
mind beyond reach, want to get the body inexpressive, and at the
same time find that I cannot quite want to, want to without re-
serve. Wittgenstein is interested in this peculiar strain of philosophy (it may be philosophy's peculiar crime) to want exactly
the impossible, thought torturing itself, language repudiating
itself. In Wittgenstein's philosophizing he seeks the source in
language of this torture and repudiation — what it is in language
that makes this seem necessary, and what about language makes it
possible. He speaks of our being bewitched by language; hence
his therapeutic procedures are to disenchant us. Lacan in a comparable way, I believe, speaks of his therapy as reading the

unreadable. (Or Shoshana Felman speaks of it for him, in "On Reading Poetry," to which, and in further matters, I am indebted.[11])

Let this serve to indicate the kind of offense the claims of ordinary language philosophy can, and should, give. It is, at any rate, the attitude or level at which I find Poe's "The Purloined Letter" to serve as their allegory.

The tale opens, I remind you, as the Prefect of the Parisian police calls upon the detective Dupin to ask his opinion about some troublesome official business. The first words of dialogue are these:

> "If it is any point requiring reflection," observed Dupin, as he forebore to enkindle the wick, "we shall examine it to better purpose in the dark."
>
> "That is another of your odd notions," said the Prefect, who had a fashion of calling everything "odd" that was beyond his comprehension, and thus lived amid an absolute legion of "oddities." . . . "The fact is, the business is *very* simple indeed, . . . but then I thought Dupin would like to hear the details of it, because it is so excessively *odd.*"
>
> "Simple and odd," said Dupin. . . . "Perhaps it is the very simplicity of the thing which puts you at fault."
>
> "What nonsense you *do* talk!" replied the Prefect, laughing heartily.
>
> "Perhaps the mystery is a little *too* plain," said Dupin.
>
> "Oh, good heavens! who ever heard of such an idea?"
>
> "A little *too* self-evident."
>
> "Ha! ha! ha! — ha! ha! ha! — ho! ho! ho!" roared [the Prefect], profoundly amused, "Oh, Dupin, you will be the death of me yet!" [12]

The narrative comes to turn on the fact that a purloined letter was hidden by being kept in plain view, as if a little too self-evident, a

---

[11] In *The Literary Freud: Mechanisms of Defense and the Poetic Will*, Joseph Smith, M.D., ed. (New Haven: Yale University Press, 1980), pp. 119–48.

[12] I use the Thomas Ollive Mabbott edition of Poe's Collected Works (Cambridge: Harvard University Press, 1978), vol. III, pp. 972–97 (including notes).

little too plain to notice, as it were beneath notice, say under the nose, and then moves to an examination of competing theories of the way to find the truth of hidden things. Now of course a reader of Wittgenstein's *Investigations* may well prick up his or her ears at the very announcement of a tale in which something is missed just because obvious. One remembers such characteristic remarks from the *Investigations* as these:

> The aspects of things that are most important for us are hidden because of their simplicity and [ordinariness, everydayness]. (One is unable to notice something — because it is always before one's eyes.) [§ 129]

> Philosophy simply puts everything before us, and neither explains nor deduces anything. — Since everything lies open to view there is nothing to explain. For what is hidden, for example, is of no interest to us. [§ 126]

But a philosopher other than one of ordinary language may make comparable claims, for example the Heidegger of *Being and Time*, whose method can be said to be meant to unconceal the obvious, the always present. The allegorical pivot from Poe's tale specifically to ordinary language philosophy is the tale's repetition of the idea of the *odd*, and specifically its associating this idea of the odd with the consequence of laughter. For the producing of examples whose oddness rouses laughter (no doubt mostly muted) is a feature of Austin's and of Wittgenstein's methods at once philosophically indispensable and (so far as I know) philosophically unique to them. Austin is the more hilarious perhaps, but here I remind you of this sound in the *Investigations*:

> Imagine someone saying: "But I know how tall I am!" and then laying his hand on top of his head to prove it. [§ 279]

> The chair is thinking to itself: . . . WHERE? In one of its parts? Or outside its body; in the air around it? Or not *any-where* at all? But then what is the difference between this chair's saying something to itself and another one's doing so, next to it? — But then how is it with man: where does *he* say things to himself? [§ 361]

> It would be possible to imagine someone groaning out: "Some-
> one is in pain — I don't know who!" — and our then hurrying
> to help him, the one who groaned. [§ 407]

But such examples only scratch the surface of the dimension of
oddness in the *Investigations*. There is, beyond them, Wittgenstein's frequent use of the word *seltsam*, characteristically translated in the English as "queer," which also translates Wittgenstein's frequent use of *merkwürdig*, as does the English "strange."
Of course they are frequent, since both exactly contrast with what
is *alltäglich*, ordinary, everyday, the appeal to which is Wittgenstein's constant method and goal. Wittgenstein sometimes explicitly undertakes to instruct us when to find something odd
("Don't take it as a matter of course, but as a remarkable fact,
that pictures and fictitious narratives give us pleasure, occupy our
minds" [§ 524]) ; as well as sometimes to give directions for overcoming a self-imposed sense of strangeness ("Sometimes a sentence only seems queer when one imagines a different language-
game for it from the one in which we actually use it." [§ 195]).
He speaks to us quite as if we have become unfamiliar with the
world, as if our mechanism of anxiety, which should signal
danger, has gone out of order, working too much and too little.

The return of what we accept as the world will then present
itself as a return of the familiar, which is to say, exactly under the
concept of what Freud names the uncanny. That the familiar is a
product of a sense of the unfamiliar and of the sense of a return
means that what returns after skepticism is never (just) the same.
(A tempting picture here could be expressed by the feeling that
"there is no way back." Does this imply that there is a way ahead?
Perhaps there are some "back's" or "once's" or pasts the presence
to which requires no "way." Then that might mean that we have
not found the way away, have never departed, have not entered
history. What has to be developed here is the idea of difference
so perfect that there is no way or feature in which the difference
consists [I describe this by saying that in such a case there is no

difference in criteria] — as in the difference between the waking world and the world of dreams, or between natural things and mechanical things, or between the masculine and the feminine, or between the past and the present. A difference in which everything and nothing differs is uncanny.)

But the angel of the odd hovers over the *Investigations* yet more persistently. The whole of the book can be seen to be contained in the book's opening of itself with a quotation from the *Confessions* of St. Augustine in which its subject describes his learning of language. This possibility depends upon seeing that the quotation contains the roots of the entire flowering of concepts in the rest of the *Investigations*. But it equally depends on seeing that the most remarkable fact about the quotation from Augustine is that anyone should find it remarkable, strange, odd, worth quoting, at all: "When they (my elders) named some object, and accordingly moved towards something, I saw this and I grasped that the thing was called by the sound they uttered when they meant to point it out. Their intention was shown by their bodily movements . . . and after I had trained my mouth to form these signs, I used them to express my own desires." (To glimpse the oddness, imagine the final sentence as from Samuel Beckett.) It presents the opening segment of countless moments in the book in which we are made uncertain whether an expression is remarkable or casual, where this turns out to be a function of whether we leave the expression ordinary or elevate it into philosophy, an elevation that depends on escaping our sense, let us say, of the ridiculous, one sense Wittgenstein undertakes to awaken. Philosophy in Wittgenstein turns out to require an understanding of how the seriousness of philosophy's preoccupations (with meaning, reference, intention, pointing, understanding, thinking, explaining, with the existence of the world, with whether my behavior consists of movements), its demand for satisfaction, its refusal of satisfaction — how this seriousness is dependent on disarming our sense of oddness and non-oddness, and therewith seeing why it is with the trivial, or superficial, that this philosophy finds itself in oscillation, as in an unearthly dance. (It was my sense of this unearthly oscillation that led me, early in my interest in Wittgenstein, to compare his writing with the writing of Beckett [for whom the extraordinary is ordinary] and with that of Chekhov [for whom the ordinary is extraordinary], who thus inescapably court the uncanny.)

I would love now to go on to a detailed working out of Poe's tale's allegory of ordinary language philosophy, but the most I can do here is flatly to assert a few claims about the issue. The second half of the tale is constituted by a narration of Dupin's narration and explanation of his powers of unconcealment. He begins by describing a childhood game of "even and odd" in which one player holds in his closed hand a number of marbles and demands of another whether that number is even or odd. An eight-year-old champion at the game explained his success to Dupin as one of determining whether his opponent was wise or stupid; and the method the boy used for this Dupin cites as the basis of the success of, among others, Tommaso Companella (whose system of mind-reading the boy has described) and of Machiavelli, no less. Lacan to my mind undervalues the relation of Dupin's story of the contest to the Prefect's opening vision of universal oddness. This relation depends on taking to heart Poe's pun, or pressure, on the English word "odd." Baudelaire does not try in his translation to preserve, or bother to note, this recurrence; he uses *bizarre* for the Prefect's "odd" and for Dupin's "even or odd" he uses *pair ou impair* — what else? Lacan of course knows this, but he seems to me over-casual in deciding (certainly correctly) that a "better" translation of "odd" in this story is a word for "singular." Singular is, elsewhere, a sensitive word for Poe, but in the text of "The Purloined Letter" the separated uses of "odd" to name what is at once funnily obvious and at the same time constitutes a possibility in a mind-reading contest with concealed counts — the untranslatable coincidence in Poe's words — should not be smoothed but kept in friction. Smoothing them would help Lacan's apparent neglect of the mind-reading contest of odd and even (masterable by a child of eight) as some kind of figure for communication, say for writing and reading, in particular for reading this text of Poe's that recounts this contest. The funny obviousness of this figure, its banality, its depth concealed in plain view, ought not to cause us not to see what it is.

Lacan's fruitful perception that Poe's tale is built on a repetition of triangular structures in the theft of the letter is the basis of the ensuing controversies about the tale, and it is only in the way he reads the repetition, or stops reading it, that my present reservation arises. Here is the sort of thing I get out of stopping over the thematization of odd and even mind-reading. When in the second triangle Dupin takes the position of the Minister in the first (the position of thief, the one who sees what the others see, namely that the King does not see the letter and that the Queen sees that the King does not see, hence falsely feels secure) and the Minister in the second triangle takes the position of the Queen in the first (the position of the one stolen from, under her very eyes, or nose), then the position of the King in the first (the one who is blind) Lacan finds to be occupied in the second by the Police (who were blind to the thing hidden in plainness). Without denying this, we should also note that in the second interview (in which Dupin robs the robber) the third party of the triangle (the Police) is present only by implication (Dupin and the Minister are fictionally alone) ; and then note further that another party is equally present there, specifically present (only) by implication, namely the reader, myself, to whom the fictional letter is also invisible. So I am to that extent both the King and the Police of Poe's letter(s). But since I am (whoever I am) after all shown the contents of the literal thing called "The Purloined Letter" (that is, Poe's tale), since they are indeed, or in art, meant for me, even as it were privately, I am the Queen from whom it is stolen, as well as the pair of thieves who remove it and return it, therapeutically, to me (for who else but myself could

have stolen *this* from myself?). And if I am to read the mind of
the one whose hand it is in (that is, mine, so my mind) but also
the mind going with the hand it is written in (that is, the author's — but which one, that of the literal "Letter" or that of the
fictional letter?), it is also to be read as the work of one who
opposes me, challenges me to guess whether each of its events is
odd or even, everyday or remarkable, ordinary or out of the ordinary. (I am here invoking not what I understand as a reader-
response theory, but something I would like to understand as a
reader-identification theory.)

So this text of Poe's "tale" presents the following representation of textuality, or constitution of a text. It is an artifact, in a
contested play of mind-reading, that is openly concealed in and
by the hand. I steal it from myself and return it to myself — steal
when I am wise or stupid (agree to play as a game of concealment)
and return when I can relate concealment and revelation, or say
repression and power (when I can know that the hand in question
does not conceal by closing). Yet I am to know that no matching
of minds can be open-handed either, that the artifact of the text is
the scene of a crime, because it is an expression of guilt, because it
is of knowledge that must be confessed, exacted, interpreted. Is
this a representation? And what crime does the hand as such re-
veal? No doubt, along with other notorious matters, it will have
to do with the circumstance that only humans have hands (with
those thumbs), and the consequent fascination of the hand for
philosophers. The writer of *Walden* confesses at the opening of
the book that the pages to follow are the work of his hands only;
and later in his opening chapter, as he enumerates the debts
he has encountered in setting out on his own life — saying that he
"thus unblushingly publishes [his] guilt" — the arithmetic is of
food, betraying the necessity of his having to eat, to preserve
himself. As if his debt is for his existence as such, for asking
acknowledgment (payable how? to whom? or is it forgivable?
by whom?).

An urgent methodological issue of ordinary language philosophy — and the issue about which this cast of thought is philosophically at its weakest — is that of accounting for the fact that we are the victims of the very words of which we are at the same time the masters. I have mentioned that one of Wittgenstein's favorite terms of criticism, or account of this recurrent failure in our possession of or by language (if failure is what it is), is to speak of our being bewitched by language. But that hardly accounts for such a crossroads as the emptiness of the word "only" in "knowing only from behavior." Perhaps my suggestion of "emptiness" and of a "will to emptiness" will prove to be an advance as a term of criticism (if, say, its invocation of Nietzsche's perception of nihilism can be made out usefully). And so perhaps will the idea of the unreadable, in the suggestion it would seem to carry, that ordinary language philosophy has not accounted for why the odd is laughable, for what it is we are laughing at philosophically, anxiously. Poe's tale imports a concrete and elaborate web of ways for conceptualizing these facts. What it may betoken that it at the same time allegorizes Lacanian psychoanalysis, together with the acts of writing and of reading, I leave open.

To complete the little topography I project for this occasion and bring Heidegger back explicitly into a bearing on the ordinary and the odd, I would have, as I indicated in putting him aside earlier, to undertake certain tasks pertaining to American transcendentalism, two in particular. First, to give an account of Thoreau's *Walden*, the major philosophical text in my life — other than the *Philosophical Investigations* — that deals in endless repetition, that begins with a vision of the extreme oddness of the everyday world, and that portrays its goal as the discovery of the day, his day, as one among others. Thoreau's guiding vision of the oddness of our everyday (its nextness, flushness, with another way) produces a response, that is, a texture of prose, hugging the border between comedy and tragedy. Second, I would

have to say what I have meant in expressing my intuition that
Thoreau, together with Emerson (having insisted upon their relation to Heidegger), underwrite the procedures of ordinary language philosophy, an intuition I have expressed by speaking of
them as inheritors of Kant's transcendentalism and as writing out
of a sense of intimacy of words with the world, or of intimacy lost.
Again there is time here only for mere assertion.

The background of the intuition is the work of mine I cited
earlier that I count on to show both the *Investigations* and *Walden*
sharing an aspiration of the *Critique of Pure Reason*, namely to
demonstrate the necessity in the world's satisfaction of the human
conditions of knowledge. *Walden*'s way of summarizing the first
Critique may be heard in its announcement that "The universe
constantly and obediently answers to our conceptions." And when
in the *Investigations* Wittgenstein calls his investigation "a grammatical one," and says "Our investigation is directed not toward
phenomena but, as one might say, toward the '*possibilities*' of
phenomena," this may be taken as saying that what he means by
grammar, or a grammatical investigation, plays the role of a transcendental deduction of human concepts. The difference relevant
for me is that in Wittgenstein's practice every word in our ordinary language requires deduction, where this means that each is
to be tracked, in its application to the world, in terms of what he
calls criteria that govern it; and our grammar is in some sense to
be understood as *a priori*.[13] (It is the sense in which human beings
are "in agreement" in their judgments.)

The mutual relation to Kant I called the background of the
intuition of American transcendentalism as underwriting ordinary
language philosophy. The foreground is the recognition that the
Investigations, like the work of Emerson and Thoreau, is written

---

[13] This is a way of putting the burden of chapters I and IV of my *The Claim
of Reason: Wittgenstein, Skepticism, Morality, and Tragedy* (New York: Oxford
University Press, 1979). This generalization, as it were, of Kant is something I
claim for Emerson in "Emerson, Coleridge, Kant," in *Raritan* 3, no. 2 (Fall 1983).

in continuous response to the threat of skepticism. It seems to me that the originality of the *Investigations* is a function of the originality of its response to skepticism, one that undertakes not to deny skepticism's power (on the contrary) but to diagnose the source (or say the possibility) of that power, to ask, as I put it a while ago, what it is about human language that allows us, even invites us, to repudiate its everyday functioning, to find it wanting. I might epitomize Wittgenstein's originality in this regard by saying that he takes the drift toward skepticism as the *discovery* of the everyday, a discovery of exactly *what* it is that skepticism would deny. It turns out to be something that the very impulse to philosophy, the impulse to take thought about our lives, inherently seeks to deny, as if what philosophy is dissatisfied by is inherently the everyday.

So the everyday is not merely one topic among others that philosophers might take an interest in, but one that a philosopher is fated to an interest in so long as he or she seeks a certain kind of response to the threat of skepticism. (It is a response that would regard science not as constituting an answer to skepticism but rather, taken as an answer, as a continuation of skepticism — as if the mad scientist in us is the double of the mad skeptic.) The everyday is what we cannot but aspire to, since it appears to us as lost to us. This is what Thoreau means when he says, after describing several of what he calls his adventures (a number of which take place while he describes himself as sitting down), "The present was my next experiment of this kind, which I purpose to describe at more length." By "the present experiment" he means of course the book in our hands, but he simultaneously means that the experiment is the present, i.e., that the book sets itself to test ways of arriving at the present, not merely at what people call "current events," which for him are not current, but old news, and are not events, but fancies. He is repeating the thought when he says "The phenomena of the year take place every day in a pond on a small scale." That is, there is nothing beyond the succession of each and every day; and grasping a day, accepting the everyday, the ordinary, is not a given but a task. This is also why Emerson says "Give me insight into today, and you may have the antique and future worlds." His words have the rhetoric of a bargain, or a prayer, as in "Give us this day our daily bread"; it is not something to take for granted.

The implication of this view of skepticism as the measure of the everyday is worked out in torturous detail in *The Claim of Reason* and I will not try to characterize it further here. Instead I will head for a conclusion by asking where Emerson and Thoreau see the answer to skepticism to lie.

I still concentrate on *Walden* and cite two foci of its conceptual elaboration. The first focus is the theme of mourning (or grieving) which, in conjunction with morning (as dawning) forms a dominating pun of *Walden* as a whole; it proposes human existence as the finding of ecstasy in the knowledge of loss. I call *Walden* a book of losses, saying of the book's creation of the region of Walden Pond, the world as an image of Paradise (Walled In), that it is everything there is to lose, and the book opens with it gone, forgone. Hume had said in the *Treatise of Human Nature* that skepticism is a malady that can never be cured. But the scene Hume thereupon portrays for us is one in which he returns from the isolation of his philosophical study into the company of his friends, where he finds welcome distraction from the sickening news his philosophical powers have uncovered. Incurable malady, as a metaphor for some grievous human condition, suggests an imaginable alternative, yet one not open to use. It would seem to have to be an alternative to the grievousness of the condition of being human. (Philosophers do sometimes suggest that the human possession of, say, the five senses is an unfortunate fact about us. It is within and against such a suggestion of the contingency of human existence that Beckett's character Hamm in *Endgame* protests when he cries, "You're on earth, you're on earth, there's no cure for that!")

Distraction (as in Hume) is one, surely understandable, reaction to these tidings. But, depending on how you take the alternative to the malady of skepticism, a more direct response, perhaps in a more acute stage, is that, as in Thoreau, of mourning — the path of accepting the loss of the world (you might say, accepting its loss of presence), accepting it as something which exists for us only in its loss (you might say its absence), or what presents itself as loss. *The Claim of Reason* suggests the moral of skepticism to be, that the existence of the world and others in it is not a matter to be known, but one to be acknowledged. And now what emerges is that what is to be acknowledged is this existence as separate from me, as if gone from me. Since I lose the world in every impulse to philosophy, say in each of the countless ways the ordinary language philosophers find that I make my expressions unreadable, the world must be regained every day, in repetition, regained as gone. Here is a way of seeing what it means that Freud too thinks of mourning as an essentially repetitive exercise. It can also be made out, in his little essay "Transience," that Freud regards mourning as the condition of the possibility of accepting the world's beauty, the condition, that is to say, of allowing its independence from me, its objectivity.[14] Learning mourning may be the achievement of a lifetime. ("I am in mourning for my life.")

In addition to distraction and mourning, Heidegger's perception of the violence of philosophical thinking, its imperative to dominance of the earth, I see as something like a competing response to, or consequence of, skepticism. One might take this violence as the response that supervenes when distraction and mourning are no longer humanly available options. Twenty years ago in an essay on *King Lear* I put the matter, or left an open suggestion for putting the matter, somewhat differently, in a way that I must interpolate here.[15] (My early suggestion originally occurs

---

[14] Standard Edition, vol. 14, pp. 305–7.
[15] "The Avoidance of Love," in *Must We Mean What We Say?*

within an interpolation in the *Lear* essay. Its recurrence here suggests, more or less impossibly, that the entire present paper could
or should have been that earlier interpolation.)

In the unbroken tradition of epistemology since Descartes
and Locke (radically questioned from within itself only in our
period), the concept of knowledge (of the world) disengages
from its connections with matters of information and skill and
learning, and becomes fixed to the concept of certainty alone,
and in particular to a certainty provided by the (by my) senses.
At some early point in epistemological investigations, the
world normally present to us (the world in whose existence,
as it is typically put, we "believe") is brought into question
and vanishes, whereupon all connection with a world is found
to hang upon what can be said to be "present to the senses";
and that turns out, shockingly, not to be the world. It is at this
point that the doubter finds himself cast into skepticism, turning the existence of the external world into a problem. Kant
called it a scandal to philosophy and committed his genius to
putting a stop to it, but it remains active in the conflicts between traditional philosophers and their ordinary language
critics, and it inhabits the void of comprehension between
continental ontology and Anglo-American analysis as a whole.
Its relevance to us at the moment is only this: The skeptic does
not gleefully and mindlessly forgo the world we share, or
thought we shared; he is neither the knave Austin took him to
be, nor the fool the pragmatists took him for, nor the simple-
ton he seems to men of culture and of the world. He forgoes
the world for just the reason that the world is important, that
it is the scene and stage of connection with the present: he
finds that it vanishes exactly with the effort to *make* it present.
If this makes him unsuccessful, that is because the presentness
achieved by certainty of the senses cannot compensate for the
presentness which had been elaborated through our old ab-
sorption in the world. But the wish for genuine connection is
there, and there was a time when the effort, however hysteri-
cal, to assure epistemological presentness was the best expression of seriousness about our relation to the world, the expression of an awareness that presentness was threatened,
gone. If epistemology wished to make knowing a substitute

for that fact, that is scarcely foolish or knavish, and scarcely some simple mistake. It is, in fact, one way to describe the tragedy *King Lear* records.

It took a good lapse of time for me to come to see how to unfold the implications in this juxtaposition, to see how tragedy is a projection or an enactment of a skeptical problematic and at the same time how skepticism traces in advance, or prophesies, a tragic structure, say a structure of revenge. What the passage I just quoted accordingly says to me now is that the loss of presentness (to and of the world) is something that the violence of skepticism deepens exactly in its desperation to correct it, a violence assured in philosophy's desperation to answer or refute skepticism, to deny skepticism's discovery of the absence or withdrawal of the world, i.e., the withdrawal of my presentness to it; which for me means the withdrawal of my presentness to language.

Perhaps something like this is what an old philosophical acquaintance, who had studied philosophy in Europe from the mid-fifties throughout the sixties, had in mind when he told me in the months after my *Must We Mean What We Say?* (which concludes with the essay on *King Lear*) appeared, that my work bore affinities with that of someone in Paris named Derrida, an observation I could not assess then and can barely begin to assess now. (Perhaps it was always, for me, too early or too late for this.) The differences, apart from the worlds of difference, are registered in my speaking of presentness (which is about me and my world) instead of (meaning what?) presence (which is about Being, not something I will ever be in a position, so far as I can judge, to judge); and my criticism of "philosophy" (by which I take myself to mean a way human beings have of being led to think about themselves, instead of something I can spell "Western metaphysics") is not, anyway not at first, that it originates in a domineering construction of (false) presence, but that it institutes an (a false) absence for which it falsely offers compensations. Even if it could be shown, and were worth someone's while to show, that these institutions are not so different, my claims do not arise from a study of classical philosophy but are limited to strands within the period of philosophy since the emergence of modern skepticism. While I take it that this radical skeptical suspicion of the "external" world as a whole, and of others in it, is not a speculation known to the classical philosophers, I also take modern skepticism to be philosophy's expression or interpretation of the thing known to literature (among other places) in melodrama and in tragedy. (By the thing known in melodrama and in tragedy I mean, roughly, the dependence of the human self on society for its definition, but at the same time its transcendence of that definition, its infinite insecurity in maintaining its existence. Which seems to mean, on this description, in determining and maintaining what "belongs" to it. "It.") Something like what we mean by melodrama and tragedy were known to the classical philosophers, hence would always have been implicated in the "Western" impulse to epistemology and metaphysics. It is perhaps this relation to tragedy that allows me the patience to put aside the metaphysical mode, in which *all* false presence is to be brought to an end before its own impossible beginning, and instead to speak within the sense that *each* impulse to metaphysical presence is to be brought to its own end by diagnosing its own beginning. In Derrida's heritage we "cannot" truly escape from the tradition of philosophy; in mine we cannot truly escape *to* philosophy. For him philosophy is apparently as primordial as language, or anyway as prose; for me it is skepticism that is thus primordial (or its possibility).

The other focus in *Walden*, in conjunction with mourning, around which skepticism tracks its answer, is constituted by the overarching narrative of the book, the building of a house, that is, the finding of one's habitation, of where it is one is at home; you can call it one's edification. The guiding thought of Heidegger's essay "Building Dwelling Thinking," [16] a companion essay to his

---

[16] In *Poetry, Language, Thought*, pp. 143–62.

"Das Ding," is that dwelling comes before building, not the other way around; and one can take this as the moral of *Walden*. But in *Walden* the proof that what you have found you have made your own, your home, is that you are free to leave it. *Walden* begins and ends with statements of departure from Walden. Emerson's complex structuring concept for this departure is *abandonment*. The significance Heidegger finds in his words, and Emerson and Thoreau find in theirs, is remarkable enough; but that in the face of this significance, to discover that their thoughts are intimately, endlessly related, has become for me unforgettably interesting. The direct historical connection (of Emerson with Heidegger) is through Nietzsche, but the intellectual conjunction has been a touchstone for me in the past few years in exploring the idea that Romanticism generally is to be understood as in struggle with skepticism, and at the same time in struggle with philosophy's responses to skepticism. (How generally this applies is not yet important. It is indicated by the figures of Coleridge and Wordsworth behind Emerson and Thoreau, and by Holderlin's shadow in Heidegger.)

With one further corner in the topography of the everyday that I am outlining, I will be ready to take up a moment of unfinished business with Heidegger's "Das Ding" and then tell you a parting story. If you take Edgar Allan Poe (together with Nathaniel Hawthorne), on some opposite side of the American mind from Emerson and Thoreau, also to be writing in response to skepticism, then it becomes significant that they too write repetitively about dwelling, settling, houses; about, call it, domestication. Since their tales, unlike the scenes of Emerson and Thoreau, typically have other people in them, they think of domestication habitually in terms of marriage or betrothal. And habitually they think not about its ecstasies but about its horrors, about houses that fall or enclose, ones which are unleavable and hence unliveable. I said that the new philosophical step in the criticism of skepticism developed in ordinary language philosophy is its discovery of skepticism's discovery, by displacement, of the everyday; hence its discovery that the answer to skepticism must take the form not of philosophical construction but of the reconstruction or resettlement of the everyday. This shows in its treatment of skepticism's threat of world-consuming doubt by means of its own uncanny homeliness, stubbornly resting within its relentless superficiality; and not, as other philosophies have felt compelled to proceed, by way of isolated, specialized, highly refined examples (Descartes' piece of wax, Kant's house, Heidegger's automobile turn signal, G. E. Moore's envelope). This is the level at which I hear Poe's declaration, at the beginning of one of his most famous tales of horror, "The Black Cat," that he "[is placing] before the world, plainly, sincerely, and without comment, a series of mere household events." [17] It stands to reason that if some image of human intimacy, call it marriage, or domestication, is the fictional equivalent of what the philosophers of ordinary language understand as the ordinary, call this the image of the everyday as the domestic; that then the threat to the ordinary that philosophy names skepticism should show up in fiction's favorite threats to forms of marriage, namely in forms of melodrama and tragedy.

This takes me back to Heidegger's "Das Ding," in which the overcoming of our distancelessness, of our loss of connection, or rather our unconnectedness, with things, our being unbethinged, *unbedingt*, that is, unconditioned (hence inhuman, monstrous, figures of a horror story), is expressed by Heidegger in terms of "the marriage of sky and earth," of the "betrothal" of "the earth's nourishment and the sky's sun." One might have imagined that this image is only accidental in Heidegger's essay, but it is essentially what goes into his extraordinary account of the thinging of the world as requiring the joining of earth, sky, gods, and mortals in what he calls "the round dance of appropriating" (*der Reigen des Ereignens*); and when he goes on to say "the round dance is the ring" that grapples and plays, he can hardly not have in mind

---

[17] In the Mabbott edition, pp. 847–59.

the wedding band (an image in this connection that he would have taken from Nietzsche's Zarathustra), something confirmed by his speaking of "the ringing of the ring" (*das Gering des Ringes*), where what he seems to want from the word *Gering* is both the intensification of the idea of being hooped together and at the same time the idea of this activity as slight, trivial, humble; it is the idea of diurnal devotedness. Thus does the idea of the everyday, which Heidegger has apparently disdained, recur, repeat itself, transformed, as the metaphysical answer to that empirical disdain.

Heidegger's idea of the humble, with its implication of cosmic radiance, may not seem very close to what Wittgenstein means in his insistence on looking for the humble use of famously philosophical words (like "language," "experience," and "world"). But the connection serves to register our sense that neither of them is as clear as their admirers would like them to be in philosophically accounting for their philosophical practice. Both wrestle against the human will to explain, but when Wittgenstein says "explanations come to an end somewhere," what he means is that philosophy must show, of each effort at philosophical explanation, the plain place at which it ends. Whereas Heidegger means to portray the shining place before which *all* explanations end. Still, we are reminded that both Wittgenstein and Heidegger were readers of Kierkegaard and that Kierkegaard's Knight of Faith exhibited what in English translates as "the sublime in the pedestrian." [18]

For the parting story I wish to tell you, I gesture toward that favorite region of mine that came up earlier for a glancing blow in Heidegger's allusion to it as symptomatic of our common, annihilating one-track thinking — the region of movies. I turn in conclusion here to a passage from a movie as also symptomatic of everyday thinking, but this time as symptomatic of the everyday

[18] Søren Kierkegaard, *Fear and Trembling*, trans. Walter Lowie, Anchor Books edition, p. 52.

recognition that our habitual modes of thought are destructive, and as an everyday effort to step back from them. The passage is from the concluding sequence of a film called *Woman of the Year* (directed by George Stevens in 1942, with Katharine Hepburn and Spencer Tracy), a relatively minor member of a genre of movie I have called "the comedy of remarriage" and that I define through certain movies from the Hollywood 1930's and 1940's. The woman in *Woman of the Year* is a world-famous, syndicated political journalist, the man a lower-class sports reporter on her house newspaper. After satisfying a number of features required by the genre (their separation and threatened divorce; the woman's particular understanding with her father and the absence of her mother; a solemn discussion of what constitutes marriage and a scene of instruction of the woman by the man which is later undermined [in this case it is instruction in the rules of baseball]; an explicit renunciation of children and the establishing of a sense that while these two may not manage to live together they are certainly not prepared to share their lives with anyone else; and a move to a smaller, more modest dwelling than they begin in), there is a final sequence in which the woman appears about dawn at her estranged husband's apartment and while he is asleep attempts, with hopeless incompetence, to cook breakfast for him. He is awakened by the noise of her incompetence, interrupts her pitiful efforts, and is treated to a humble declaration from her which begins, significantly for the genre of remarriage, "I love you, Sam. Will you marry me?" He treats this outburst from his wife with a mocking tirade of disbelief, to which she replies: "You don't think I can do the ordinary things that any idiot can do, do you?" He says no; she asks why not; upon which he delivers a long remarkable lecture which begins, "Because you're incapable of doing them," and ends by saying that she is trained to do things incompatible with the training that doing those ordinary things demands. All I call attention to here is that this proves to be all right with him, with both of them; that for example in this genre of movie if anyone is seen to cook it is the man, never the woman (or never without him); that, uniquely in this genre of comedy, so far as I know, the happiness of marriage is dissociated from any *a priori* concept of what constitutes domesticity (you might also call marriage in these films the taking of mutual pleasure without a concept — whether two people are married does not necessarily depend on what age they are, or what gender, or whether legally). Marriage here is being presented as an estate meant not as a distraction from the pain of constructing happiness from a helpless, absent world, but as the scene in which the chance for happiness is shown as the mutual acknowledgment of separateness, in which the prospect is not for the passing of years (until death parts us) but for the willing repetition of days, willingness for the everyday (until our true minds become unreadable to one another).

The Moral First Aid Manual

DANIEL C. DENNETT

THE TANNER LECTURES ON HUMAN VALUES

Delivered at
The University of Michigan

November 7 and 8, 1986

DANIEL C. DENNETT was born in Boston in 1942 and received his B.A. from Harvard and his D. Phil. from Oxford. After six years at the University of California at Irvine, he moved to Tufts University in 1971, where he is now distinguished Arts and Sciences Professor, and Director of the Center for Cognitive Studies. In addition to his books on the philosophy of mind, *Content and Consciousness* (1969), *Brainstorms* (1978), and *The Intentional Stance* (1987), he has written on free will (*Elbow Room*, 1984) and co-edited, with Douglas Hofstadter, *The Mind's I: Fantasies and Reflections on Self and Soul* (1981).

I was very pleased to be invited to give the Tanner Lecture this year, not just because of the honor of being included in this most distinguished series, and not just because of my Ann Arbor friendships, but also because of the bracing opportunity it offered to indulge in what might be called "licensed poaching." According to the letter of invitation, "The purpose of the Tanner Lectures is to advance and reflect upon the scholarly and scientific learning relating to human values and valuation."

I decided to take this seriously, and thus have been lured a little further into ethics — human values and valuation — than I belong. I was not at all unwilling to be a poacher, since I have long harbored dissatisfactions and skepticisms about what I took to be being done in ethics, in particular about the wildly unrealistic idealizations being used, and this was to be an occasion for me to express them. But poaching is a dangerous business, and as I began doing my homework I discovered that the very themes I had hoped to hold forth on have already found expression in recent work in ethics, and in just about every case were developed with subtlety and precision that went beyond my amateur ruminations. I was an ill-read floater with the *Zeitgeist*, not the pioneer I had hoped to be.

With time running out, it became less and less clear to me that I had anything, beyond some selective applause, to offer to the

NOTE: In this lecture I revise and expand on material presented in the Kathryn Fraser McKay Lecture, St. Lawrence University, September 1986, the George Brantl Lecture, Montclair St. College, February 1986, a Distinguished Lecture to the MIT Laboratory for Computer Science, March 1986, published as "Information, Technology, and the Virtues of Ignorance," *Daedalus*, Summer 1986, pp. 135–53, and a Humanities Lecture at the University of Kansas, November 1986. In addition to the discussions prompted by those lectures, I am particularly indebted to my colleagues Stephen White, Norman Daniels, and Hugo Bedau for their discussions with me, and also to Gordon Brittan, Richmond Campbell, Bo Dahlbom, Robert French, Douglas Hofstadter, Charles Karelis, Onora O'Neill, and Connie Rosati for their comments and advice.

current groundswell of reaction against the misuse of theoretical idealizations in ethics. In the end, however, I concluded that the current salutary trend has not gone far enough in certain respects, and that — unless I am deceived by the felt need to say something "new" — I may provide something of a fresh perspective on the issues. As you will soon learn, there is a certain poetic justice in my confessing that what you are about to hear is the somewhat misshapen product of time-pressured problem-solving.

1. MILL'S NAUTICAL METAPHOR

A hundred and twenty-five years ago, John Stuart Mill felt called upon to respond to an annoying challenge to his *utilitarianism*: ". . . defenders of utility often find themselves called upon to reply to such objections as this — that there is not time, previous to action, for calculating and weighing the effects of any line of conduct on the general happiness." His reaction was quite fierce:

> Men really ought to leave off talking a kind of nonsense on this subject, which they would neither talk nor listen to on other matters of practical concernment. Nobody argues that the art of navigation is not founded on astronomy because sailors cannot wait to calculate the Nautical Almanac. Being rational creatures, they go to sea with it ready calculated; and all rational creatures go out upon the sea of life with their minds made up on the common questions of right and wrong, as well as on many of the far more difficult questions of wise and foolish. And this, as long as foresight is a human quality, it is to be presumed they will continue to do.
>
> [*Utilitarianism*, 1861, p. 31]

This haughty retort has found favor with many — perhaps most — ethical theorists, but in fact it papers over a crack that has been gradually widening under an onslaught of critical attention. The naïve objector was under the curious misapprehension that a system of ethical thinking *was supposed to work* and noted that Mill's system was highly impractical — at best. This is no objection, Mill insists; utilitarianism is supposed to be practical, but not *that* practical. Its true role is as a background justifier of the foreground habits of thought of real moral reasoners. This background role for ethical theory (and not only utilitarians have sought it) has proven, however, to be ill-defined and unstable. Just how practical is a system of ethical thinking *supposed* to be? What is an ethical theory for? Tacit differences of opinion about this issue, and even a measure of false consciousness among the protagonists, have added to the inconclusiveness of the subsequent debate.

For the most part philosophers have been content to ignore the practical problems of real-time decision-making, regarding the brute fact that we are all finite and forgetful, and have to rush to judgment, as a real but irrelevant element of friction in the machinery whose blueprint they are describing. It is as if there might be two disciplines — ethics proper, which undertakes the task of calculating the principles of what the ideal agent ought to do under all circumstances — and then the less interesting, "merely practical" discipline of *Moral First Aid*, or *What to Do Until the Doctor of Philosophy Arrives*, which tells, in rough-and-ready terms, how to make "on line" decisions under time pressure.

In practice, philosophers acknowledge, we overlook important considerations — considerations that we really shouldn't overlook — and we bias our thinking in a hundred idiosyncratic — and morally indefensible — ways; but *in principle*, what we ought to do is what the ideal theory (one ideal theory or another) says we ought to do. Philosophers have then concentrated, not unwisely, on spelling out what that ideal theory is. The theoretical fruits of deliberate oversimplification through idealization are not to be denied — in philosophy or in any scientific discipline; reality in all its messy particularity is too complicated to theorize about taken straight. The issue is rather (since every idealization is a strategic choice): which idealizations might really shed some light on the nature of morality, and which will just land us with diverting fairy tales.

It is easy to forget just how impractical ethical theories actually are, but we can make the truth vivid by reflecting on what is implicit in Mill's use of a metaphor drawn from the technology of his own day. The *Nautical Almanac* is a book of tables, calculated and published annually, from which one can easily and swiftly derive the exact position in the skies of the sun, the moon, the planets, and the major stars for *each second* of the forthcoming year. The precision and certainty of this annual generator of expectations was, and still is, an inspiring instance of the powers of human foresight, properly disciplined by a scientific system *and directed upon a sufficiently orderly topic*. Armed with the fruits of such a system of thought, the rational sailor can indeed venture forth confident of his ability to make properly informed real-time decisions about navigation. The practical methods devised by the astronomers actually work.

Do the utilitarians have a similar product to offer to the general public? Mill seems at first to be saying so. Today we are inured to the inflated claims made on behalf of dozens of high-tech systems — of cost–benefit analysis, computer-based expert systems, etc. — and from today's perspective we might suppose Mill to be engaging in an inspired bit of advertising: suggesting that utilitarianism can provide the moral agent with a foolproof Decision-Making Aid. ("We have done the difficult calculations for you! All you need do is just fill in the blanks in the simple formulae provided.")

Jeremy Bentham, the founder of utilitarianism, certainly aspired to just such a "felicific calculus," complete with mnemonic jingles, like the systems of practical celestial navigation that every sea captain memorized.[1]

---

[1] From chapter IV of Bentham's *Introduction to the Principles of Morals and Legislation*, 1789:

Intense, long, certain, speedy, fruitful, pure —
Such marks in *pleasures* and in *pains* endure.
Such pleasures seek if *private* be thy end:
If it be *public*, wide let them *extend*.

This myth of practicality has been part of the rhetoric of utilitarianism from the beginning, but in Mill we see already the beginning of the retreat up the ivory tower to ideality, to what is calculable "in principle" but not in practice.

Mill's idea, for instance, was that the best of the homilies and rules of thumb of everyday morality — the formulae people *actually considered* in the hectic course of their deliberations — had received (or would receive in principle) official endorsement from the full, laborious, systematic utilitarian method. The faith placed in these formulae by the average rational agent, based as it was on many lifetimes of experience accumulated in cultural memory, could be justified ("in principle") by being formally derived from the theory. But no such derivation has ever been achieved.[2]

It will help us appreciate this obvious fact about consequentialist theories such as utilitarianism if we compare them, not to the productions of the Astronomer Royal, as Mill did, but to a more contemporary technique of expectation-generation: computer-aided weather forecasting.

The current North American data-gathering grid divides the atmosphere into cells approximately thirty miles on a side and ten thousand feet in height. This yields in the neighborhood of 100,000 cells, each characterized by less than a dozen intensities: temperature, barometric pressure, wind direction and velocity, etc. How these intensities change as a function of the intensities in the neighboring cells is fairly well understood, but computing these changes in temporal increments small enough to keep some significance in the answers challenges today's largest supercomputers. Obviously, a weather prediction must be both accurate and timely;

---

[2] It is arguable that Robert Axelrod's *The Evolution of Cooperation* (New York: Basic Books, 1984), achieves a derivation of the Tit For Tat rule: Cooperate at the outset, punish defections with a defection, but respond to further cooperation with cooperation. As Axelrod himself points out, however, the rule's provable virtues assume conditions that are only intermittently (and controversially) realized. In particular, the "shadow of the future" must be "sufficiently great," a condition about which reasonable people might disagree indefinitely, it seems.

achieving accuracy at the cost of taking thirty-six hours to calculate a twenty-four-hour prediction is no solution.

It is not clear yet whether reliable long-range weather forecasting is possible, since the weather may prove to be too chaotic to permit *any* feasible computation. The behavior of the weather is strikingly unlike the behavior of the heavenly bodies. Suppose though, for the sake of illustration, that there were a *proven* forecasting algorithm — one that could successfully "predict" tomorrow's weather if allowed to engage in a *month* of number crunching on a bank of supercomputers. This would be scientifically very interesting, but not very useful. We can imagine taking the tour of the weather bureau and being shown the gleaming giants at their work. "How do you actually *use* the algorithm in figuring out the forecasts you are obliged to issue every day?" we ask. "Oh, we don't use the algorithm at all. We sort of eyeball the maps and the local conditions and then apply our favorite maxims. Jones is partial to 'red sky at night, sailor's delight' while I am more into aching joints and looking for the groundhog's shadow. We vote, in the end, and our track record is pretty good."

That is the way it is with ethics too — only with ethics, things are worse. At least with meteorology, there is an uncontroversial and widely accepted ideal background theory — however infeasible it might be in practical calculations. Now we can see that there are actually three ways in which Mill's metaphor is misleading. First, as just mentioned, no ethical theory enjoys the near-universal acceptance of astronomy or meteorology, in spite of vigorous campaigns by the partisans. Second, there are no feasible algorithms or decision procedures for ethics as there are for celestial navigation. Third, the informal rules of thumb people actually use have never been actually derived from a background theory, but only guessed at, in an impressionistic derivation rather like that of our imagined meteorologists.

And unlike the weather, which *may* turn out not to be a chaotic and incalculable system (but may rather asymptote on some ball-park trends), the ethically relevant effects of our contemplated actions are bound to be incalculable unless we place *arbitrary* limits on them.

Why? Because of what might be called the Three Mile Island Effect. Was the melt-down at Three Mile Island a good thing to have happened or a bad thing? If, in planning some course of action, one encountered the melt-down as a sequel of probability p, what should one assign to it as a weight? Is it a strongly negative or strongly positive effect? We can't yet say, and it is not clear that *any* particular long run would give us the answer.

Compare the problem facing us here with the problems confronting the designers of computer chess programs. One might suppose that the way to respond to the problem of real time pressure for ethical decision-making techniques is the way one responds to time pressure in chess: heuristic search-pruning techniques. But there is no checkmate in life, no point at which we get a definitive result, positive or negative, from which we can calculate, by retrograde analysis, the actual values of the alternatives that lay along the path taken. How deep should one look before settling on a weight for a position? In chess, what looks positive from ply 5 may look disastrous from ply 7. There are ways of tuning one's heuristic search procedures to minimize (but not definitively) the problem of misevaluating anticipated moves. Is the anticipated capture a strongly positive future to be aimed at, or the beginning of a brilliant sacrifice for your opponent? A *principle of quiescence* will help to resolve that issue: always look a few moves beyond any flurry of exchanges to see what the board looks like when it quiets down. But in real life, there is no counterpart principle that deserves reliance.

Three Mile Island has been followed by quite a long intervening period of consolidation and quiescence, but we *still* have no idea whether it is to be counted among the good things that have happened or the bad.

The suspicion that there is no stable and persuasive resolution to such impasses has long lain beneath the troubled surface of

criticism to consequentialism, which looks to many skeptics like
a thinly veiled version of the classically vacuous stock market
advice: buy low and sell high — a great idea in principle, but
systematically useless as advice to follow.[3]

So not only have utilitarians never made an actual practice of
determining their specific moral choices by calculating the expected utilities of (all) the alternatives (there not being time,
as our original objector noted), they have never achieved stable
"off-line" *derivations* of partial results — "landmarks and direction posts," as Mill puts it — to be exploited on the fly by those
who must cope with "matters of practical concernment."

What, then, of the utilitarians' chief rivals, the various sorts
of Kantians? Their rhetoric has likewise paid tribute to practicality — largely via their indictments of the impracticality of the
utilitarians.[4]

What, though, do the Kantians put in the place of the unwork-
able consequentialist calculations? Kantian decision-making typi-

---

[3] Judith Jarvis Thomson has objected that neither "buy low and sell high" nor
its consequentialist counterpart, "do more good than harm," is strictly vacuous; both
presuppose something about ultimate goals, since the former would be bad advice
to one who sought to lose money, and the latter would not appeal to the ultimate
interests of all morally-minded folk. I agree. The latter competes, for instance, with
the advice the Pirate King gives to Frederick, the self-styled "slave of duty," in
Pirates of Penzance: "Aye me lad, always do your duty — and chance the consequences!" Neither slogan is *quite* vacuous.

[4] A Kantian who presses the charge of practical imponderability against utilitarianism with particular vigor and clarity is Onora O'Neill in "The Perplexities of
Famine Relief," in *Matters of Life and Death*, Tom Regan, ed. (New York: Random House, 1980). She shows how two utilitarians, Garrett Hardin and Peter
Singer, armed with the same information, arrive at opposite counsels: we should
take drastic steps to prevent short-sighted efforts to feed famine victims (Hardin),
or we should take drastic steps to provide food for today's famine victims (Singer).
For a more detailed consideration, see her *Faces of Hunger* (Boston: Allen and
Unwin, 1986). An independent critic is Bernard Williams, who claims in *Utilitarianism For and Against*, p. 137, that utilitarianism makes

> enormous demands on supposed empirical information, about peoples' prefer-
> ences, and that information is not only largely unavailable, but shrouded in
> conceptual difficulty; but that is seen in the light of a technical or practical
> difficulty, and utilitarianism appeals to a frame of mind in which technical
> difficulty, even insuperable technical difficulty, is preferable to moral unclarity,
> no doubt because it is less alarming. (That frame of mind is in fact deeply
> foolish . . . .)

cally reveals that rather different idealizations — departures from reality in other directions — are doing all the work. For instance, unless some *deus ex machina* is handy to whisper in one's ear, it is far from clear just how one is to figure out how to limit the scope of the "maxims" of one's contemplated actions before putting them to the litmus test of the Categorical Imperative. There seems to be an inexhaustible supply of candidate maxims.

Certainly the quaint Benthamite hope of a fill-in-the-blanks decision procedure for ethical problems is as foreign to the spirit of modern Kantians as it is to sophisticated utilitarians. All philosophers can agree, it seems, that real moral thinking takes insight and imagination, and is not to be achieved by any mindless application of formulae.[5]

This is not meant to be a shocking indictment, but just a reminder of something quite obvious: no remotely compelling system of ethics has ever been made *computationally tractable*, even indirectly, for real-world moral problems. So even though there has been no dearth of utilitarian (and Kantian, and contractarian, etc.) *arguments* in favor of particular policies, institutions, practices, and acts, these have all been heavily hedged with *ceteris paribus* clauses and plausibility claims about their idealizing assumptions. These hedges are designed to overcome the combinatorial explosion of calculation that threatens if one actually attempts — as theory says one must — to *consider all things*. And as arguments — not derivations — they have all been controversial (which is not to say that none of them could be sound in the last analysis).

If there is a *Moral Almanac* actually in use, then, it is less like the *Nautical Almanac* than it is like *The Old Farmer's Almanac*— an unsystematic collection of wise sayings, informal precepts, tra-

---

[5] As Mill himself puts it, still in high dudgeon, "There is no difficulty in proving any ethical standard whatever to work ill if we suppose universal idiocy conjoined with it" (*Utilitarianism*, p. 31). This bit of rhetoric is somewhat at war with his earlier analogy, since one of the legitimate claims of the systems of practical navigation was that just about any idiot could master them.

ditional policies, snatches of taboo, and the like, a vade mecum
vaguely approved of by the experts — who, after all, rely on it
themselves — but so far lacking credentials.

There is not now any ethical theory that stands in the same
relation to practical ethical decision-making as astronomy stands
to practical navigation. That is hardly controversial. The hope of
achieving such a theory has not been entirely abandoned, however. Theorists have attempted to salvage a close relation to practice by creating various brands of *indirect* utilitarianism, for instance, which factor in rules, dispositions, habits, institutions, and
the like to "govern" our actual practices after receiving their
credentials from the idealized theory. The general form of such
licensing is an argument to show why and how, after all, *it is
rational* or *it is optimizing* or *it is better* for agents to adopt (or
just follow) these rules, inculcate (or just have) these dispositions, given some facts about the actual predicaments of such
agents. This is still very much in the spirit of the "all things considered" tradition; for the proponents can claim that among *all*
the things to be considered are certain crucial facts about agents'
actual circumstances that were simply overlooked in the earlier
idealizations. It is rather as if the earlier astronomers had ne-
glected to notice the need for navigators to apply a variable
"height-of-eye correction" to their sextant readings.

While I have learned a great deal from the recent work in
this spirit, and even more from the critics of that work (I have
in mind such authors as Gauthier, Gibbard, Hare, Parfit, Slote,
and Williams), I will try to show that it still idealizes away from
the heart of the problems. And while I think that compelling
arguments can be (and have been) given to show that the hope
of an astronomical foundation — an "Archimedean point," in
Bernard Williams' phrase — should be abandoned as confused, I
will simply assume in what follows that this is so.

Suppose, then, that we try to write the *Moral First Aid
Manual*, but suppose further that we should write it with no

expectation that the Doctor of Philosophy will ever arrive with the Ultimate Right Answer.[6]

I should say at the outset that the job I envision, if done right, would involve systematic empirical studies and experiments by psychologists in addition to my informal and anecdotal explorations, and formal analyses of the task domains and the useful heuristics for them (of the sort sometimes produced by people in artificial intelligence), in addition to my intuitive guesswork. I am not ready to do this work, but — as philosophers are wont — I am ready to talk about why it would be interesting work for somebody to do. (And I should also add that previous Tanner Lecturers in Ann Arbor include two of the real pioneers in this endeavor: Herbert Simon and Thomas Schelling.)

2. JUDGING THE COMPETITION

To get a better sense of the difficulties that contribute to actual moral reasoning, let us give ourselves a smallish moral problem and see what we do with it. While a few of its details are exotic, the problem I am setting exemplifies a familiar structure.

Your Philosophy Department has been chosen to administer a munificent bequest: a Twelve-year Fellowship to be awarded in open competition to the most promising graduate student in philosophy in the country. You duly announce the award and its conditions in the *Journal of Philosophy*, and then to your dismay

---

[6] I will mention, but pass over, two other well-known reactions to the recognition that there is no hope of astronomy-like foundations for ethics: the defeatist banalities of "situation ethics" and other dreary relativisms of laziness on the one hand, and the useful — but, I think, only marginally useful — retreat to an "ethics of virtue" on the other. It is all very well to say, more or less with Aristotle, that if we concentrate our theoretical attentions on Virtue, the process of decision-making will take care of itself (since the Virtuous Person will know how to make morally wise decisions without any need to consult a Manual). This just passes the buck; how, exactly, is the paragon of Virtue supposed to do this? This "design" question remains achingly open — it is both theoretically and practically interesting, since few of us take ourselves to be beyond improvement in this regard — even if we agree (as we should not, in fact) that the ideally virtuous agent needs no help from our designers.

you receive, by the deadline, 250,000 legal entries, complete with lengthy dossiers, samples of written work and testimonials. A quick calculation convinces you that living up to your obligation to evaluate all the material of all the candidates by the deadline for announcing the award would not only prevent the Department from performing its primary teaching mission, but — given the costs of administration and hiring additional qualified evaluators — bankrupt the award fund itself, so that all the labor of evaluation would be wasted; no one would gain.

What to do? If only you had anticipated the demand, you could have imposed tighter eligibility conditions, but it is too late for that: every one of the 250,000 candidates has, we will suppose, a right to equal consideration, and in agreeing to administer the competition you have undertaken the obligation to select the best candidate.[7]

When I have put this problem to colleagues, I find that after a brief exploratory period, they tend to home in on one version or another of a mixed strategy, such as:

> choose a small number of *easily checked* and *not entirely unsymptomatic* criteria of excellence — such as grade point average, number of philosophy courses completed, weight of the dossier (eliminating the too light and the too heavy) — and use this to make a first cut. Conduct a lottery with the remaining candidates, cutting the pool down randomly to some manageably small number of finalists — say 50 or 100 — whose dossiers will be carefully screened by a committee, which will then vote on the winner.

There is no doubt that this procedure is very unlikely to find the best candidate. Odds are, in fact, that more than a few of the losers, if given a day in court, could convince a jury that they

---

[7] I don't mean to beg any questions with this formulation in terms of rights and obligations. If it makes a difference to you, recast the setting of the problem in terms of the overall disutility of violating the conditions set forth in your announcement of the competition. My point is that you would find yourself in a bind, whatever your ethical persuasion.

were *obviously* superior to the elected winner. But, you might want to retort, that's just tough; you did the best you could. It is quite possible, of course, that you would lose the lawsuit, but you might still feel, rightly, that you could have arrived at no better decision at the time.

My example is meant to illustrate, enlarged and in slow motion, the ubiquitous features of real-time decision-making. First, there is the simple physical impossibility of "considering all things" in the allotted time. Note that "all things" doesn't have to mean *everything* or even *everybody in the world*, but just "everything in 250,000 readily available dossiers." You have all the information you need "at your fingertips"; there need be no talk of conducting further investigations. Second, there is the ruthless and peremptory use of some distinctly second-rate cut rules. No one thinks *grade point average* is a remotely foolproof indicator of promise, though it is probably somewhat superior to *weight of dossier*, and clearly superior to *number of letters in surname*. There is something of a trade-off between ease of application and reliability, and if no one can *quickly* think of any easily applied criteria that one can have *some* faith in, it would be better to eliminate the first cut step and proceed straight to the lottery for all candidates. Third, the lottery illustrates a partial abdication of control, giving up on a part of the task and letting something else — nature or chance — take over for awhile, while still assuming responsibility for the result. (That is the scary part.) Fourth, there is the phase where you try to salvage something presentable from the output of that wild process; having *over*-simplified your task, you count on a meta-level process of self-monitoring to correct or renormalize or improve your final product to some degree.[8] Fifth, there is the endless vulnerability to second-guessing and

---

[8] See my "A Route to Intelligence: Oversimplify and Self-monitor" (CCM-85-4, Center for Cognitive Studies, Tufts), forthcoming in J. Khalfa, ed., *Can Intelligence Be Explained?* (Oxford University Press); and "Designing Intelligence" (CCM-86-4, Center for Cognitive Studies, Tufts), British Association for Advancement of Science, September 2, 1986.

hindsight wisdom about what you should have done — but done is done. You let the result stand and go on to other things.

The decision process just described is an instance of the fundamental pattern first explicitly analyzed by Herbert Simon, who named it "satisficing." [9] Notice how the pattern repeats itself, rather like a fractal curve, as we trace down through the sub-decisions, the sub-sub-decisions, and so forth until the process becomes invisible. At the departmental meeting called to consider how to deal with this dilemma, (1) everyone is bursting with suggestions — more than can be sensibly discussed in the two hours allotted, so (2) the chairman becomes somewhat peremptory, deciding not to recognize several members who might well, of course, have some very good ideas, and then (3) after a brief free-for-all "discussion" in which — for all anyone can tell — timing, volume, and timbre may count for more than content, (4) the chairman attempts to summarize by picking a few highlights that somehow strike him as the operative points, and the strengths and weaknesses of these are debated in a rather more orderly way, and then a vote is taken. After the meeting, (5) there are those who still think that better cut rules could have been chosen, that the department could have afforded the time to evaluate 200 finalists (or only 20), etc., but done is done. They have learned the important lesson of how to live with the sub-optimal decision-making of their colleagues, so after a few minutes or hours of luxuriating in clever hindsight, they drop it.

"But *should* I drop it?" you ask yourself, just as you asked yourself the same question in the midst of the free-for-all when the chairman wouldn't call on you. Your head was teeming at that moment (1) with reasons why you should insist on being heard, competing with reasons why you should go along with your colleagues quietly, and all this was competing with your attempts to follow what others were saying, and so forth — more informa-

---

[9] *Models of Man*, 1957; "Theories of Decision-Making in Economics and Behavioral Science," *The American Economic Review* XLIX (1959), pp. 253–83.

tion at your fingertips than you could handle, so (2) you swiftly, arbitrarily, and unthinkingly blocked off some of it — running the risk of ignoring the most important considerations, and then (3) you gave up trying to *control* your thoughts; you relinquished meta-control and let your thoughts lead wherever they might for awhile. After a bit you somehow (4) resumed control, attempted some ordering and improving of the materials spewed up by the free-for-all, and made the decision to drop it — suffering (5) instant pangs of dubiety and toying with regret, but, because you are wise, you shrugged these off as well.

And how, precisely, did you go about dismissing that evanescent and unarticulated micro-wonder ("should I have dropped it?")? Here the processes become invisible to the naked eye of introspection, but if we look at cognitive science models of "decision-making" and "problem-solving" *within* such swift, unconscious processes as perception and language comprehension, we see further tempting analogues of our phases in the various models of heuristic search and problem-solving.[10]

My suggestion, then, is that time-pressured decision-making is like that *all the way down*. Satisficing extends even back behind the fixed biological design of the decision-making agent, to the design "decisions" that Mother Nature — the process of natural selection — settled for when designing us and other organisms. There may be dividing lines to be drawn somehow between biological, psychological, and cultural manifestations of this structure, but not only are the structures — and their powers and vulnerabilities — basically the same; the particular contents of "deliberation" are probably not locked into any one level in the overall process but can migrate. Under suitable provocation, for instance, one can dredge up some virtually subliminal consideration and elevate

---

[10] The suggestion of temporal ordering in the five phases is not essential, of course. The arbitrary pruning of randomly explored search trees, the triggering of decision by a partial and non-optimal evaluation of results, and the suppression of second-guessing need not follow the sequence in time I outline in the initial example.

it for self-conscious formulation and appreciation — it becomes an "intuition" — and then express it so that others can consider it as well. Moving in the other direction, a reason for action perennially mentioned and debated in committee can eventually "go without saying" — at least out loud — but continue to shape the thinking, both of the group and the individuals, from some more subliminal base (or bases) of operations in the process. And as Donald Campbell and Richard Dawkins have argued, cultural institutions can sometimes be interpreted as compensations or corrections of the "decisions" made by natural selection.[11]

3. THE PANGLOSSIAN SLIDE

The fundamentality of satisficing — the fact that it is the *basic* structure of all real decision-making, moral, prudential, economic, or even evolutionary — gives birth to a familiar and troubling slipperiness of claim that bedevils theory in several quarters. To begin with, notice that merely claiming that this structure is basic is not necessarily saying that it is best, but that conclusion is certainly invited — and inviting. We began this exploration, remember, by looking at a moral *problem* and trying to *solve* it: the problem of designing a *good* (justified, defensible, sound) candidate evaluation process. Suppose we decide that the system we designed is about as good as it could be, given the constraints. A group of roughly rational agents — us — decide that this is the right way to design the process, and we have reasons for choosing the features we did.

Given this genealogy, we might muster the *chutzpah* to declare that this is optimal design — the best of all possible designs. This apparent arrogance might have been imputed to me as soon as I set the problem, for did I not propose to examine how *anyone*

---

[11] Donald Campbell, "On the Conflicts Between Biology and Social Evolution and Between Psychology and Moral Tradition," in *American Psychologist* (December 1975), pp. 1103–26; Richard Dawkins, *The Selfish Gene* (Oxford: Oxford University Press, 1976), ch. 11.

ought to make moral decisions by examining how *we in fact* make a particular moral decision? Who are we to set the pace?[12]

Optimality claims have a way of evaporating, however; it takes no *chutzpah* at all to make the modest admission that this was the best solution *we* could come up with, given our limitations.[13]

I call this the Panglossian slide, after Voltaire's optimistic Dr. Pangloss, who claimed that this is the best of all possible worlds, only to find that the pessimist agreed with him: no better world was possible, alas. The Panglossian slide is ubiquitous. In philosophy it regularly appears in debates about what is rational, in epistemology and in ethics. When it comes to defining *knowledge* as opposed to mere true belief, is "good enough" ever good enough? When it comes to doing the right thing, is it ever right to live by a rule you know to be sub-optimizing or non-maximizing? Can it be rational to opt on occasion for irrationality? This same question reappears in the interpretation of experiments in psychology, sometimes provoking quite hostile debates (for instance, between L. Jonathan Cohen and Amos Tversky about whether human irrationality can be experimentally demonstrated).[14] In

---

[12] Well, who else should we trust? If we can't rely on our own good judgment, it seems we can't get started: "Thus, what and how we do think is evidence for the principles of rationality, what and how we ought to think. This itself is a methodological principle of rationality; call it the *Factunorm Principle*. We are (implicitly) accepting the Factunorm Principle whenever we try to determine what or how we ought to think. For we must, in that very attempt, think. And unless we can think that what and how we do think there is correct — and thus is evidence for what and how we ought to think — we cannot determine what or how we ought to think." R. Wertheimer, "Philosophy on Humanity," in R. L. Perkins, ed., *Abortion: Pro and Con* (Cambridge, Mass.: Schenkman, 1974), pp. 110–11. See also Nelson Goodman, *Fact, Fiction and Forecast*, 2d ed., 1965, p. 63.

[13] Compare that with the claim: "Mother Nature isn't perfect, but she does the best she can." Is that a Panglossian statement or not? See my "Intentional Systems in Cognitive Ethology: The 'Panglossian Paradigm' Defended," *Behavioral and Brain Sciences* 6 (1983), pp. 343–90.

[14] L. J. Cohen, "Can Human Irrationality Be Experimentally Demonstrated?" *Behavioral and Brain Sciences* 4 (1981), pp. 317–70; see also "Continuing Commentary," *Behavioral and Brain Sciences* 6 (1983), pp. 487–517. Commentary by Tversky and others and replies by Cohen are included in these references.

biology it appears in the debate between the adaptationists, who make use of optimality assumptions, and their opponents, who claim — mistakenly — to be innocent of such ideology.[15]

The mistake that is sometimes made is to suppose that there is or must be a single (best or highest) perspective from which to assess ideal rationality. Does the ideally rational agent have the all-too-human problem of not being able to remember certain crucial considerations when they would be most telling, most effective in resolving a quandary? If we stipulate, as a theoretical simplification, that our imagined ideal agent is immune to such disorders, then we don't get to ask the question of what the ideal way might be to cope with them.

The *Moral First Aid Manual* should thus be considered not merely as a grubby compromise with practicality, but itself just as pure an ideal vision as any other in ethics: if you like, it is the book the ideally rational agent would write as his own vade mecum, written in the light of his perfect self-knowledge about his many limitations.

Any such exercise presupposes that certain features — the "limitations" — are fixed, and other features are malleable; the latter are to be adjusted so best to accommodate the former. But one can always change the perspective and ask about one of the presumably malleable features whether it is not, in fact, fixed in one position — a constraint to be accommodated. And one can ask about each of the fixed features whether it is something one would want to tamper with in any event; perhaps it is for the best as it is. Addressing that question requires one to consider still

---

[15] See note 13. A recent clear expression of the claim — which also clearly reveals its confusion, in my opinion — is Stephen Jay Gould, "Cardboard Darwinism," *New York Review of Books*, Sept. 25, 1986, pp. 47–52. Gould's long-term fascination with what he calls the "paradox" inherent in the unavoidable mixture of teleology and tinkering — *bricolage* or *satisficing* versus a God's-eye view of what is best — provides philosophers with a valuable guide to the pitfalls encountered in these issues. See also my "Evolution, Error, and Intentionality," forthcoming in my collection *The Intentional Stance*, from Bradford Books/MIT Press.

further ulterior features as fixed, in order to assess the wisdom of
the feature under review. There is no Archimedean point here,
either; if we suppose the readers of the *Moral First Aid Manual*
are *complete* idiots, our task is impossible, while if we suppose
they are saints our task is too easy to shed any light.[16]

4. SOME SUGGESTIONS FOR THE MORAL FIRST AID MANUAL

If *The Moral First Aid Manual* is to be optimally (or at least
pretty well) addressed to a time-pressured decision-maker, it may
help us design it if we slow the process down once more and look
at what makes for good decision-making at the departmental level.
First, of course, you want to have good colleagues: people who
can be relied upon to come up with the right sorts of considerations right away, without wasting precious time on irrelevancies.[17]

This crucial component is often idealized away in ethical discussions via the introduction of what amounts to a Master of Cere-

---

[16] This comes out graphically in the slippery assumptions about rationality in
theoretical discussions of the Prisoner's Dilemma; there is no problem if you are
entitled to assume that the players are saints; saints always cooperate, after all.
Near-sighted jerks always defect, so they are hopeless. What does "the ideally
rational" player do? Perhaps, as some say, he sees the rationality in adopting the
meta-strategy of turning himself into a less than ideally rational player — in order
to cope with the less than ideally rational players he knows he is apt to face. But
then in what sense *is* that new player less than ideally rational? It is a mistake to
suppose this instability can be made to go away if we just think carefully enough
about what ideal rationality is. That is the *truly* Panglossian fallacy. (Cf. the reflections along these lines in A. Gibbard, "Moral Judgment and the Acceptance of
Norms," Nicholas Sturgeon, "Moral Judgment and Norms," and A. Gibbard, "Reply
to Sturgeon," in *Ethics* 96 [October 1985], pp. 5–41.)

[17] This "translates" readily into the discussions among utilitarians, familiar
since Mill's day, of the value of inculcating good *habits of thought*. But the hunch
that there is any straightforward way of getting such habits to *work* is of a piece
with the complacent assumptions among *epistemologists* that hid the Frame Problem
from them. See my "Cognitive Wheels: An Introduction to the Frame Problem
of AI," in Christopher Hookway, ed., *Minds, Machines and Evolution: Philosophical Studies* (Cambridge: Cambridge University Press, 1984).

monies who handily *provides a frame*, by telling the agent exactly what the available options are.

"Your two choices *this* hour, Mr. Dennett, are

(A) stuff envelopes for Oxfam OR

(B) go to a movie!

What do you choose?"

Well, what happened to the option of watching the evening news, thereby informing myself of national and international problems, or answering some long-overdue letters, or spending the hour chatting with my daughter, or . . . ?

We need to have "alert," "wise" habits of thought — colleagues who will regularly, if not infallibly, draw our attention in directions we will not regret in hindsight. There is no point having more than one colleague if they are clones of each other, all wanting to raise the same consideration, so we may suppose them to be specialists, each somewhat narrow-minded and preoccupied with protecting a certain set of interests.

Now how shall we avert a cacophony of colleagues? We need some *conversation-stoppers*. In addition to our timely and appropriate generators of considerations, we need consideration-generator-squelchers. We need some ploys that will arbitrarily terminate reflections and disquisitions by our colleagues, and cut off debate independently of the specific content of current debate. Why not just a *magic word*? Magic words work fine as control-shifters in artificial intelligence programs, but we're talking about controlling intelligent colleagues here, and they are not apt to be susceptible to magic words, as if they were under post-hypnotic suggestion. That is, good colleagues will be reflective and rational, and open-minded within the limits imposed by their specialist narrow-mindedness. (They could take their motto from the philosophical journal *Nous*: *Nihil philosophicum a nobis alienum putamus* [We deem nothing philosophical to be foreign to us].)

They need to be hit with something that will appeal to their rationality, while discouraging further reflection.

It will not do at all for these people to be *endlessly* philosophizing, endlessly calling us back to first principles and demanding a justification for these apparently (and actually) quite arbitrary principles. What could possibly protect an arbitrary and somewhat second-rate conversation-stopper from such relentless scrutiny? A meta-policy that forbids discussion and reconsideration of the conversation-stoppers? But, our colleagues would want to ask, is *that* a wise policy? Can it be justified? It will not always yield the best results, surely and . . . and so forth.

This is a matter of delicate balance, with pitfalls on both sides. On one side, we must avoid the error of thinking that the solution is *more rationality*, more rules, more justifications, for there is no end to that demand. Any policy *may* be questioned, so unless we provide for some brute and a-rational termination of the issue, we will design a decision process that spirals fruitlessly to infinity. On the other side, no mere brute fact about the way we are built is — or should be — entirely beyond the reach of being undone by further reflection.[18] Although such fixed and hence sphexish (Hofstadter's term; for a discussion see *Elbow Room*, p. 11ff) features of our lives are unavoidable — indeed even sometimes essential — elements in our competence, no one of them is exempt from rational assessment, and we can always at least imagine what it would be like for the feature to be otherwise.

One cannot expect there to be a single stable solution to such a design problem, but rather a variety of uncertain and temporary equilibria, with the conversation-stoppers tending to accrete pearly layers of supporting dogma which themselves cannot withstand

---

[18] Stephen White, in "Self-Deception and Responsibility for the Self," forthcoming in a volume on self-deception, edited by A. Rorty, discusses Strawson's well-known attempt ("Freedom and Resentment," Proc. Brit. Acad., 1962) to terminate the demand for a justification of "our reactive attitudes" in a brute fact about our way of life about which "we have no choice." He shows that this conversation-stopper cannot resist a further demand for justification (which White provides in an ingeniously indirect way).

extended scrutiny, but which do actually serve on occasion, blessedly, to deflect and terminate consideration.

Here are some promising examples:

    "But that would do more harm than good."

    "But that would be murder."

    "But that would be to break a promise."

    "But that would be to use someone merely as a means."

    "But that would violate a person's *right*."

Bentham once rudely dismissed the doctrine of "natural and imprescriptible rights" as "nonsense upon stilts" and we might now reply that perhaps he was right; perhaps talk of rights *is* nonsense upon stilts, but *good* nonsense — and good only because it is on stilts, only because it happens to have the "political" power to keep rising above the meta-reflections, not indefinitely, but usually "high enough," to reassert itself as a compelling — that is, conversation-stopping — "first principle."

It might seem then that "rule worship" of a certain kind is a good thing, at least for agents designed like us. It is good not because there is a certain rule, or set of rules, which is provably the best, or which always yields the right answer, but because having rules works — somewhat — and not having rules doesn't work at all.

But this cannot be all there is to it — unless we really mean "worship," i.e., a-rational allegiance, because just *having* rules, or *endorsing* or *accepting* rules is no design solution at all. Stephen White has suggested to me that a good bumper-sticker slogan for act utilitarians would be "Rules don't punish people; people do!" He goes on to point out that we can reinterpret this slogan as a reminder about the mistake he calls the Nominalist Fallacy: there is nothing magical, or even forcing, about the mere presence of a rule — or other intellectual property, such as a proposition — in a rational agent.[19] Having the rules, all the

---

[19] More secure than a-rational allegiance, White argues ("Self-Deception"), is a "self-supporting disposition" which flows from a set of "noninstrumental desires

information, and even good intentions does not suffice, by itself, to guarantee the right action; the agent must find all the right stuff and use it, even in the face of contrary rational challenges designed to penetrate the conviction.

Having, and recognizing the force of, rules is not enough, and sometimes the agent is better off with less. Douglas Hofstadter draws attention to a phenomenon he calls "reverberant doubt," which is stipulated out of existence in most idealized theoretical discussions. In what Hofstadter calls Wolf's Dilemma, an "obvious" non-dilemma is turned into a serious dilemma by nothing but the passage of time and the possibility of reverberant doubt.

> Imagine that twenty people are selected from your high school graduation class, you among them. You don't know which others have been selected, . . . All you know is that they are all connected to a central computer. Each of you is in a little cubicle, seated on a chair and facing one button on an otherwise blank wall. You are given ten minutes to decide whether or not to push your button. At the end of that time, a light will go on for ten seconds, and while it is on, you may either push or refrain from pushing. All the responses will then go to the central computer, and one minute later, they will result in consequences. Fortunately, the consequences can only be good. If you pushed your button, you will get $100, no strings attached. . . . If *nobody* pushed their button, then *everybody* will get $1,000. But if there was even a single button-pusher, the refrainers will get nothing at all.[20]

Obviously, you do not push the button, right? But what if just one person were just a little bit overcautious or dubious and began wondering whether this was obvious after all? Everyone should allow that this is an outside chance, and everyone should recog-

---

in Ideal Reflective Equilibrium" — a disposition which no rational criticism can challenge, because the subject has no desire to which a critical appeal can be directed.

[20] "Dilemmas for Superrational Thinkers, Leading Up to a Luring Lottery," in Hofstadter, *Metamagical Themas* (New York: Basic Books, 1984), pp. 739–55.

nize that everyone should allow this. As Hofstadter notes, it is a situation "in which the tiniest flicker of a doubt has become amplified into the gravest avalanche of doubt. . . . And one of the annoying things about it is that the brighter you are, the more quickly and clearly you see what there is to fear. A bunch of amiable slowpokes might well be more likely to unanimously refrain and get the big payoff than a bunch of razor-sharp logicians who all think perversely recursively reverberantly" (p. 753).[21]

Faced with a world in which such predicaments are not unknown, we can recognize the appeal of a little old-time religion, some unquestioning dogmatism that will render agents impervious to the subtle invasions of hyperrationality. Creating something rather like that dispositional state is indeed one of the goals of the *Moral First Aid Manual*, which, while we imagine it to be framed as *advice* to a rational, heeding audience, can also be viewed as not having achieved its end unless it has the effect of changing the "operating system" — not merely the "data," not merely the contents of belief or acceptance — of the agents it addresses. For it to succeed in such a special task, it will have to address its target audiences with pinpoint accuracy.

There might, then, be several different *Moral First Aid Manuals*, each effective for a different type of audience. This opens up a disagreeable prospect to philosophers, for two reasons. First,

---

[21] Robert Axelrod has pointed out to me that what Hofstadter calls Wolf's Dilemma is formally identical to Jean-Jacques Rousseau's Parable of the Stag Hunt (in the *Discourse on the Origin and Foundations of Inequality Among Men*). There is a good discussion of the Stag Hunt in Russell Hardin, *Collective Action* (Baltimore and London: Johns Hopkins University Press, 1982), pp. 167ff, from which it appears that Hofstadter's point has been missed in previous discussions, such as those of David Lewis, in *Convention* (Cambridge: Harvard University Press, 1969), and Kenneth Waltz, in *Man, the State, and War* (New York: Columbia University Press, 1965). On Lewis's discussion, "the problem of social cooperation [in Stag Hunt circumstances] does not seem intractable" — because Lewis ignores the prospect of imperfection in the agents, and while Waltz focuses on the possibility that agents with "limited time horizons" will turn such occasions into Prisoners' Dilemmas, there is no appreciation of the further point — Hofstadter's — that even if one supposes that such imperfections are extremely unlikely, the tiniest doubt — even a *groundless* doubt — can undo the stability of the solution.

it suggests, contrary to their austere academic tastes, that there is reason to pay more attention to rhetoric and other only partly or impurely rational means of persuasion; the ideally rational *audience* to whom the ethicist may presume to address his or her reflections is yet another dubiously fruitful idealization. And more important, it suggests that what Williams calls the ideal of "transparency" of a society — "the working of its ethical institutions should not depend on members of the community misunderstanding how they work" — is an ideal that may be politically inaccessible to us.[22] Recoil as we may from elitist mythmaking, and such systematically disingenuous doctrines as the view Williams calls "Government House utilitarianism," [23] we may find — this is an open empirical possibility after all — that we will be extremely lucky to find any rational and transparent route from who we are now to who we would like to be.

Rethinking the *practical* design of a moral agent, via the process of writing various versions of the *Moral First Aid Manual*, might nevertheless allow us to make sense of some of the phenomena traditional ethical theories wave their hands about. For one thing, we might begin to understand our current moral position — by that I mean yours and mine, at this very moment. Here we are, devoting an hour to my meta-meta-meta-reflection on values and valuation. Is this time well spent? Shouldn't we all be out raising money for Oxfam or picketing the Pentagon or writing letters to our senators and representatives about various matters? Did you consciously decide, on the basis of calculations, that the time was ripe for a little sabbatical from real-world engagement, a period "off line" for maintenance and inventory control? Or was your process of decision — if that is not too grand a name for it — much more a matter of your *not* tampering with some current "default" principles that virtually ensure that you

[22] *Ethics and the Limits of Philosophy*, p. 101. Williams notes that this is the ideal Rawls calls "publicity" in *A Theory of Justice*.

[23] Ibid., p. 108.

will ignore all but the most galvanizing potential interruptions to your rather narrow, personal lives?

If so, is that itself a lamentable feature, or something we finite beings could not conceivably do without? Consider a traditional bench test which most systems of ethics can pass with aplomb: solving the problem of what you should do if you are walking along, minding your own business, and you hear a cry for help from a drowning man. That is the easy problem, a conveniently delimited, already well-*framed* local decision. The hard problem is: how do we get there from here? How can we *justifiably* find a route from our actual predicament to that relatively happy and straightforwardly decidable predicament? Our prior problem, it seems, is that every day, while trying desperately to mind our own business, we hear a thousand cries for help, complete with volumes of information on how we might oblige. How on earth could anyone prioritize that cacophony? Not by any systematic process of considering all things, weighing expected utilities, and attempting to maximize. Nor by any systematic generation and testing of Kantian maxims — there are too many to consider.

Yet we do get there from here. Few of us are paralyzed by such indecision for long stretches of time. By and large, we must solve this decision problem by allowing an utterly "indefensible" set of defaults to shield our attention from all but our current projects. Disruptions of those defaults can only occur by a process that is bound to be helter-skelter heuristics, with arbitrary and unexamined conversation-stoppers bearing most of the weight.

That arena of competition encourages escalations, of course. With our strictly limited capacity for attention, the problem faced by others who want us to consider their favorite consideration is essentially a problem of advertising — of attracting the attention of the well-intentioned. This is the same problem whether we view it in the wide-scale arena of politics, or in the close-up arena of personal deliberation. The role of the traditional formulae of ethical discussion as directors of attention, or as shapers of habits of moral imagination, is thus a subject for further scrutiny.

For better or for worse, your attention got attracted to my considerations for more than my share of time. I am grateful for it, and hope it proves to have been time well spent.

The Significance of Choice

T. M. SCANLON, JR.

THE TANNER LECTURES ON HUMAN VALUES

Delivered at
Brasenose College, Oxford University

May 16, 23, and 28, 1986

T. M. SCANLON is Professor of Philosophy at Harvard University. He was educated at Princeton, Brasenose College, Oxford, and Harvard, and taught philosophy at Princeton from 1966 until 1984. Professor Scanlon is the author of a number of articles in moral and political philosophy and was one of the founding editors of *Philosophy and Public Affairs*.

Lecture 1

1. INTRODUCTION

Choice has obvious and immediate moral significance. The fact that a certain action or outcome resulted from an agent's choice can make a crucial difference both to our moral appraisal of that agent and to our assessment of the rights and obligations of the agent and others after the action has been performed. My aim in these lectures is to investigate the nature and basis of this significance. The explanation which I will offer will be based upon a contractualist account of morality — that is, a theory according to which an act is right if it would be required or allowed by principles which no one, suitably motivated, could reasonably reject as a basis for informed, unforced general agreement.[1]

I believe that it is possible within this general theory of morality to explain the significance of various familiar moral notions such as rights, welfare, and responsibility in a way that preserves their apparent independence rather than reducing all of them to one master concept such as utility. The present lectures are an attempt to carry out this project for the notions of responsibility and choice.

This is a revised version of three lectures presented at Brasenose College, Oxford, on May 16, 23, and 28, 1986. I am grateful to the participants in the seminars following those lectures for their challenging and instructive comments. These lectures are the descendants of a paper, entitled "Freedom of the Will in Political Theory," which I delivered at a meeting of the Washington, D.C., Area Philosophy Club in November 1977. Since that time I have presented many intervening versions to various audiences. I am indebted to members of those audiences and to numerous other friends for comments, criticism, and helpful suggestions.

[1] I have set out my version of contractualism in "Contractualism and Utilitarianism," in Amartya Sen and Bernard Williams, eds., *Utilitarianism and Beyond* (Cambridge: Cambridge University Press, 1982), pp. 103–28. What follows can be seen as an attempt to fulfill, for the case of choice, the promissory remarks made at the end of section III of that paper.

2. The Problems of Free Will

Quite apart from this general theoretical project, however, there is another, more familiar reason for inquiring into the basis of the moral significance of choice. This is the desire to understand and respond to the challenge to that significance which has gone under the heading of the problem of free will. This problem has a number of forms. One form identifies free will with a person's freedom to act otherwise than he or she in fact did or will. The problem, on this view, is the threat to this freedom posed by deterministic conceptions of the universe. A second, related problem is whether determinism, if true, would deprive us of the kind of freedom, whatever it may be, which is presupposed by moral praise and blame. This version of the problem is closer to my present concern in that it has an explicitly moral dimension. In order to address it one needs to find out what the relevant kind of freedom is, and this question can be approached by asking what gives free choice and free action their special moral significance. Given an answer to this question, which is the one I am primarily concerned with, we can then ask how the lack of freedom would threaten this significance and what kinds of unfreedom would do so.

The challenge I have in mind, however, is not posed by determinism but by what I call the Causal Thesis. This is the thesis that the events which are human actions, thoughts, and decisions are linked to antecedent events by causal laws as deterministic as those governing other goings-on in the universe. According to this thesis, given antecedent conditions and the laws of nature, the occurrence of an act of a specific kind follows, either with certainty or with a certain degree of probability, the indeterminacy being due to chance factors of the sort involved in other natural processes. I am concerned with this thesis rather than with determinism because it seems to me that the space opened up by the falsity of determinism would be relevant to morality only if it were filled by something other than the cumulative effects of indeterministic physical processes. If the actions we perform result from the fact that we have a certain physical constitution and have been subjected to certain outside influences, then an apparent threat to morality remains, even if the links between these causes and their effects are not deterministic.

The idea that there is such a threat is sometimes supported by thought experiments such as the following: Suppose you were to learn that someone's present state of mind, intentions, and actions were produced in him or her a few minutes ago by the action of outside forces, for example by electrical stimulation of the nervous system. You would not think it appropriate to blame that person for what he or she does under such conditions. But if the Causal Thesis is true then all of our actions are like this. The only differences are in the form of outside intervention and the span of time over which it occurs, but surely these are not essential to the freedom of the agent.

How might this challenge be answered? One strategy would be to argue that there are mistakes in the loose and naive idea of causality to which the challenge appeals or in the assumptions it makes about the relation between mental and physical events. There is obviously much to be said on both of these topics. I propose, however, to follow a different (but equally familiar) line. Leaving the concepts of cause and action more or less unanalyzed, I will argue that the apparent force of the challenge rests on mistaken ideas about the nature of moral blame and responsibility.[2]

---

[2] In his admirably clear and detailed defense of incompatibilism, Peter van Inwagen observes that if one accepts the premises of his argument for the incompatibility of determinism and free will (in the sense required for moral responsibility) then it is "puzzling" how people could have the kind of freedom required for moral responsibility even under indeterministic universal causation. (See *An Essay on Free Will* [Oxford: Oxford University Press, 1983], pp. 149–50.) On the other hand, he takes it to be not merely puzzling but inconceivable that free will should be impossible or that the premises of his arguments for incompatibilism should be false or that the rules of inference which these arguments employ should be invalid. This leads him, after some further argument, to reject determinism: "If incompatibilism is true, then either determinism or the free-will thesis is false.

It has sometimes been maintained that even if the Causal Thesis holds, this does not represent the kind of unfreedom that excuses agents from moral blame. That kind of unfreedom, it is sometimes said, is specified simply by the excusing conditions which we generally recognize: a person is acting unfreely in the relevant sense only if he or she is acting under posthypnotic suggestion, or under duress, is insane, or falls under some other generally recognized excusing condition. Since the Causal Thesis does not imply that people are always acting under one or another of these conditions, it does not imply that moral praise and blame are generally inapplicable.

I am inclined to think that there is something right about this reaffirmation of common sense. But in this simple form it has been rightly rejected as question begging. It begs the question because it does not take account of the claim that commonsense morality itself holds that people cannot be blamed for what they do when their behavior is the result of outside causes, a claim which is supported by our reactions to imaginary cases like the thought experiment mentioned above and by more general reflection on what a world of universal causality would be like.

In order to show that moral praise and blame are compatible with the Causal Thesis, it is necessary to rebut this claim. The most promising strategy for doing so is to look for a general account of the moral significance of choice, an account which, on

---

To deny the free-will thesis is to deny the existence of moral responsibility, which would be absurd. Moreover, there seems to be no good reason to accept determinism (which, it should be recalled, is *not* the same as the Principle of Universal Causation). Therefore, we should reject determinism" (p. 223).

My response is somewhat different. Determinism is a very general empirical thesis. Our convictions about moral responsibility seem to me an odd basis for drawing a conclusion one way or the other about such a claim. In addition, whatever one may decide about determinism, it remains puzzling how moral responsibility could be compatible with Universal Causation. I am thus led to wonder whether our initial assumptions about the kind of freedom required by moral responsibility might not be mistaken. Rather than starting with a reinterpretation of the principle of alternative possibilities (along the lines of the conditional analysis), my strategy is to ask first, Why does the fact of choice matter morally? and then, What kind of freedom is relevant to mattering in that way?

the one hand, explains why the significance of choice is undermined both by commonly recognized excusing conditions and by
factors such as those imagined to be at work in the thought experiment described above and, on the other hand, explains why the
moral significance of choice will not be undermined everywhere
if the Causal Thesis is true. Such an account, if convincing, would
provide a basis for arguing that our initial response to the Causal
Thesis was mistaken. At the very least, it would shift the burden
of argument to the incompatibilist, who would need to explain
why the proffered account of the moral significance of choice was
inadequate. Before beginning my search for an account of the
significance of choice, however, I will take a moment to examine
some other forms of the free-will problem.

The problem of free will is most often discussed as a problem
about moral responsibility, but essentially the same problem arises
in other forms as well. It arises in political philosophy, for example, as a problem about the significance of choice as a legitimating
condition. We generally think that the fact that the affected
parties chose or assented to an outcome is an important factor in
making that outcome legitimate. But we also recognize that there
are conditions under which acquiescence does not have this legitimating force. These include conditions like those listed above:
hypnosis, brain stimulation, mental incapacity, brainwashing, and
so on. To many, at least, it seems plausible to maintain that these
conditions deprive choice of its moral significance because they are
conditions under which the agent's action is the result of outside
causes. But if the Causal Thesis holds, this is true of all actions,
and it would follow that choice never has moral significance as a
legitimating factor.

Let me turn to a different example, drawn from John Rawls's
book, *A Theory of Justice.*[3] (I believe the example involves a
misinterpretation of Rawls, albeit a fairly natural one, but I will

[3] *A Theory of Justice* (Cambridge, Mass.: Harvard University Press, 1971),
pp. 72–74, 104.

try to correct that later.) Replying to an argument for the justice of a purely laissez-faire economy, Rawls observes that in such a system economic rewards would be unacceptably dependent on factors such as innate talents and fortunate family circumstances, which are, as he puts it, "arbitrary from a moral point of view." In particular, he says that even such factors as willingness to exert oneself will depend to a large extent on family circumstances and upbringing. Therefore we cannot say, of those who might have improved their economic position if they had exerted themselves, that because their predicament is their own doing they have no legitimate complaint. Their lack of exertion has no legitimating force because it is the result of "arbitrary factors."

But this argument, if successful, would seem to prove too much. Consider a society satisfying Rawls's Difference Principle. This principle permits some inequalities, such as those resulting from incentives which improve productivity enough to make everyone better off. When such inequalities exist, they will be due to the fact that some people have responded to these incentives while others have not. If the Causal Thesis is correct, however, there will be some causal explanation of these differences in behavior. They will not be due to gross differences in economic status, since, by hypothesis, these do not exist. But they must be due to something, and it seems clear that the factors responsible, whatever they are, are likely to be as "morally arbitrary" in at least one sense of that phrase as the factors at work in the case of the laissez-faire society to which Rawls was objecting. To sustain Rawls's argument, then, we need a better explanation of how "morally arbitrary" background conditions can undermine the legitimating force of choice, an explanation which will not deprive all choice of moral force if the Causal Thesis is correct.

Let me mention a further, slightly different case. We think it important that a political system should, as we say, "leave people free to make up their own minds," especially about important political questions and questions of personal values. We regard certain conditions as incompatible with this important freedom and therefore to be avoided. Brainwashing is one extreme example, but there are also more moderate, and more common, forms of manipulation, such as strict control of sources of information, bombardment with one-sided information, and the creation of an environment in which people are distracted from certain questions by fear or other competing stimuli. What is it that is bad about these conditions? If they count as conditions of unfreedom simply because they are conditions under which people's opinions are causal products of outside factors, then there is no such thing as "freedom of thought" if the Causal Thesis is correct. It would follow that defenders of "freedom of thought" who accept the Causal Thesis could rightly be accused of ideological blindness: what they advocate as "freedom" is really just determination by a different set of outside factors, factors which are less rational and no more benign than those to which they object. There may be good reasons to favor some determining factors over others, but the issue cannot be one of "freedom." Here again, then, the problem is to show that "determination by outside causes" is not a sufficient condition for unfreedom. To do this we need to come up with some other explanation of what is bad about the conditions which supporters of freedom of thought condemn.[4]

These are versions of what I will call the political problem of free will. As I have said, they have much the same structure as the more frequently discussed problem about moral praise and blame. In addition to these problems there is what might be called the personal problem of free will. If I were to learn that one of my past actions was the result of hypnosis or brain stimulation, I would feel alienated from this act: manipulated, trapped, reduced to the status of a puppet. But why, if the Causal Thesis is correct, should we not feel this way about all of our acts? Why should

---

[4] I have said more about this version of the problem in section IIB of "Freedom of Expression and Categories of Expression," *University of Pittsburgh Law Review* 40 (1979).

we not feel trapped all the time? This is like the other problems in that what we need in order to answer it is a better explanation of why it is proper to feel trapped and alienated from our own actions in cases like hypnosis, an explanation which goes beyond the mere fact of determination by outside factors. But while this problem is like the others in its form, it differs from them in not being specifically a problem about morality: the significance with which it deals is not *moral* significance. This makes it a particularly difficult problem, much of the difficulty being that of explaining what the desired but threatened form of significance is supposed to be. Since my concern is with moral theory I will not address this problem directly, though the discussion of the value of choice in lecture 2 will have some bearing on it.

I will be concerned in these lectures with the first two of these problems and with the relation between them: to what degree can the "better explanation" that each calls for be provided within the compass of a single, reasonably unified theory? My strategy is to put forward two theories which attempt to explain why the conditions which we commonly recognize as undermining the moral significance of choice in various contexts should have this effect. These theories, which I will refer to as the Quality of Will theory and the Value of Choice theory, are similar to the theories put forward in two famous articles, P. F. Strawson's "Freedom and Resentment," [5] and H. L. A. Hart's "Legal Responsibility and Excuses." [6] My aim is to see whether versions of these two approaches — extended in some respects and modified in others to fit within the contractualist theory I espouse — can be put together into a single coherent account. We can then see how far this combined theory takes us toward providing a satisfactory account of the moral significance of choice across the range of cases I have listed above.

[5] In Strawson, ed., *Studies in the Philosophy of Thought and Action* (Oxford: Oxford University Press, 1968), pp. 71–96.

[6] Chapter 2 of Hart, *Punishment and Responsibility* (Oxford: Oxford University Press, 1968).

3. THE INFLUENCEABILITY THEORY

Before presenting the Quality of Will theory, it will be helpful to consider briefly an older view which serves as a useful benchmark. This view, which I will call the Influenceability theory, employs a familiar strategy for explaining conditions which excuse a person from moral blame.[7] This strategy is first to identify the purpose or rationale of moral praise and blame and then to show that this rationale fails when the standard excusing conditions are present. According to the Influenceability theory, the purpose of moral praise and blame is to influence people's behavior. There is thus no point in praising or blaming agents who are not (or were not) susceptible to being influenced by moral suasion, and it is this fact which is reflected in the commonly recognized excusing conditions.

The difficulties with this theory are, I think, well known.[8] I will not go into them here except to make two brief points. The first is that the theory appears to conflate the question of whether moral judgment is applicable and the question of whether it should be *expressed* (in particular, expressed to the agent). The second point is that difficulties arise for the theory when it is asked whether what matters is influenceability at or shortly before the time of action or influenceability at the (later) time when moral judgment is being expressed. The utilitarian rationale for praise and blame supports the latter interpretation, but it is the former which retains a tie with commonsense notions of responsibility.

[7] See J. J. C. Smart, "Freewill, Praise, and Blame," *Mind* 70 (1961): 291–306; reprinted in G. Dworkin, ed., *Determinism, Free Will, and Moral Responsibility* (Englewood Cliffs, N.J.: Prentice-Hall, 1970; page references will be to this edition). The theory was stated earlier by Moritz Schlick in chapter 7 of *The Problems of Ethics*, trans. D. Rynin (New York: Prentice-Hall, 1939), reprinted as "When Is a Man Responsible?" in B. Berofsky, ed., *Free Will and Determinism* (New York: Harper and Row, 1966; page references will be to this edition).

[8] Some are set forth by Jonathan Bennett in section 6 of "Accountability," in Zak van Staaten, ed., *Philosophical Subjects* (Oxford: Oxford University Press, 1980).

The Influenceability theory might explain why a utilitarian system of behavior control would include something like what we now recognize as excusing conditions. What some proponents of the theory have had in mind is that commonsense notions of responsibility should be given up and replaced by such a utilitarian practice. Whatever the merits of this proposal, however, it is clear that the Influenceability theory does not provide a satisfactory account of the notions of moral praiseworthiness and blameworthiness as we now understand them. The usefulness of administering praise or blame depends on too many factors other than the nature of the act in question for there ever to be a good fit between the idea of influenceability and the idea of responsibility which we now employ.[9]

4. QUALITY OF WILL: STRAWSON'S ACCOUNT

The view which Strawson presents in "Freedom and Resentment" is clearly superior to the Influenceability theory. Like that theory, however, it focuses less on the cognitive content of moral judgments than on what people are doing in making them. The centerpiece of Strawson's analysis is the idea of a reactive attitude. It is the nature of these attitudes that they are reactions not simply to what happens to us or to others but rather to the attitudes toward ourselves or others which are revealed in an agent's actions. For example, when you tread on my blistered toes, I may feel excruciating pain and greatly regret that my toes were stepped on. In addition, however, I am likely to resent the malevolence or callousness or indifference to my pain which your action indicates. This resentment is what Strawson calls a "personal reactive attitude": it is my attitudinal reaction to the attitude toward me which is revealed in your action. Moral indignation, on the other

---

[9] Broadening the theory to take into account the possibility of influencing people other than the agent will produce a better fit in some cases, but at the price of introducing even more considerations which are intuitively irrelevant to the question of responsibility.

hand, is what he calls a "vicarious attitude": a reaction to the attitude toward others in general (e.g., lack of concern about their pain) which your action shows you to have. All of these are what Strawson calls "participant attitudes." They "belong to involvement or participation with others in inter-personal human relationships." [10] This is in contrast to "objective attitudes," which involve seeing a person "as an object of social policy; as an object for what in a wide range of senses might be called treatment; as something certainly to be taken account, perhaps precautionary account, of; to be managed or handled or cured or trained." [11]

It follows from this characterization that the discovery of new facts about an action or an agent can lead to the modification or withdrawal of a reactive attitude in at least three ways: (a) by showing that the action was not, after all, indicative of the agent's attitude toward ourselves or others; (b) by showing that the attitude indicated in the act was not one which makes a certain reactive attitude appropriate; (c) by leading us to see the agent as someone toward whom objective, rather than participant, attitudes are appropriate.

Commonly recognized excusing conditions work in these ways. The most extreme excusing conditions sever any connection between an action (or movement) and the attitudes of the agent. If your stepping on my toes was a mere bodily movement resulting from an epileptic seizure, then it shows nothing at all about your concern or lack of concern about my pain. It would therefore be inappropriate for me to resent your action or for someone else, taking a more impartial view, to feel moral disapproval of you on that account.

Other excusing conditions have the less extreme effect of modifying the quality of will which an action can be taken to indicate, thus modifying the reactive attitudes which are appropri-

[10] Strawson, "Freedom and Resentment," p. 79.
[11] Ibid.

ate. If I learn, for example, that you stepped on my foot by accident, then I can no longer resent your callousness or malevolence,
but I may still, if conditions are right, resent your carelessness. If
I learn that you (reasonably) believed that the toy spider on my
boot was real, and that you were saving my life by killing it before
it could bite me, then I can no longer *resent* your action at all,
although it remains indicative of a particular quality of will on
your part.

Actions produced by posthypnotic suggestion are a less clear
case. Much depends on what we take the hypnosis to do. Hypnosis might lead you to perform the intentional act of stamping your
foot on mine but without any malice or even any thought that you
are causing me harm. In this case a criticizable attitude is indicated by your act: a kind of complacency toward touching other
people's bodies in ways that you have reason to believe are unwanted. But this attitude is not really attributable to *you*. *You*
may not lack any inhibition in this regard: it is just that your
normal inhibition has been inhibited by the hypnotist. The case is
similar if the hypnotist implants in you a passing hatred for me
and a fleeting but intense desire to cause me pain. Here again
there is a criticizable attitude — more serious this time — but it is
not yours. It is "just visiting," so to speak.

Strawson's account of why conditions such as insanity and
extreme immaturity excuse people from moral blame is less satisfactory. The central idea is that these conditions lead us to take an
"objective attitude" toward a person rather than to see him or her
as a participant in those interpersonal human relationships of
which the reactive attitudes are a part. Strawson's claim here can
be understood on two levels. On the one hand there is the empirical claim that when we see someone as "warped or deranged,
neurotic or just a child . . . all our reactive attitudes tend to be pro-
foundly modified." [12] In addition to this, however, there is the

---

[12] Ibid. My appreciation of this straightforwardly factual reading of Strawson's
argument was aided by Jonathan Bennett's perceptive analysis in "Accountability."

suggestion that these factors render reactive attitudes such as resentment and indignation *inappropriate*. But Strawson's theory does not explain the grounds of this form of inappropriateness as clearly as it explained the grounds of the other excusing conditions. In fact, aside from the references to interpersonal relationships, which are left unspecified, nothing is said on this point.

In other cases, however, Strawson's theory succeeds in giving a better explanation of commonly recognized excusing conditions than that offered by the idea that a person is not to be blamed for an action which is the result of outside causes. The mere fact of causal determination seems to have little to do with the most common forms of excuse, such as accident and mistake of fact. It is a distinct advantage of Strawson's analysis that it accounts for the force of more extreme excuses such as hypnosis and brain stimulation in a way that is continuous with a natural explanation of these less extreme cases as well. Moreover, his theory can explain the relevance of "inability to do otherwise" in several senses of that phrase. Sometimes, as in the case of brain stimulation, the factors which underlie this inability sever any connection between an action and the agent's attitudes. In other cases, "inability to do otherwise" in the different sense of lack of *eligible* alternatives can modify the quality of will indicated by an agent's willingness to choose a particular course of action. For example, if you stamp on my toes because my archenemy, who is holding your child hostage next door, has ordered you to do so, this does not make you less *responsible* for your act. The act is still fully yours, but the quality of will which it indicates on your part is not blameworthy.

As Strawson observes, these appeals to "inability to do otherwise" do not generalize. The truth of the Causal Thesis would not mean that either of these forms of inability obtained generally or that actions never indicated the presence in the agent of those attitudes or qualities of will which make resentment or moral indignation appropriate.

Like the unsuccessful defense of common sense mentioned above, Strawson's analysis is internal to our moral concepts as we now understand them. Its explanation of the conditions which negate or modify moral responsibility rests on a claim that, given the kind of thing that moral indignation is, it is an appropriate response only to actions which manifest certain attitudes on the part of the agent. This internal character may be thought to be a weakness in Strawson's account, and he himself considers an objection of this sort. The objection might be put as follows: You have shown what is and is not appropriate given the moral notions we now have; but the question is whether, if the Causal Thesis is correct, it would not be irrational to go on using those concepts and holding the attitudes they describe. Strawson's direct response to this objection is to say that the change proposed is "practically inconceivable."

> The human commitment to participation in ordinary interpersonal relationships is, I think, too thoroughgoing and deeply rooted for us to take seriously the thought that a general conviction might so change our world that, in it, there were no longer any such things as inter-personal relationships as we normally understand them; and being involved in inter-personal relationships as we normally understand them precisely is being exposed to the range of reactive attitudes and feelings that is in question.[13]

But there is another reply which is suggested by something that Strawson goes on to say and which seems to me much stronger.[14] This reply points out that the principle "If your action was a causal consequence of prior factors outside your control then you cannot properly be praised or blamed for performing it" derives its strength from its claim to be supported by commonsense morality. Consequently, if an analysis such as Strawson's succeeds

[13] Strawson, "Freedom and Resentment," p. 82.

[14] Ibid., p. 83.

in giving a convincing account of the requirements of freedom implicit in our ordinary moral views — in particular, giving a systematic explanation of why commonly recognized excusing conditions should excuse — then this is success enough. Succeeding this far undermines the incompatibilist challenge by striking at its supposed basis in everyday moral thought.[15]

Plausible and appealing though it is, there are several respects in which Strawson's analysis is not fully satisfactory. One of these has already been mentioned in connection with insanity. Strawson suggests that the attitudes which moral judgments express are appropriately held only toward people who are participants in certain interpersonal relationships and that these attitudes are therefore inhibited when we become aware of conditions which render a person unfit for these relationships. But one needs to know more about what these relationships are, about why moral reactive attitudes depend on them, and about how these relationships are undermined or ruled out by factors such as insanity.

A second problem is more general. Strawson explains why certain kinds of unfreedom make moral praise and blame inapplicable by appealing to a fact about interpersonal reactive attitudes in general (and moral ones in particular), namely the fact that they are attitudes toward the attitudes of others, as manifested in their actions. But one may wonder whether anything further can be said about why attitudes of moral approval and disapproval are of this general type. Moreover, it is not clear that moral judgments need always involve the *expression* of any par-

---

[15] Compare Thomas Nagel's comments on Strawson's theory in *The View from Nowhere* (Oxford: Oxford University Press, 1986), pp. 124–26. The response I am advocating here does not deny the possibility of what Nagel has called "external" criticism of our practices of moral evaluation. It tries only to deny the incompatibilist critique a foothold in our ordinary ideas of moral responsibility. It claims that a commitment to freedom which is incompatible with the Causal Thesis is not embedded in our ordinary moral practices in the way in which a commitment to objectivity which outruns our experience is embedded in the content of our ordinary empirical beliefs. The incompatibilist response, obviously, is to deny this claim. My point is that the ensuing argument, which I am trying to advance one side of, is internal to the system of our ordinary moral beliefs.

ticular reactive attitude. For example, I may believe that an action of a friend, to whom many horrible things have recently happened, is morally blameworthy. But need this belief, or its expression, involve a feeling or expression of moral indignation or disapproval on my part? Might I not agree that what he did was wrong but be incapable of feeling disapproval toward him?

Here Strawson's analysis faces a version of one of the objections to the Influenceability theory: it links the content of a moral judgment too closely to *one* of the things that may be done in expressing that judgment. Of course, Strawson need not claim that moral judgment always involves the expression of a reactive attitude. It would be enough to say that such a judgment always makes some attitude (e.g., disapproval) appropriate. But then one wonders what the content of this underlying judgment is and whether the requirement of freedom is not to be explained by appeal to this content rather than to the attitudes which it makes appropriate.

In order to answer these questions one needs a more complete account of moral blameworthiness. A number of different moral theories might be called upon for this purpose, but what I will do is to sketch briefly how a Quality of Will theory might be based on a contractualist account of moral judgment.

5. QUALITY OF WILL: A CONTRACTUALIST ANALYSIS

According to contractualism as I understand it, the basic moral motivation is a desire to regulate one's behavior according to standards that others could not reasonably reject insofar as they, too, were looking for a common set of practical principles. Morality, on this view, is what might be called a system of co-deliberation. Moral reasoning is an attempt to work out principles which each of us could be expected to employ as a basis for deliberation and to accept as a basis for criticism. To believe that one is morally at fault is just to believe that one has not regulated one's behavior in the way that such standards would

require. This can be so either because one has failed to attend
to considerations that such standards would require one to take
account of or because one has consciously acted contrary to what
such standards would require. If one is concerned, as most people
are to at least some extent, to be able to justify one's actions to
others on grounds they could not reasonably reject, then the
realization that one has failed in these ways will normally produce
an attitude of serious self-reproach. But this attitude is distinct
from the belief which may give rise to it. Similarly, to believe that
another person's behavior is morally faulty is, at base, to believe
that there is a divergence of this kind between the way that person
regulated his or her behavior and the kind of self-regulation that
mutually acceptable standards would require. For reasons like
those just mentioned, this belief will normally be the basis for
attitudes of disapproval and indignation. This view of morality
grounds the fact that moral appraisal is essentially concerned with
"the quality of an agent's will" in an account of the nature of
moral reasoning and moral motivation. The analysis of moral
judgment which it supports is essentially cognitivist. It can explain
why moral judgments would normally be accompanied by certain
attitudes, but these attitudes are not the basis of its account of
moral judgment.

Contractualism also gives specific content to the idea, suggested by Strawson, that moral judgments presuppose a form of
interpersonal relationship. On this view, moral judgments apply
to people considered as possible participants in a system of co-
deliberation. Moral praise and blame can thus be rendered inapplicable by abnormalities which make this kind of participation
impossible. (The implications of this idea for excusing conditions
such as insanity will be discussed below.)

6. THE SPECIAL FORCE OF MORAL JUDGMENT

Insofar as it goes beyond Strawson's theory in committing itself
to a fuller account of the nature of moral blameworthiness, the

contractualist view I have described leaves itself open to the objection that this notion of blameworthiness requires a stronger form of freedom, a form which may be incompatible with the Causal Thesis. In order to assess this objection, it will be helpful to compare the contractualist account of blame with what Smart calls "praise and dispraise." According to Smart, we commonly use the word "praise" in two different ways.[16] On the one hand, praise is the opposite of blame. These terms apply only to what a person does or to aspects of a person's character, and they are supposed to carry a special force of moral approval or condemnation. But we also praise things other than persons and their character: the California climate, the flavor of a melon, or the view from a certain hill. In this sense we also praise features of persons which we see as "gifts" beyond their control: their looks, their coordination, or their mathematical ability. Praise in this sense is not the opposite of blame, and Smart coins the term "dispraise" to denote its negative correlate. Praise and dispraise lack the special force of moral approval or condemnation which praise and blame are supposed to have. To praise or dispraise something is simply to grade it.

Smart takes the view that the kind of moral judgment involved in praise and blame as these terms are normally used must be rejected because it presupposes an unacceptable metaphysics of free will. However, we can praise and dispraise actions and character just as we can grade eyes and skill and mountain peaks. The primary function of praise in this "grading" sense, according to Smart, is just "to tell people what people are like."[17] However, since people like being praised and dislike being dispraised, praise and dispraise also have the important secondary function of serving to encourage or discourage classes of actions. Smart suggests that "clear-headed people," insofar as they use the terminology of praise and blame, will use it only in this "grading" sense and will

---

[16] Smart, "Freewill, Praise, and Blame," p. 210.
[17] Ibid., p. 211.

restrict its use to cases in which this important secondary function can be fulfilled.

Most people would agree that moral praise and blame of the kind involved when we "hold a person responsible" have a force which goes beyond the merely informational function of "telling people what people are like." The problem for a compatibilist is to show that judgments with this "additional force" can be appropriate even if the Causal Thesis is true. The prior problem for moral theory is to say what this "additional force" is. What is it that an account of moral judgment must capture in order to be successfully "compatibilist"?

As I have said, Smart's analysis is not compatibilist. His aim is to replace ordinary moral judgment, not to analyze it. Strawson, on the other hand, is offering a compatibilist analysis of (at least some kinds of) moral judgment, and his analysis clearly satisfies one-half of the compatibilist test. The expression of interpersonal reactive attitudes is compatible with the Causal Thesis for much the same reason that Smart's notions of praise and dispraise are. These attitudes are reactions to "what people are like," as this is shown in their actions. As long as the people in question really are like this — as long, that is, as their actions really do manifest the attitudes in question — these reactive attitudes are appropriate.

Strawson's theory is more appealing than Smart's because it offers a plausible account of moral judgment as we currently understand it, an account of how moral judgment goes beyond merely "saying what people are like" and of how it differs from mere attempts to influence behavior. But his theory is like Smart's in locating the "special force" of moral judgment in what the moral judge is *doing*. The contractualist account I am offering, on the other hand, locates the origin of this distinctive force in what is claimed about the person judged. It is quite compatible with this analysis that moral judgments should often be intended to influence behavior and that they should often be made as expressions of reactive attitudes; but such reforming or expressive intent is not essential. What is essential, on this account, is that a judgment of moral blame asserts that the way in which an agent decided what to do was not in accord with standards which that agent either accepts or should accept insofar as he or she is concerned to justify his or her actions to others on grounds that they could not reasonably reject. This is description, but given that most people care about the justifiability of their actions to others, it is not *mere* description.

This account of the special force of moral judgment may still seem inadequate. Given what I have said it may seem that, on the contractualist view, this special force lies simply in the fact that moral judgments attribute to an agent properties which most people are seriously concerned to have or to avoid. In this respect moral judgments are like judgments of beauty or intelligence. But these forms of appraisal, and the pride and shame that can go with accepting them, involve no attribution of responsibility and hence raise no question of freedom. To the extent that moral appraisal is different in this respect, and does raise a special question of freedom, it would seem that this difference is yet to be accounted for.

One way in which freedom is relevant to moral appraisal on the Quality of Will theory (the main way mentioned so far) is this: insofar as we are talking about praising or blaming a person on the basis of a particular action, the freedom or unfreedom of that action is relevant to the question whether the intentions and attitudes seemingly implicit in it are actually present in the agent. This evidential relevance of freedom is not peculiar to moral appraisal, however. Similar questions can arise in regard to assessments of intelligence or skill on the basis of particular pieces of behavior. (We may ask, for example, whether the occasion was a fair test of her skill, or whether there were interfering conditions.) The objection just raised does not dispute the ability of the Quality of Will theory to explain *this* way in which moral judgments may depend on questions of freedom, but it suggests that this is not enough. It assumes that "blameworthy" intentions and attitudes are correctly attributed to an agent and then asks how, on the analysis I have offered, this attribution goes beyond welcome or unwelcome description. Behind the objection lies the idea that going "beyond description" in the relevant sense would involve holding the agent *responsible* in a way that people are not (normally) responsible for being beautiful or intelligent and that this notion of responsibility brings with it a further condition of freedom which my discussion of the Quality of Will theory has so far ignored.

I do not believe that in order to criticize a person for behaving in a vicious and callous manner we must maintain that he or she is responsible for becoming vicious and callous. Whether a person is so responsible is, in my view, a separate question. Leaving this question aside, however, there is a sense in which we are responsible for — or, I would prefer to say, *accountable for* — our intentions and decisions but not for our looks or intelligence. This is just because, insofar as these intentions and decisions are *ours*, it is appropriate to ask us to justify or explain them — appropriate, that is, for someone to ask, Why do you think you can treat me this way? in a way that it would not be appropriate to ask, in an accusing tone, Why are you so tall? This is not to say that these mental states are the kinds of thing which have reasons *rather than causes* but only that they are states for which requests for reasons are in principle relevant.

Moral criticism and moral argument, on the contractualist view, consist in the exchange of such requests and justifications. Adverse moral judgment therefore differs from mere unwelcome description because it calls for particular kinds of response, such as justification, explanation, or admission of fault. In what way does it "call for" these responses? Here let me make three points. First, the person making an adverse moral judgment is often literally asking for or demanding an explanation, justification, or apology. Second, moral criticism concerns features of the agent for which questions about reasons, raised by the agent him or herself, are appropriate. Insofar as I think of a past intention, decision, or action as *mine*, I think of it as something which was sensitive to my assessment, at the time, of relevant reasons. This makes it appropriate for me to ask myself, Why did I think or do that? and Do I still take those reasons to be sufficient? Third, the contractualist account of moral motivation ties these two points together. A person who is concerned to be able to justify him- or herself to others will be moved to respond to the kind of demand I have mentioned, will want to be able to respond positively (i.e., with a justification) and will want to carry out the kind of first-person reflection just described in a way that makes such a response possible. For such a person, moral blame differs from mere unwelcome description not only because of its seriousness but also because it engages in this way with an agent's own process of critical reflection, thus raising the questions Why did I do that? Do I still endorse those reasons? Can I defend the judgment that they were adequate grounds for acting?

Whether one accepts this as an adequate account of the "special force" of moral judgments will depend, of course, on what one thinks that moral judgment in the "ordinary" sense actually entails. Some have held that from the fact that a person is morally blameworthy it follows that it would be a good thing if he or she were to suffer some harm (or, at least, that this would be less bad than if some innocent person were to suffer the same harm).[18] I do not myself regard moral blame as having this implication. So if a compatibilist account of moral judgment must have this consequence, I am content to be offering a revisionist theory. (The problem of how the fact of choice may make harmful consequences more justifiable will, however, come up again in lecture 2.)

---

[18] This idea was suggested to me by Derek Parfit in the seminar following the presentation of this lecture in Oxford.

7. BLAMEWORTHINESS AND FREEDOM

It remains to say something about how this contractualist version of the Quality of Will theory handles the difficult question of moral appraisal of the insane. Discussion of this matter will also enable me to draw together some of the points that have just been made and to say more about the kind of freedom which is presupposed by moral blameworthiness according to the theory I have been proposing.

As I said earlier, to believe that one's behavior is morally faulty is to believe either that one has failed to attend to considerations which any standards that others could not reasonably reject would require one to attend to or that one has knowingly acted contrary to what such standards would require. Let me focus for a moment on the first disjunct. Something like this is a necessary part of an account of moral blameworthiness, since failure to give any thought at all to what is morally required can certainly be grounds for moral criticism. But the purely negative statement I have given above is too broad. The class of people who simply fail to attend to the relevant considerations includes many who do not seem to be candidates for moral blame: people acting in their sleep, victims of hypnosis, young children, people suffering from mental illness, and so on. We need to find, within the notion of moral blame itself, some basis for a nonarbitrary qualification of the purely negative criterion.

According to contractualism, thought about right and wrong is a search for principles "for the regulation of behavior" which others, similarly motivated, have reason to accept. What kind of "regulation" is intended here? Not regulation "from without" through a system of social sanctions but regulation "from within" through critical reflection on one's own conduct under the pressure provided by the desire to be able to justify one actions to others on grounds they could not reasonably reject. This idea of regulation has two components, one specifically moral, the other not. The specifically moral component is the ability to reason about what could be justified to others. The nonmoral component is the more general capacity through which the results of such reasoning make a difference to what one does. Let me call this the capacity for critically reflective, rational self-governance — "critically reflective" because it involves the ability to reflect and pass judgment upon one's actions and the thought processes leading up to them; "rational" in the broad sense of involving sensitivity to reasons and the ability to weigh them; "self-governance" because it is a process which makes a difference to how one acts.

The critical reflection of a person who has this capacity will have a kind of coherence over time. Conclusions reached at one time will be seen as relevant to critical reflection at later times unless specifically overruled. In addition, the results of this reflection will normally make a difference both in how the person acts given a certain perception of a situation and in the features of situations which he or she is on the alert for and tends to notice.

This general capacity for critically reflective, rational self-governance is not specifically moral, and someone could have it who was entirely unconcerned with morality. Morality does not tell one to have this capacity, and failing to have it in general or on a particular occasion is not a moral fault. Rather, morality is addressed to people who are assumed to have this general capacity, and it tells them how the capacity should be exercised. The most general moral demand is that we exercise our capacity for self-governance in ways that others could reasonably be expected to authorize. More specific moral requirements follow from this.

Since moral blameworthiness concerns the exercise of the general capacity of self-governance, our views about the limits of moral blame are sensitive to changes in our views about the limits of this capacity. We normally believe, for example, that very young children lack this capacity and that it does not govern our actions while we are asleep. Nor, according to some assumptions about hypnosis, does it regulate posthypnotic suggestion, and it is generally believed to be blocked by some forms of mental illness. These assumptions could be wrong, but given that we hold them it is natural that we do not take people in these categories to be morally blameworthy for their actions. (Whether we think it is useful to blame them is of course another question.) It is important to our reactions in such cases, however, that what is impaired or suspended is a *general* capacity for critically reflective, rational self-governance. If what is "lost" is more specifically moral — if, for example, a person lacks any concern for the welfare of others — then the result begins to look more like a species of moral fault.

As a "higher order" capacity, the capacity for critically reflective, rational self-governance has an obvious similarity to the capacities for higher-order desires and judgments which figure in the analyses of personhood and freedom offered by Harry Frankfurt and others.[19] I have been led to this capacity, however, not through an analysis of general notions of freedom and personhood but rather through reflection on the nature of moral argument and moral judgment. Basic to morality as I understand it is an idea of agreement between individuals *qua* critics and regulators of their own actions and deliberative processes. Critically reflective, rational self-governance is a capacity which is required in order for that idea not to be an idle one. It follows that moral criticism is restricted to individuals who have this capacity and to actions which fall within its scope.[20]

---

[19] See Harry Frankfurt, "Freedom of the Will and the Concept of a Person," *Journal of Philosophy* 68 (1971): 5–20; Wright Neely, "Freedom and Desire," *Philosophical Review* 83 (1974): 32–54; and Gary Watson, "Free Agency," *Journal of Philosophy* 72 (1975): 205–20.

[20] The idea that moral criticism is applicable only to actions which are within the scope of a capacity of self-governance which normally makes a difference in what a person does marks a point of tangency between the Influenceability theory and the analysis I am offering. I am not suggesting, however, that particular acts of moral criticism are aimed at influencing people or that moral criticism is always inappropriate when there is no hope of its making any difference to what people do. Morality as I am describing it is in a general sense "action guiding" — moral argument concerns principles for the general regulation of behavior. But moral

In Frankfurt's terms, these restrictions correspond roughly to a restriction to persons (as opposed to "wantons") and a restriction to actions which are performed freely. In my view, however, this last characterization is not entirely apt. Aside from external impediments to bodily motion, what is required for moral appraisal on the view I am presenting is the "freedom," whatever it may be, which is required by critically reflective, rational self-governance. But this is less appropriately thought of as a kind of freedom than as a kind of intrapersonal responsiveness. What is required is that what we do be importantly dependent on our process of critical reflection, that that process itself be sensitive to reasons, and that later stages of the process be importantly dependent on conclusions reached at earlier stages. But there is no reason, as far as I can see, to require that this process itself not be a causal product of antecedent events and conditions.[21] Calling the relevant condition a form of freedom suggests this requirement, but this suggestion is undermined by our investigation into the moral significance of choice.

8. CONCLUSION

The contractualist version of the Quality of Will theory which I have described seems to me to provide a satisfactory explanation of the significance of choice for the moral appraisal of agents.

"ought" judgments need not be intended as action guiding, and insofar as they do guide action they need not do so by being prescriptive in form. Rather, they guide action by calling attention to facts about the justifiability of actions — facts which morally concerned agents care about. In these respects my view differs from R. M. Hare's prescriptivism, though we would say some of the same things about free will. See his "Prediction and Moral Appraisal," in P. French, T. Uehling, and H. Wettstein, eds., *Midwest Studies in Philosophy*, vol. III (Minneapolis: University of Minnesota Press, 1978), pp. 17–27.

21 For more extended discussion of this issue, see Daniel Dennett's *Elbow Room* (Cambridge, Mass.: MIT Press, 1984), especially chs. 3–5. I make no claim to be advancing beyond what other compatibilists have said about the nature of deliberation and action. My concern is with the question of moral responsibility. Here I differ with Dennett, who goes much further than I would toward accepting the Influenceability theory. See ch. 7 of *Elbow Room* and Gary Watson's criticisms of it in his review in *Journal of Philosophy* 83 (1986): 517–22.

This theory offers a convincing and unified account of familiar excusing conditions, such as mistake of fact and duress, and explains our reactions to questions about moral appraisal of very young children, the insane, and victims of hypnosis. It can explain the special critical force which moral judgments seem to have, and it does this without presupposing a form of freedom incompatible with the Causal Thesis. But the theory applies only to what I called earlier the moral version of the free-will problem. A parallel account may, as I will suggest later, have some relevance to the case of criminal punishment, but it does not offer a promising approach to the other problems I have mentioned. The significance of a person's choices and other subjective responses for questions of economic justice and freedom of thought may have something to do with the fact that these responses reflect what might loosely be called "the quality of the person's will," but this is not because what we are doing in these cases is judging this "quality" or expressing attitudes toward it (since this is not what we are doing.) So, in search of an explanation that might cover these other cases, I will look in a different direction.

Lecture 2

1. THE VALUE OF CHOICE

It would have been natural to call these lectures an investigation into the significance of voluntariness. I have spoken of "choice" instead because this term applies not only to something that an agent does — as in "She made a choice" — but also to what an agent is presented with — as in "She was faced with this choice." It thus encompasses both an action and a situation within which such an action determines what will happen: a set of alternatives, their relative desirabilities, the information available to the agent, and so on. My main concern in these lectures is with the significance of choice in the first of these senses: the moral significance of the choices people make. In this lecture, however, I will present a theory which exploits the ambiguity just mentioned by seeking to explain one kind of moral significance of the choices people make in terms of the value of the choices they have. I will call this the Value of Choice theory.[22]

This theory starts from the idea that it is often a good thing for a person to have what will happen depend upon how he or she responds when presented with the alternatives under the right conditions. To take a banal example, when I go to a restaurant, it is generally a good thing from my point of view to have what appears on my plate depend on the way in which I respond when presented with the menu. The most obvious reason why choice has value for me in this situation is simply instrumental: I would like what appears on my plate to conform to my preferences at the time it appears, and I believe that if what appears then is made to depend on my response when faced with the menu then the result is likely to coincide with what I want. This reason for valuing choice is both conditional and relative. It is conditional in that the value of my response as a predictor of future satisfaction depends on the nature of the question and the conditions under which my response is elicited. It is relative in that it depends on the reliability of the available alternative means for selecting the outcomes in question. In the restaurant case this value depends on how much I know about the cuisine in question and on my condition at the time the menu arrives: on whether I am drunk or overeager to impress my companions with my knowledge of French

---

[22] As I have said, the basic idea of this theory was presented by Hart in "Legal Responsibility and Excuses." Since Hart's article others have written in a similar vein, although they have been concerned mainly with the theory of punishment. See, for example, John Mackie, "The Grounds of Responsibility," in P. M. S. Hacker and J. Raz, eds., *Law, Morality, and Society: Essays in Honour of H. L. A. Hart,* (Oxford: Oxford University Press, 1977), and C. S. Nino, "A Consensual Theory of Punishment," *Philosophy and Public Affairs* 12 (1983): 289–306. Like Hart, Nino links the significance of choice (in his terms, consent) as a condition of just punishment with its significance elsewhere in the law, e.g., in contracts and torts. His view of this significance, however, is closer than my own to what I refer to below as the Forfeiture View.

or my ability to swallow highly seasoned food. Thus the same interest which sometimes makes choice valuable — the desire that outcomes should coincide with one's preferences — can at other times provide reasons for wanting outcomes to be determined in some other way. When I go to an exotic restaurant with my sophisticated friends, the chances of getting a meal that accords with my preferences may be increased if someone else does the ordering.

What I have described so far is what might be called the "predictive" or "instrumental" value of choice. In the example I have given, choice is instrumental to my own future enjoyment, but the class of states which one might seek to advance by making outcomes dependent on choices is of course much broader. Aside from such instrumental values, however, there are other ways in which having outcomes depend on my choice can have positive or negative value for me. One of these, which I will call "demonstrative" value, can be illustrated as follows. On our anniversary, I want not only to have a present for my wife but also to have chosen that present myself. This is not because I think this process is the one best calculated to produce a present she will like (for that, it would be better to let her choose the present herself). The reason, rather, is that the gift will have special meaning if I choose it — if it reflects my feelings about her and my thoughts about the occasion. On other occasions, for reasons similar in character but opposite in sign, I might prefer that outcomes *not* be dependent on my choices. For example, I might prefer to have the question of who will get a certain job (my friend or a stranger) not depend on how I respond when presented with the choice: I want it to be clear that the outcome need not reflect my judgment of their respective merits or my balancing of the competing claims of merit and loyalty.

The features of oneself which one may desire to demonstrate or see realized in action are highly varied. They may include the value one attaches to various aims and outcomes, one's knowledge, awareness, or memory, or one's imagination and skill. Many of these are involved in the example cited: I want to make the choice myself because the result will then indicate the importance I attach to the occasion (my willingness to devote time to choosing a gift); my memory of, attention to, and concern for what she likes; as well as my imagination and skill in coming up with an unusual and amusing gift. The desire to see such features of oneself manifested in actions and outcomes is of course not limited to cases in which one's feelings for another person are at issue. I want to choose the furniture for my own apartment, pick out the pictures for the walls, and even write my own lectures despite the fact that these things might be done better by a decorator, art expert, or talented graduate student. For better or worse, I want these things to be produced by and reflect my own taste, imagination, and powers of discrimination and analysis. I feel the same way, even more strongly, about important decisions affecting my life in larger terms: what career to follow, where to work, how to live.

These last examples, however, may involve not only demonstrative but also what I will call "symbolic" value. In a situation in which people are normally expected to determine outcomes of a certain sort through their own choices unless they are not competent to do so, I may value having a choice because my not having it would reflect a judgment on my own or someone else's part that I fell below the expected standard of competence. Thus, while I might like to have the advantage of my sophisticated friends' expertise when the menu arrives tonight, I might prefer, all things considered, to order for myself, in order to avoid public acknowledgment of my relative ignorance of food, wine, and foreign cultures.

I make no claim that these three categories of value are mutually exclusive or that, taken together, they exhaust the forms of value that choice can have. My aim in distinguishing them is simply to illustrate the value that choice can have and to make clear that this value is not always merely instrumental: the reasons people have for wanting outcomes to be (or sometimes not to be) dependent on their choices has to do with the significance that choice itself has for them, not merely with its efficacy in promoting outcomes which are desired on other grounds.

The three forms of value which I have distinguished (predictive, demonstrative, and symbolic) would all figure in a full account of the problem of paternalism. Legal restriction of people's freedom "for their own good" is likely to seem justified where (a) people who make a certain choice are likely to suffer very serious loss; (b) the instrumental value of choice as a way of warding off this loss is, given the circumstances under which that choice would be exercised, seriously undermined; (c) the demonstrative value that would be lost by being deprived of this choice is minimal; and (d) the tendency to "make the wrong choice" under the circumstances in question is widely shared, so that no particular group is being held inferior in the argument for legal regulation. The pejorative ring of "paternalism" and the particular bitterness attaching to it stem from cases in which either the seriousness of the loss in question or the foolishness of the choice leading to it is a matter of controversy. Those who are inclined to make a particular choice may not see it as mistaken and may attach demonstrative value to it. Consequently, they may resent paternalistic legislation, which brands them as less than fully competent when, in their view, they merely differ from the majority in the things they value. But this kind of resentment need not properly extend to other kinds of legislation sometimes called "paternalistic," such as wage and hour laws. Whether there is any reason at all for such resentment will depend on the reasons supporting a piece of legislation and also on the reasons people actually have for valuing freedom of choice which they would lose.

As controversies about paternalism illustrate, people can disagree sharply about the value of particular choices. They disagree, for example, about how important it is to have whether one wears a seat belt depend on how one reacts (in the absence of any coercion) when setting off in a car. Some regard it as a significant loss when some form of coercion or even mild duress (the threat of a fine, or even the monitory presence of a brief buzzer) is introduced. Others, like me, regard this loss as trivial, and see the "constrained" choice as significantly more valuable than the unconstrained one. This disagreement reflects differences in the instrumental, demonstrative, and symbolic value we attach to these choices.

The existence of such differences raises the question of what is to count as "the value" of a choice as I have been using this phrase. One possibility is what I will call "fully individualized value." This is the value of the choice to a particular individual, taking into account the importance that individual attaches to having particular alternatives available, the difference that it makes to that individual which of these alternatives actually occurs, the importance which the individual attaches to having this be determined by his or her reactions, and the skill and discernment with which that individual will choose under the conditions in question. This fully individualized value may not be the same as the value which the individual actually assigns to the choice in question; rather, it is the *ex ante* value which he or she *should* assign given his or her values and propensities.

Fully individualized value is not what normally figures in moral argument, however. Appeals to the value of choice arise in moral argument chiefly when we are appraising moral principles or social institutions rather than when we are discussing particular choices by specific individuals. In these contexts we have to answer such general questions as How important is it to have the selection among these alternatives depend on one's choice? How bad a thing is it to have to choose under these conditions? When we address these questions, fully individualized values are not known. We argue instead in terms of what might be called the "normalized value" of a choice: a rough assignment of values to categories of choice which we take to be a fair starting point for justification. Thus, for example, we take it as given for purposes of moral argument that it is very important that what one wears and whom one lives with be dependent on one's choices and much less important that one be able to choose what other people wear, what they eat, and how they live. And we do this despite the fact that there may be some who would not agree with this assignment of values.

This phenomenon — the use in moral argument of nonunanimously held "normalized" standards of value — is familiar and by no means limited to the case of choice. The status and justification of such standards is a difficult problem in moral theory. I will not address the general question here but will mention briefly two points about the case of choice. First, "giving people the choice" — for example, the opportunity to transfer goods through market trading—is one way to deal with the problem of divergent individual preferences. What has just been indicated, however, is that it is at best a partial solution. "Having a choice" among specified alternatives under specified conditions is itself a good which individuals may value differently — as is "having the choice whether to have the choice" and so on.[23] Second, differences in individualized valuations of choices result not only from differences in preference but also from differences in the personal characteristics which make a choice valuable: differences in foresight, in self-control, in self-understanding, and so on. Moral argument commonly refers to "normal" levels of these capacities as well as to "normal" valuations of outcomes and of demonstrative and symbolic values.

Let me turn now to the question of how the value of choice is related to the Quality of Will theory, discussed above. Like

---

[23] The variability of the value of choice is pointed out clearly by Gerald Dworkin in "Is More Choice Better Than Less?" in P. French, T. Uehling, and H. Wettstein, eds., *Midwest Studies in Philosophy*, vol. VII (Minneapolis: University of Minnesota Press, 1982), pp. 47–62.

what I have here called predictive and demonstrative value, the
form of appraisal underlying the Quality of Will theory starts
from the obvious fact that subjective responses can indicate or
express continuing features of a person and from the equally
obvious fact that these responses are better indicators under some
conditions than under others. Even in this common starting point,
however, there is a difference: the features of the person with
which the Quality of Will theory is concerned constitute a narrow
subset of those that give choice its value for the agent. For example, I want to choose my own food largely because my choices
will be good indicators of what will please me, but my being pleased
more by fish than by liver is not part of the quality of my will
with which moral judgment is concerned.

Where the two theories differ most importantly, however, is
in the way in which they assign moral significance to this indicative aspect of choice. The Quality of Will theory takes the point
of view of the moral judge. Variations in the indicative value of
subjective responses are significant from this point of view because
moral judgment involves an inference from behavior to quality of
will. The Value of Choice theory, on the other hand, begins with
the value for an agent of having outcomes depend (or not depend) on his or her subjective responses under certain conditions.
This (so far purely personal) value takes on moral significance
by being the basis for a claim against social institutions (or against
other individuals). In my view, to show that a social institution
is legitimate one must show that it can be justified to each person
affected by it on grounds which that person could not reasonably
reject. One thing which people may reasonably demand, however,
is the ability to shape their lives and obligations through the exercise of choice under reasonably favorable conditions. Moral principles or social institutions which deny such opportunities when
they could easily be provided, or which force one to accept the
consequences of choice under extremely unfavorable conditions
which could be improved without great cost to others, are likely

to be reasonably rejectable for that reason. Let me illustrate by considering some examples.

2. JUSTICE AND CHOICE

Consider first the economic justice example which I mentioned earlier. Suppose a society, not marked by significant economic inequalities, decides that it needs to have a significant proportion of its workforce work overtime at a particular job. To this end, a bonus is offered to anyone willing to undertake the work, at an amount calculated to elicit the required number of volunteers. The choice between extra pay and extra leisure has obvious instrumental value for the people involved, and giving people this choice makes it overwhelmingly likely that those who prefer additional income (with additional labor) will get it, while those who prefer the opposite will get what *they* prefer. If overtime work was not made dependent on choice the scheme would be very difficult to justify; with this feature, justification is much easier. Nonetheless, whether or not a given worker winds up among those with extra pay will no doubt depend on some "morally arbitrary" facts about his or her background. Why then is this situation any better than the one criticized by Rawls?

The difference does not lie in the "fact" that the choices made in one case have causal antecedents while those made in the other case do not. In the egalitarian case, however, we can say that by placing the people in those circumstances, offering them that choice, and letting the outcome be determined by the choice they make under those conditions, we have done as much for them as could reasonably be required. In the other case it may be argued that we cannot say this: once the people are placed in disadvantageous circumstances, circumstances which themselves make it very unlikely that anyone would make the choices necessary to escape, offering these people the opportunity to exert themselves does little to improve their position.

The background conditions under which choices are made in the laissez-faire system are "arbitrary from a moral point of view" in this sense: they could be almost anything. All we know is that they will be conditions which arose from a series of voluntary transactions, and this does nothing to ensure that they will be good conditions under which to choose. Consequently, there is no assurance that these conditions will have the moral property of being conditions under which choices confer legitimacy on their outcomes.

This interpretation of Rawls's objection to the laissez-faire "system of natural liberty" provides the basis for a reply to one line of criticism raised by Nozick and others. Nozick interprets Rawls as arguing that the fact that some people exert themselves, take risks, and excel while others do not do so cannot by itself justify different economic rewards for the two groups because these differences in motivation may be the result of causal factors outside the control of the agents themselves. He goes on to object that

> this line of argument can succeed in blocking the introduction of a person's autonomous choices and actions (and their results) only by attributing *everything* noteworthy about the person completely to certain sorts of "external" factors. So denigrating a person's autonomy and prime responsibility for his actions is a risky line to take for a theory that founds so much (including a theory of the good) upon persons' choices.[24]

The problem which Nozick raises here is a version of the "political problem of free will" as I presented it in my first lecture. My reply (I do not claim that this was also Rawls's intention) is that it is not mere attributability to "external" factors that undermines the legitimating force of the choices in a "system of natural liberty." The problem, rather, is that such a system

[24] Robert Nozick, *Anarchy, State, and Utopia* (New York: Basic Books, 1974), p. 214.

provides no assurance that these factors will not be ones which undermine the value of choice for many people in the society. Suppose that I exert myself to develop my talents and become wealthy. You, on the other hand, suffering the psychological effects of your unfortunate starting position, fail to exert yourself, and as a consequence remain poor. Can I "claim credit" for my initiative and perseverance, given that they resulted from "fortunate family and social circumstances for which [I] can claim no credit"? [25] If to "claim credit" means simply to consider these traits and actions "mine" in the sense required in order to take pride in them, then the answer is clearly yes. My accomplishments reflect personal qualities which I really do have. If, however, what is meant is that these differences in our behavior can be taken to justify my having more income and your having less, then the answer may be no. This is not because my actions, being caused by outside factors, are not "mine," or because your actions, similarly caused by other factors, are therefore not "yours," but rather because presenting a person with a choice of the kind you had is not doing enough for that person.

Of course, Rawls and Nozick disagree over what constitutes "doing enough" for a person. For Nozick, one has "done enough" as long as the person's Lockean rights have not been violated; for Rawls, the standard is set by the principles which would be accepted behind the Veil of Ignorance. As a result, Rawls's remarks about "factors arbitrary from a moral point of view," as I have interpreted them, may seem not to advance his argument against Nozick but merely to restate the disagreement between them. But this restatement seems to me to have several virtues. First, it locates the disagreement in what seems, intuitively, to be the right place — in a question of justice rather than in a separate (and I believe spurious) question of causal determination. Second, framing the argument in terms of the value of choice has

[25] Rawls, *A Theory of Justice*, p. 104; quoted by Nozick, *Anarchy, State, and Utopia*, p. 214.

the effect of disentangling the idea of individual liberty from Nozick's particular system of Lockean rights. This allows opponents of that system to make clear that they, too, value individual choice and liberty and gives them a chance to put forward their alternative interpretations of these values. The argument can then proceed as a debate about the merits of competing interpretations of the moral significance of liberty and choice rather than as a clash between defenders of liberty and proponents of equality or some other pattern of distribution.

The Value of Choice theory represents a general philosophical strategy which is common to Hart's analysis of punishment and Rawls's theory of distributive justice as I have just interpreted it. In approaching the problems of justifying both penal and economic institutions we begin with strong pretheoretical intuitions about the significance of choice: voluntary and intentional commission of a criminal act is a necessary condition of just punishment, and voluntary economic contribution can make an economic reward just and its denial unjust. One way to account for these intuitions is by appeal to a preinstitutional notion of desert: certain acts deserve punishment, certain contributions merit rewards, and institutions are just if they distribute benefits and burdens in accord with these forms of desert.

The strategy I am describing makes a point of avoiding any such appeal. The only notions of desert which it recognizes are internal to institutions and dependent upon a prior notion of justice: if institutions are just then people deserve the rewards and punishments which those institutions assign them. In the justification of institutions, the notion of desert is replaced by an independent notion of justice; in the justification of specific actions and outcomes it is replaced by the idea of legitimate (institutionally defined) expectations.[26]

In order for this strategy to succeed, the conception of justice by which institutions are to be judged must adequately represent

---

[26] Rawls, *A Theory of Justice*, p. 313.

our intuitions about the significance of choice without falling back on a preinstitutional concept of desert. This is where the idea of the value of choice comes in. Just institutions must make outcomes depend on individuals' choices because of the importance which individuals reasonably attach to this dependence. But there is a serious question whether this strategy can account for the distinctive importance which choice appears to have. Insofar as choice-dependence is merely one form of individual good among others, it may seem that the Value of Choice theory will be unable to explain our intuition that the moral requirement that certain outcomes be made dependent on people's choices is not to be sacrificed for the sake of increases in efficiency, security, or other benefits.

Several defenses can be offered against this charge. The first is to point out the distinctiveness of the value of choice as compared with other elements in a person's welfare. As I have indicated above, the value of choice is not a purely instrumental value. People reasonably attach intrinsic significance to having outcomes depend on their choices. In addition, the moral requirements which this value gives rise to within a contractualist moral theory are not corollaries of a more general duty to look out for people's welfare. In fact, the demand to make outcomes depend on people's choices and the demand to promote their welfare are quite independent, and they can often pull in opposite directions.

A second defense — parallel to Rawls's argument for the priority of liberty — is to argue that in appraising social institutions people would reasonably set a particularly high value on having certain kinds of outcomes be dependent on their choices.[27] A third, more pragmatic defense is to argue that the distinctive significance which choice appears to have is in part an artifact of the position from which we typically view it. This is a position internal to institutions, and one in which choices have special salience because they are the last justifying elements to enter the

[27] See section 82 of *A Theory of Justice*.

picture. When the relevant background is in place — when conditions are right, necessary safeguards have been provided, and so
on — the fact that a person chooses a certain outcome may make
that outcome one that he or she cannot reasonably complain of.
But choice has this effect only when these other factors are present.
Because they are relatively fixed features of the environment, these
background conditions are less noticeable than the actions of the
main actors in the drama, but this does not mean that they are less
important.

These defenses are most convincing in those cases in which the
first argument is strongest — that is, in cases like the economic
justice example just discussed, in which people's desire to shape
their own lives gives choice an important, positive value. The
Value of Choice theory looks weaker in cases where the only reason for wanting to have a choice is that it makes certain unwanted
outcomes (such as punishment) less likely. Here choice has no
positive value — rather than have the choice, one would prefer to
eliminate these outcomes altogether if that were possible — yet
the fact of choice seems to retain its special significance as a
justifying condition. Let me turn, then, to an example of this kind.

3. Choice and Protection

Suppose that we, the officials of a town, must remove and
dispose of some hazardous waste. We need to dig it up from the
illegal dump near a residential area where it has lain for years and
move it to a safer spot some distance away. Digging it up and
moving it will inevitably release dangerous chemicals into the
atmosphere, but this is better than leaving it in its present location, where it will in the long run seep into the water supply.
Obviously we must take precautions to minimize the risks involved
in this operation. We need to find a safe disposal site, far away
from where people normally have to go. We should build a high
fence around the new site, and another around the old one where

the excavation is to be done, both of them with large signs warning of the danger. We should also arrange for the removal and transportation to be carried out at times when few people are around, in order to minimize the number potentially exposed, and we must be sure to have the material wetted down and transported in covered trucks to minimize the amount of chemicals released into the air. Inevitably, however, enough chemicals will escape to cause lung damage to those who are directly exposed if, because of past exposure or genetic predisposition, they happen to be particularly sensitive, but not enough to pose a threat to anyone who stays indoors and away from the excavation site. Given that this is so, we should be careful to warn people, especially those who know that they are at risk, to stay indoors and away from the relevant area while the chemicals are being moved.

Suppose that we do all of these things but that nonetheless some people are exposed. A few of these, who did not know that they were particularly sensitive to the chemical, suffer lung damage. Let me stipulate that with respect to all of these people we did all that we could reasonably be expected to do to warn and protect them. So in that sense they "can't complain" about what happened. The question which concerns me, however, is what role the signs and warnings play in making this the case. These are the factors which make outcomes depend on people's choices. Are they, like the fences, the careful removal techniques, and the remote location of the new site, just further means through which the likelihood of someone's being injured is reduced? This is what the Value of Choice theory seems to imply. For after all, since no one wants to have the opportunity to be exposed to this chemical, the only value which choice can have in this case is that of making exposure less likely. This may be an adequate explanation of why we would want to be warned and hence "given the choice" whether to be exposed or not. But it may not account for the full moral significance of the fact that those who were injured "knew what they were getting into." Consider the following two cases.

Suppose that one person was exposed because, despite the newspaper stories, mailings, posted signs, radio and television announcements, and sound trucks, he never heard about the danger. He simply failed to get the word. So he went for his usual walk with no idea what was going on. A second person, let us suppose, heard the warnings but did not take them seriously. Curious to see how the task was being done, she sneaked past the guards and climbed the fence to get a better look.

There seems to be a clear difference between these two cases. In the first, we have "done enough" to protect the person simply because, given what we have done, it was extremely unlikely that anyone would be directly exposed to contamination, and we could not have made this even more unlikely without inordinate expense. There is, after all, a limit to the lengths to which we must go to protect others. The second person, on the other hand, bears the responsibility for her own injury, and it is this fact, rather than any consideration of the cost to us of doing more, which makes it the case that she has no claim against us. By choosing, in the face of all our warnings, to go to the excavation site, she laid down her right to complain of the harm she suffered as a result.

4. THE FORFEITURE VIEW

This familiar and intuitively powerful idea about the significance of choice, which I will call "the Forfeiture View," is not captured by either of the theories I have been considering. It is distinct from the Value of Choice theory, since on that theory what matters is the value of the choice a person is presented with: once a person has been placed in a sufficiently good position, the outcome which emerges is legitimate however it may have been produced. On the Forfeiture View, on the other hand, it matters crucially that an outcome actually resulted from an agent's conscious choice, the agent having intentionally passed up specific alternatives. This is why that view accounts so well for our reaction to the person in the second example: not only does she have no one else to blame for her fate; she has *herself* to blame. We could account for this sense of blame by appealing to a prudential version of the Quality of Will theory: the process of deliberation leading to a decision to climb over the fence "just to see what they are doing" is obviously faulty. But the Quality of Will theory is an account of the moral appraisal of agents, while what we are concerned with here is the justification of outcomes. It may be natural to suppose that a difference in the first translates into or supports a difference in the second, but on reflection it is by no means obvious how this is so.

Moreover, the idea of fault is in fact irrelevant here. The intuition to which the Forfeiture View calls attention concerns the significance of the fact of choice, not the faultiness of that choice. We can imagine a person who, unlike the imprudently curious woman in my example, did not run the risk of contamination foolishly or thoughtlessly. Suppose this third person found, just as the excavation was about to begin, that the day was a perfect one for working on an outdoor project to which she attached great value. Aware of the danger, she considered the matter carefully and decided that taking into account her age and condition it was worth less to her to avoid the risk than to advance her project in the time she was likely to have remaining. Surely this person is as fully "responsible for her fate" as the imprudent woman whom I originally described. But her decision is not a foolish or mistaken one.

This illustrates the fact that what lies behind the Forfeiture View is not an idea of desert. That is, it is not an idea according to which certain choices, because they are foolish, immoral, or otherwise mistaken, positively merit certain outcomes or responses. The idea is rather that a person to whom a certain outcome was available, but who knowingly passed it up, cannot complain about not having it: *volenti non fit iniuria*.

It is important to remember here that the challenge of the Forfeiture View lies in the suggestion that the Value of Choice theory gives an inadequate account of the significance of choice *in the justification of institutions, policies, and specific moral principles*. Once we have accepted as justified an institution or policy attaching specific consequences to particular choices, there is no disagreement about whether these choices have the kind of special force which the Forfeiture View claims. This force can be accounted for by appeal to the institutions, principles, or policies in question. The disagreement concerns the way in which such institutions, principles, and policies themselves are to be justified. When the Forfeiture View says that people who make certain choices "cannot complain" about the harms they suffer as a result, what is meant is that these harms lack the force in this process of justification which otherwise comparable harms would have.

It may seem that a view of this kind is in fact forced on us by contractualism. According to contractualism the crucial question about a proposed moral principle is whether anyone could reasonably reject it. In order for rejecting a principle to be reasonable it must at least be reasonable from the point of view of the person doing the rejecting, that is, the person who would bear the burden of that principle. It may seem, therefore, that a harm which an agent has the opportunity to avoid (without great sacrifice) could never serve as a ground for reasonable rejection of a moral principle. Consider the following argument. From the point of view of an agent, an action which he has the choice of performing must be seen as available to him. Suppose that an agent will run the risk of suffering a certain harm if he follows one course of action but that he would avoid this harm if he were to follow an alternative course which is available to him and does not involve significant sacrifice. Given, then, that the harm is from his point of view costlessly avoidable, how could the agent appeal to this harm as grounds for objecting, for example, to a principle freeing others from any duty to prevent such harms from occurring? It would seem that such harms can have no weight in moral argument.

But this conclusion is not forced on us. In moral argument we are choosing principles to apply in general to situations in which we may be involved. Even if we know that actions avoiding a certain unwanted outcome will be available to us in a given situation, we also know that our processes of choice are imperfect. We often choose the worse, sometimes even in the knowledge that it is the worse. Therefore, even from the point of view of an agent looking at his own actions over time, situations of choice have to be evaluated not only for what they make "available" but for what they make it likely that one will choose. It is not unreasonable to want to have some protection against the consequences of one's own mistakes.

5. REJECTING THE FORFEITURE VIEW

The appeal of the Forfeiture View can and should be resisted. Note, first, that the Value of Choice theory can account for the apparent difference between the two victims of hazardous waste removal described above. We may have "done enough" to protect the first person, who failed to hear of the danger, in the sense that we have gone to as much effort and expense as could be expected. But because we did not succeed in making him aware of the danger we did not make what happened depend on his choice. Given that this kind of "choice-dependence" is something which we all would want for ourselves — we want such risks to be, as far as possible, "under our control" — we did not make this person as well off as we would reasonably want to be. The second person, on the other hand, did have the benefit of "having the choice," even though this turned out to be worth less to her than it would be to most of us. (There was in this case a divergence between "individualized" and "normalized" value.) Given that she had the choice, however, and was provided with the other protections, it was true of her in a way that it was not of the first person that she was placed in as good a position as one could ask for.

From the fact that a person chose, under good conditions, to take a risk, we may conclude that he alone is responsible for what happens to him as a result. But this conclusion need not be seen as a reflection of the special legitimating force of voluntary action. Rather, the fact that an outcome resulted from a person's choice under good conditions *shows* that he was *given* the choice and provided with good conditions for making it, and it is these facts which make it the case that he alone is responsible. A conscious decision to "take the risk" is not necessary. Consider, here, the case of a person who was informed of the risk of contamination but then simply forgot. As a result, he was out in his yard exercising, breathing hard, when the trucks went by. If enough was done to protect and warn him, then this person is responsible for what happens to him and "cannot complain of it" even though he made no conscious decision to take the risk.

The central element of truth in the Forfeiture View is thus a consequence of the Value of Choice theory rather than an alternative to it. Putting this truth in terms of the Forfeiture View, however, has the distorting effect of suggesting that choice has independent deontic force in the justification of institutions and principles. It also exaggerates the importance of the fact of choice relative to that of the conditions under which the choice was made. The Forfeiture View suggests that these conditions are important only insofar as they bear on the voluntariness of the choice. This is a mistake. The fact that a choice was voluntary does not always establish that we "did enough" for an agent by placing him or her in the position from which the choice was made. Nor does the fact that an agent did not voluntarily choose an outcome, or choose to take a certain risk, establish that what resulted was not his fault. Giving him the *opportunity* to choose may have constituted "doing enough" to protect him. It is thus an important virtue of the Value of Choice theory that it gives the conditions of choice their appropriate independent weight and forces us to keep them clearly in view.

6. RESPONSIBILITY AND THE MORAL DIVISION
OF LABOR: BEYOND CHOICE

Within the Value of Choice theory, ideas of responsibility arise as a derived (and often only implicit) moral division of labor. Because most people take themselves to be more actively concerned with the promotion of their own safety and well-being than others are, they want outcomes to be dependent on their choices even when this has only "avoidance value." Given this concern, "giving people the choice" under favorable conditions makes it extremely unlikely that they will suffer easily avoidable harms. We do not want the trouble and expense of supervising others' choices more closely, and do not want them to be supervising us. Therefore, we take the view that giving people the opportunity of avoiding a danger, under favorable conditions, often constitutes "doing enough" for them: the rest is their responsibility. So stated, this is not a principle but only a description of a general tendency in our moral thought. In particular, the idea of "favorable conditions," here left vague, must be filled in before any specific principle of responsibility is obtained, and this filling in will be done differently in the case of different risks and dangers.

This general analysis does, however, shed light on appeals to responsibility in cases in which the notion of choice seems out of place. The idea of freedom of thought, mentioned in my first lecture, is one such case. Another, which I will discuss briefly here, is the idea of responsibility for one's preferences.

This idea arises in the context of debates as to whether, for purposes of assessing claims of justice, people's welfare should be measured in terms of preference satisfaction or in terms of some objective standard of well-being such as what Rawls has called Primary Social Goods. Objective standards of this kind may seem unfair, since the same bundle of objective goods can yield quite different levels of satisfaction for people with different preferences. Rawls has replied that someone who makes this objection "must argue in addition that it is unreasonable, if not unjust, to hold such persons responsible for their preferences and to require them to make out as best they can." To argue this, he says, "seems to presuppose that citizens' preferences are beyond their control as propensities or cravings which simply happen." The use of an objective standard like primary goods, on the other hand, "relies on a capacity to assume responsibility for our ends." The conception of justice which Rawls advocates thus

> includes what we may call a social division of responsibility: society, the citizens as a collective body, accepts responsibility for maintaining the equal basic liberties and fair equality of opportunity, and for providing a fair share of the other primary goods for everyone within this framework, while citizens (as individuals) and associations accept the responsibility for revising and adjusting their ends and aspirations in view of the all-purpose means they can expect, given their present and foreseeable situation. This division of responsibility relies on the capacity of persons to assume responsibility for their ends and to moderate the claims they make on their social institutions in accordance with the use of primary goods. Citizens' claims to liberties, opportunities and all-purpose means are made secure from the unreasonable demands of others.[28]

I am strongly inclined to agree with Rawls here, and I have defended a similar position myself.[29] Nonetheless, I find this argument somewhat worrisome, because it is easily misinterpreted as involving an appeal to the idea of forfeiture which I argued against above. On this interpretation, the argument is that the imagined objection to objective measures of welfare overlooks the fact that people's preferences are under their control. Given this

[28] John Rawls, "Social Unity and Primary Goods," in Amartya Sen and Bernard Williams, eds., *Utilitarianism and Beyond* (Cambridge: Cambridge University Press, 1982), pp. 168, 169, 170.

[29] In "Preference and Urgency," *Journal of Philosophy* 72 (1975): 655–69. The following discussion concerns issues dealt with in my reply to "the voluntariness objection" on pp. 664–66 of that article.

fact, and in view of the basic moral truth that one cannot complain of harms one could have avoided, the objection is no objection at all: people whose preferences are particularly difficult to satisfy have only themselves to blame.

There are two difficulties with this argument. First, for reasons I have already discussed, the "basic moral truth" to which it appeals seems open to serious doubt. Second, even if this "truth" is correct, the argument appears to exaggerate the degree of control which people have over their preferences. To be sure, the argument does not suggest that people can alter their preferences by simply deciding what to prefer; the kind of control which is envisaged is to be exercised through decisions affecting the development of one's preferences over time. Even so, it is questionable how much control of this kind people can realistically be assumed to exercise.

This leads me to look for an alternative interpretation under which the argument avoids these difficulties while still retaining its force. Following the general strategy which I have been advocating in this lecture, this alternative interpretation takes the idea of responsibility for one's preferences to be part of the view being defended rather than an independent moral premise. As Rawls says, the conception of justice which he is defending *includes* "what we may call a social division of responsibility." The question is how this combination — an objective standard of welfare and the idea of responsibility which it entails — can be defended without appeal to anything like the notion of forfeiture.

The issue here is the choice between two types of public standards of justice, objective standards of the sort just described, according to which institutions are judged on the degree to which they provide their citizens with good objective conditions for the development and satisfaction of their preferences, and subjective standards, under which institutions are also judged on the basis of the levels of preference satisfaction which actually result from their policies. In our earlier discussion of individual choice, the argument for a "moral division of labor" rested on three claims: the value which we attach to having outcomes depend on our own choices (even when this is only "avoidance value"), our reluctance to have our choices supervised by others, and our reluctance to bear the costs of protecting others beyond a certain point. The case for the "social division of responsibility" entailed by objective standards of welfare rests on three analogous claims. We reasonably attach a high value to forming our own preferences under favorable conditions, and one reason for this is our expectation that we will to *some* extent be steered away from forming preferences when we can see that they will be difficult to satisfy and will lead mainly to frustration. Second, we do not want others to be taking an active role in determining what we will prefer. And third, we do not want to be burdened with the costs of satisfying other people's preferences when these are much more costly than our own.

The first of these claims accounts for the (limited) force of the idea, to which Rawls appeals, that people can to some extent avoid "costly" preferences. But it does this without invoking a preinstitutional notion of forfeiture, and without assuming the degree of conscious and deliberate control which the Forfeiture View would require.

The second claim is especially important. Particularly in a society marked by sharp disagreements about what is worth preferring, a public standard of justice requiring government policy to be aimed at raising individual levels of satisfaction is an open invitation to unwelcome governmental intervention in the formation of individuals' values and preferences. The "social division of responsibility" which goes with an objective standard of welfare is therefore an attractive alternative.

The case for an objective standard of welfare is thus largely defensive. Giving up the claim to a greater share of resources in the event that one's preferences turn out to be particularly difficult to satisfy is the price one pays for greater security against governmental interference and greater freedom from the possibly burdensome demands of other people's preferences. The role of the possibility of modifying one's preferences (or of avoiding the formation of preferences which are difficult to satisfy) is just to make this price smaller and not, as the Forfeiture View would have it, to license the result.

7. CONCLUSION

In this lecture I have presented the idea of the Value of Choice as part of a general strategy explaining the moral significance of choice in the justification of social institutions and policies. As compared with its main rival, the Forfeiture View, this strategy has the advantage of assigning choice an important positive value without exaggerating its role and significance in justification. It remains to be seen what kind of freedom the Value of Choice theory presupposes and how it fits together with the Quality of Will theory to account for the significance of choice across a range of cases. These questions will be addressed in my next lecture.

Lecture 3

1. PUNISHMENT AND PROTECTION

Let me begin with a schematic comparison of the institution of punishment and the policy of hazardous waste disposal which I discussed in my last lecture. In each case we have the following elements. First, there is an important social goal: protecting the water supply in the one case; protecting ourselves and our possessions in the other. Second, there is a strategy for promoting that goal which involves the creation of another risk: the risk of contamination in the one case, the risk of punishment in the other. Third, the effect of this strategy is to make it the case that there is, literally or metaphorically, a certain affected area which one can no longer enter without danger. In the one case this is the area of excavation, transport, and disposal, in the other the "area" of activities which have been declared illegal. Fourth, although we introduce certain safeguards to reduce exposure to the risk created, it remains the case that many of those who choose to enter the affected area, and perhaps a few others, will suffer harm. Some of these safeguards (such as requirements of due process, and careful methods of excavation and transport) have the effect of protecting those who choose to stay out of the affected area. Other safeguards enhance the value of choice as a protection by making it less likely that people will choose to enter. In the hazardous waste case these include signs, warnings, and publicity to inform people about the nature of the risk, as well as fences, guards, and the choice of an obscure disposal site where no one has reason to go. Analogous features in the case of punishment are education, including moral education, the dissemination of basic information about the law, and the maintenance of social and economic conditions which reduce the incentive to commit crime by offering the possibility of a satisfactory life within the law. Restrictions on "entrapment" by law enforcement officers also belong in this category of safeguards which make it less likely that one will choose badly. Without such safeguards the value of choice as a protection would be reduced to an unacceptable level.

In each case, in order to defend the institution in question we need to claim that the importance of the social goal justifies creating the risk and making the affected area unusable and that, given the prevailing conditions and the safeguards we have put in place, we have done enough to protect people against suffering harm from the threat that has been created.

Now let me turn to some of the differences between the two cases. First, insofar as the activities which make up "the affected area" in the case of punishment are ones which it is morally wrong to engage in, being deprived of the ability to "enter this area" without risk cannot be counted as a morally cognizable loss. This makes the task of justification easier than in the example of hazardous waste.

A second difference makes this task more difficult, however. In neither case is it our aim that people should suffer the new harm, though in both cases the possibility of their doing so is created by our policy. But in the case of punishment this harm, when it occurs, is intentionally inflicted on particular people. It is an essential part of that institution that people who run afoul of the law should be punished; but it is no part of our waste-removal policy that those who enter the affected area should suffer contamination. If, as I believe, intentionally inflicting harm is in most cases more difficult to justify than merely failing to prevent harm, it follows that an institution of punishment carries a heavier burden of justification.

When such an institution *is* justified, however, this justification entails the kind of "forfeiture" which we looked for but did not find in the hazardous waste case. A person who intentionally commits a crime lays down his or her right not to suffer the prescribed punishment. This forfeiture is a consequence of the justification of the institution of punishment, however, not an element in that justification. It is a consequence, specifically, of the "heavier justificatory burden" just mentioned: because the institution assigns punishment to those who fulfill certain conditions, justifying the institution involves justifying the infliction of these penalties. If the conditions for punishment include having made a certain kind of choice, then a justification for the institution justifies making that choice a necessary and, when the other conditions are fulfilled, sufficient condition for punishment. No such assignment and hence no such forfeiture is involved in the justification of the policy of hazardous waste removal. A person who recklessly chooses to enter the affected area does not lay down a right to further protection against contamination: she has already received all the protection she is entitled to. She does not lay down her right to treatment (or rescue) unless this has been pre-

scribed and the policy including this prescription is justified. Forfeiture, like economic desert, is the creature of particular social
institutions and relatively specific moral principles (such as those
governing promising). It is not a moral feature of choice in general. As I argued in my last lecture, the moral aspect of choice
which figures in the justification and criticism of such institutions
and principles is not forfeiture but the less-sharp-edged notion of
the value of choice.

I have been assuming that "the affected area" is so defined
that one can "enter" it only by conscious choice. This will be so
if we identify "entering" that area with committing a crime whose
definition involves conditions of voluntariness and intent. But a
system of criminal law incorporating elements of strict liability
could also fit the abstract model I have described. If a legal penalty
is attached to selling adulterated milk (not merely to doing so
knowingly, recklessly, or negligently), then one "enters the
affected area" simply by going into the milk business, and if such
a law is justified then doing this involves laying down one's right
not to be penalized if the milk one sells turns out to be impure.
This enlargement of the affected area is one reason (perhaps not
the only one) why such laws are more difficult to justify, especially
since the newly affected area includes activities, such as conscien-
tious engagement in the milk business, which people are morally
entitled to engage in. Having them entail forfeiture of the right
not to be punished is a morally cognizable loss.

2. Excuses and the Value of Choice

I said in my first lecture that an acceptable account of the significance of choice should be able to explain standardly recognized excusing conditions in a way that will not generalize to
undermine the moral significance of all choice if the Causal Thesis
is true. Let me now say something about how the Value of Choice
theory fulfills this assignment. My aim here is not to derive particular excusing conditions or to define the notion of voluntariness

appropriate to particular social institutions and moral principles. This would be an extremely time-consuming task, since it is reasonable to suppose that these conditions will vary in detail from case to case. My present purpose is merely to point out in a more general way how the Value of Choice theory would account for these conditions and for their variation.

The general point is obvious. If the justification for a principle or institution depends in part on the value of the choices it presents people with, and if the value of these choices in turn can vary greatly depending on the presence or absence of certain conditions, then in order to be justifiable the institution will have to qualify the consequences it attaches to choices by explicitly requiring the presence or absence of the most important of these conditions.

Lack of knowledge of the nature of the alternatives available, lack of time to consider them, and the disruptive effects of fear or emotional distress can all weaken the connection between a person's reaction at a given time and his or her more stable preferences, values, and sensitivities, thus undermining both the predictive and demonstrative value of choice. Coercion and duress can have similar disrupting effects on the process of choice, but also and more often they diminish the value of choice simply by contracting or altering the set of alternatives between which one can choose. Diminishing the set of alternatives or weighting some with penalties can sometimes increase the value of choice — or so those of us must believe who sign up to give lectures we have not yet written and buy automobiles with seat belt buzzers. But this is not usually the case.

Even when duress, false belief, or other conditions clearly diminish the value of choice, however, it does not immediately follow that these conditions must be recognized as negating a particular obligation or liability. Whether it does or not will depend on, among other things, the costs to others of introducing such an exception into the principle or institution in question. This is a further reason why, on the present theory, it is possible for excusing conditions to vary from principle to principle and institution to institution.

Here there is a clear contrast with the genesis of excusing conditions under the Quality of Will theory. Once we learn that an agent acted under duress or under the influence of a mistaken belief, this immediately alters the "will" attributable to that agent. There is no need to ask what the effect would be of recognizing this "excuse." Of course, such considerations are relevant to the further question of which "qualities of will" should be regarded as morally deficient. But the Quality of Will theory plays no role in answering this question; it is an account only of the process of moral appraisal.

A second contrast between the two theories is this. The Value of Choice theory treats changes in the set of alternatives available to a person and changes in the conditions under which he or she chooses among them as factors contributing to the answer to a single question: how good or bad a thing is it to be presented with that choice? Under the Quality of Will theory, on the other hand, there is an important difference here. Some conditions affect the degree to which a "will" can be imputed to the agent; others modify the nature of that will. This difference may explain Hart's remark that while continental jurisprudence has traditionally distinguished between imputability and fault he sees little to be gained by observing this rigid distinction.[30] This difference is to be expected insofar as Hart is speaking as a Value of Choice theorist while the continental tradition may be more concerned with aspects of the law akin to quality of will.

3. The Value of Choice and the Causal Thesis

I turn now to the question of whether choice will retain the moral significance which the Value of Choice theory assigns it if the Causal Thesis is true. Whether it does so or not will depend on

---

[30] *Punishment and Responsibility,* p. 218.

whether choice will retain its value for an individual if the Causal Thesis is true. This is at least part of what I called in my first lecture "the personal problem of free will." So it seems that the most that the Value of Choice theory could accomplish would be to reduce the political problem of free will to the personal problem.

The mere truth of the Causal Thesis would not deprive choice of its predictive value: a person's choices could remain indicative of his or her future preferences and satisfactions even if they had a systematic causal explanation. Nor, it seems to me, need the demonstrative value of choice be undermined. A person's choices could still reflect continuing features of his or her personality such as feelings for others, memory, knowledge, skill, taste, and discernment.

This is how things seem to me, perhaps because I am in the grip of a theory. It is difficult to support these intuitions by argument because it is difficult, for me at least, to identify clearly the basis of the intuitions which move one toward the opposite conclusion. It might be claimed that what I have called the demonstrative value of choice would be undermined because the feelings, attitudes, and so on which a person's choices might be taken to "reflect" will no longer "belong" to that person if the Causal Thesis is true, but it is not clear why this should be the case. It is easy to see that particular kinds of causal history might make a belief or desire "alien." This would happen when, as in the "implantation" examples mentioned above, the special causal genesis of a belief meant also that it lacked connection with the person's other conscious states — that it was not all dependent on other beliefs and desires for support and not subject to modification through the agent's process of critical reflection. But it does not seem that this kind of loss of connection need hold generally if the Causal Thesis is correct.

One can certainly imagine a form of causal determination which would make this kind of alienation hold generally and would make it inappropriate to speak of a person's holding beliefs and attitudes at all. A person's conscious states might be caused to occur in a pattern which made no sense at all "from the inside," following one another in a random and meaningless sequence preserving no continuity of belief or attitude. It might be argued that the "normal case" is more like this than we are inclined to suppose: that our idea of the coherence and regularity of our conscious life is to a large degree an illusion. This might undermine the sense of self on which the value of choice depends. But this, if true, would be the result of a particular substantive claim about the order and coherence of the events that make up our "mental lives." It would not be a consequence of the bare Causal Thesis itself.

4. FREEDOM AND OVERDETERMINATION

The kind of freedom required by the Value of Choice theory is in one respect more extensive than that required for moral appraisal of the kind discussed in my first lecture. This difference can be brought out by considering how the ideas of quality of will and value of choice apply to overdetermination cases of the kind introduced by Harry Frankfurt.[31] Frankfurt's central example involves two drug addicts. It is assumed that neither is capable of resisting the pull of his addiction: both will take the drug when it is offered, and neither could do otherwise. But while one, the "unwilling addict," would prefer that the desire to take the drug not be the one which he acts on, the other, "the willing addict," not only has a desire for the drug but also has the "second-order desire" to act on that desire. Frankfurt believes that the latter addict acts freely in the sense required for moral responsibility but that the former does not. What interests me here is the fact that the two theories I have presented appear to give different answers to the question of freedom in cases like that of Frankfurt's willing addict — that is to say, cases in which (for reasons which may or

---

[31] In "Freedom of the Will and the Concept of a Person."

may not be like those in Frankfurt's particular example) a person has no alternative to doing a certain thing but nonetheless gets what he wants or does what he is inclined to do. If the question is whether the action reflects the agent's quality of will, then cases like that of Frankfurt's willing addict seem to be cases of freedom. (This answer agrees with Frankfurt, which is not surprising given that he is concerned specifically with moral responsibility.) If, on the other hand, the question is whether the agent has been given a fair chance to make outcomes conform to or exhibit his or her preferences and abilities, then the answer seems to be no, and the cases count as instances of unfreedom.

It may seem that this difference is illusory. The question under the Value of Choice theory is whether there was the right kind of opportunity for the person's disposition to choose to be discovered and registered. Insofar as it is predictive value we are concerned with, the assumption is that "we" do not generally know in advance what a person's preference is: we are trying to set up a social mechanism to discover this and react to it. In Frankfurt's cases, however, it is assumed that *we* know the addicts' (first- and second-order) preferences. Indeed, we are assumed to know more about this than agents themselves normally do. The question of how these preferences might be discovered is not at issue in Frankfurt's discussion. But this question can arise with respect to moral responsibility. Administering praise and blame is something *we* do, and it is relevant to ask whether we have adequate grounds for doing so: whether it is fair to judge a person on the basis we have. This is like the question which arose in application of the Value of Choice theory: whether there was adequate opportunity for the person's preferences, whatever they may have been, to be revealed.

This same question of fairness can also be raised when we are only forming an opinion about an agent's blameworthiness, without intending to express it. But the question whether the agent is blame*worthy* goes beyond these questions of adequate grounds, and it is the question which is fundamental: if the person's will in doing the action was of the appropriate sort, then a certain moral judgment is in fact applicable, whether or not any particular person is in a position to make it. Insofar as this is the case, the difference between the two theories that was pointed out above still stands.

Of course, parallel to the fact that a person "really was blameworthy" in acting a certain way, there is the fact that a person "really did want X, which was what he got," and this too might be held to be the fundamental fact, on the basis of which we could ask, How can he complain, since he got what he wanted? But this fact of preference is not fundamental in the way that the fact of blameworthiness is: the two facts are differently related to the moral ideas on which the theories in which they figure are based. The Quality of Will theory is based on the idea that the applicability of moral praise and blame depends on what the quality of will expressed in an action actually was. In determining this quality we may need to know what the agent believed the alternatives to be, but the question of which of these were actually available is in at least some cases irrelevant. Under the Value of Choice theory, however, the basic moral idea is not simply that people should get what they want but that things should be set up so that outcomes are made dependent on people's choices. In overdetermination cases this demand may not have been met, even though, as it happens, the person is in certain respects no worse off as a result.

5. The Two Theories Combined

I have described two theories and said something about how they are related to one another. It remains to be seen how these two theories, when combined, cover the territory. I have so far employed the Value of Choice theory mainly to give an account of the significance of choice in "political" cases, and I have relied upon the Quality of Will theory in discussing moral responsibility.

But this division of labor is overly simple. In fact, both analyses are required to account for the significance of choice in morality, and both are required to explain its force in the law.

Let me take the moral case first. Suppose you think that I promised on Monday to pick up your child at school on Tuesday but then failed to do this. There are two ways in which considerations of voluntariness and choice might enter into an assessment of how blameworthy I am on this account. First, such considerations could undermine my blameworthiness by making it the case that I had no obligation to pick up your child in the first place. It could be that I never assented to your request: when I said yes, it was to something else, and I never heard your request at all. Or perhaps I did assent to your request but only because you threatened me or concealed from me the fact that I would have to wait three hours beyond the normal end of the school day. Factors such as these could erase or modify my obligation.

On the other hand, it could be that while I did indeed incur an obligation to you, my not meeting your child was not due to any failure on my part to take my obligation seriously and try to fulfill it. It might be that I was hit over the head and knocked unconscious just before I was to leave, or that my car broke down on the way, leaving me stranded in a deserted spot.

These two kinds of excusing conditions are quite different. Something like the Value of Choice theory seems to provide the best explanation of why moral obligations are qualified by restrictions of the first sort. As Hart suggested, a system for the making of binding agreements, whether moral or legal, is defensible only if it is constrained by restrictions to ensure that the obligations one acquires are obligations one judges to be worth acquiring. The assessment of quality of will has at most a secondary role here.

Things are reversed in a case of involuntary nonfulfillment of a valid obligation. Here the natural value of choice analysis (modeled on that analysis of the choice requirement for criminal punishment) would be that a morality which held agents liable to blame in such cases would be objectionable because it gave people insufficient "protection" against incurring the sanction of moral blame. This is clearly not the right explanation. It is wrong because it treats moral blame simply as a "sanction" which people would like to avoid, which we attach to certain actions although it could just as well be attached to others (e.g., to things that are done involuntarily). This ignores the distinctive content of moral blame, in virtue of which it is not simply another kind of unpleasant treatment, like being shunned. Morality is, at base, a system of mutually authorizable deliberation. To feel oneself subject to moral blame is to be aware of a gap between the way one in fact decided what to do and the form of decision which others could reasonably demand. The absence of such a gap is by itself a sufficient explanation of why blame is inapplicable in cases like that of the person who, despite his or her best efforts, fails to pick up the child. There is no need to refer to the kind of question which the Value of Choice theory addresses.

This internal connection between the nature of "the moral sanction" and the content of morality — between the nature of blame and the things one can be blamed for — differentiates morality from a social institution set up to serve certain extrinsic purposes. Of course there could be a social practice according to which people would be subject to scolding and shunning in cases for actions involving no faulty willing or deliberation, but what was expressed by this behavior would not be moral blame. Even without such a practice there is a question, distinct from that of blameworthiness, of whether one has good reason to engage in "blaming behavior" toward a given person on a given occasion. As I mentioned in my first lecture, even when people are blameworthy it might be callous to scold them, and the reverse may also be true. For example, even though very young children are not blameworthy it may be important for their moral education to treat them as if they were.

The issues raised here are similar to those which arise in connection with what Hart called the "definitional stop" argument against exemplary or vicarious punishment of persons known to be innocent of any offense.[32] A utilitarian justification of punishment, insofar as it is a justification of *punishment*, could not justify such practices, this argument ran, because these practices do not count as punishment, which, by definition, must be of an offender for an offense. The obvious response to this argument is that it is not important what we call it; the question is why it would not be permissible to subject people, known to be innocent, to unpleasant treatment (prison, fines, etc.) as part of a scheme to intimidate others into obeying the law. As I have said above, I agree with Hart that the Value of Choice theory provides a good (though perhaps not fully satisfying) answer to this question. With respect to moral blame, however, I have responded in effect that it matters a great deal what you call it, because blameworthi-*ness*, rather than any form of "blaming behavior," is the central issue. There is also, of course, a question of the desirability and permissibility of expressing or administering blame in a certain way, but this is a separate question and a secondary one.

In the case of criminal punishment this emphasis is reversed: the main question is whether we can justify depriving people of their property, their liberty, or even their lives.[33] Despite the

---

[32] *Punishment and Responsibility*, pp. 5–6.

[33] In a recent article, R. B. Brandt put forward something like the Quality of Will theory as a limitation on legal punishment. See "A Motivational Theory of Excuses in the Criminal Law," in J. R. Pennock and J. W. Chapman, eds., *NOMOS XXVII: Criminal Justice* (New York: New York University Press, 1985), pp. 165–98. Specifically, Brandt defends the principle that a condition should be recognized as excusing a person from legal blame if the presence of that condition "blocks the normal inference" from the fact that the agent performed a certain act to the conclusion that the agent's motivation is defective. His defense of this principle appeals to the value of assuring people that if they lack "defective motivation" they will almost certainly not be punished. This is reminiscent of Hart and the Value of Choice theory, but Brandt's defense is avowedly rule-utilitarian: he sees the value in question merely as a contribution to the general welfare, not as fulfilling a special requirement of fairness to the individual. Moreover, he sees the requirement of "defective motivation" as a replacement for Hart's notion of "capac-

changed emphasis, however, both elements are still present, and consequently it does "matter what you call it" even if this consideration does not settle the crucial question of justification. The law is not just an organized system of threats. It also provides rules and standards which good citizens are supposed to "respect," that is, to employ as a way of deciding what to do — not simply as a way of avoiding sanctions but as a set of norms which they accept as reason-giving. This important feature of law offers a further reason why the Value of Choice theory was not completely satisfying as an explanation of the choice requirement for criminal punishment. Insofar as punishment is in part an expression of "legal blame," as Feinberg and others have pointed out,[34] there is a special inappropriateness in having it fall on persons who have deliberated and acted just as the law says they should. The Value of Choice theory thus fails to be a complete account of the significance of choice in the law for much the same reason that it fails to be a complete account in the case of morality. In each case there is *something* to the "definitional stop."

Something, perhaps, but in the case of the law, how much? Pointing out "the expressive function of punishment" helps us to understand our reactions to punishing particular kinds of people, but what role if any does it have in the justification of punishment? It seems to have no positive role in justifying hard treatment of the legally blameworthy. Insofar as expression is our aim, we could just as well "say it with flowers" or, perhaps more appropriately, with weeds. Nor, it seems, is this idea the central explanation of the apparent wrongfulness of punishing, say, young children or the mentally ill. Assuming that these people lack the

---

ity and fair opportunity" to avoid punishment (*ibid.*, p. 180). My analysis is similar to Brandt's in a number of respects, but, unlike him, I see quality of will and the value of choice as two independent (though related) *reasons* for the limits of moral and legal blameworthiness. Since they are related, it is not surprising that these two kinds of reasons often support the same limits. But they do not always do so.

34 Joel Feinberg, "The Expressive Function of Punishment," in *Doing and Deserving* (Princeton: Princeton University Press, 1970).

capacity for critically reflective, rational self-governance, we could argue, as we did in the case of morality, that they cannot be legally blameworthy. But even in the case of morality, the justification of "blaming behavior" is a separate issue from that of blameworthiness, and here it is a much weightier one in view of the losses that the law can inflict.

The Value of Choice theory offers a more plausible explanation. According to that theory the lack of the normal capacity for critically reflective, rational self-governance is relevant because people who lack it are so unlikely to be deterred. This may or may not make punishment pointless for us, but it certainly makes it unfair to them: we must protect them against punishment just as, in my other example, we must post barriers or guards to keep people with Alzheimer's disease away from the hazardous waste. But within the Value of Choice theory the normal capacity for critically reflective, rational self-governance lacks the *distinctive* importance which it has when moral (or legal) blameworthiness is at issue. There are many people who have this capacity yet will not be deterred. It is easy to say why they are blameworthy, but why should we respond differently to their suffering than to that of the mentally ill? We can say that, because they have this normal capacity for self-governance, deterrence is a plausible strategy for us to use in dealing with them and that the possibility of their being deterred is, from their point of view, *some* measure of protection. If it turns out not to be enough, then the best we can say, if it is true, is that we did as much as we could be expected to do to protect them.

At some moments it seems to me that we must be able to say more — that choice has a further significance not captured by either of the theories I have considered, perhaps something more like what the Forfeiture View is straining toward. At other times, however, it seems to me an advantage of the combined theory I have been defending, and a natural consequence of its aspiration to be compatible with the Causal Thesis, that it leaves us in this position: moral and (if there is such a thing) legal indignation toward lawbreakers is entirely in order, and the sufferings we inflict upon them may be justified. But in justifying these sufferings, and inflicting them, we have to say not "You asked for this" but "There but for the grace of God go I."

Law and Morality

JÜRGEN HABERMAS

Translated by Kenneth Baynes
Boston University

THE TANNER LECTURES ON HUMAN VALUES

Delivered at
Harvard University

October 1 and 2, 1986

Dr. Jürgen Habermas was born June 18, 1929, in Düsseldorf. He studied in Göttingen, Zürich, and Bonn and completed his doctoral research with a dissertation on Schelling. He was professor of philosophy at Heidelberg, and for ten years he was the director of the Max Plank Institute for Research of Living Conditions in a Scientific and Technical World. He is the recipient of many honors, prizes, and degrees, as well as professor of philosophy at Johann Wolfgang Goethe-Universität in Frankfurt.

LECTURE ONE: HOW IS LEGITIMACY POSSIBLE ON THE BASIS OF LEGALITY?

Max Weber regarded the political systems of modern Western societies as forms of "legal domination." Their legitimacy is based upon a belief in the legality of their exercise of political power. Legal domination acquires a rational character in that, among other things, belief in the legality of authorities and enacted regulations has a quality different from that of belief in tradition or charisma. It is the rationality intrinsic to the form of law itself that secures the legitimacy of power exercised in legal forms.[1] This thesis has sparked a lively discussion. With it Weber supported a positivistic concept of law: law is precisely what the political legislator — whether democratic or not — enacts as law in accordance with a legally institutionalized procedure. Under this premise the form of law cannot draw its legitimating force from an alliance between law and morality. Modern law has to be able to legitimate power exercised in a formally legal manner through its own formal properties. These are to be demonstrated as "rational" without any reference to practical reason in the sense of Kant or Aristotle. According to Weber, law possesses its own rationality, independent of morality. In his view, any fusion of law and morality threatens the rationality of law and thus the basis of the legitimacy of legal domination. Weber diagnosed such a fatal moralization of law in contemporary developments, which he described as the "materialization" of bourgeois formal law.

Today there is a debate concerning legal regulation (or juridification: *Verrechtlichung*), which is connected to Weber's diag-

[1] Max Weber, *Wirtschaft und Gesellschaft* (Cologne, 1964), ch. 3, pp. 2, 160ff.

nosis.[2] I would like to develop my own reflections on law and morality in this context. First, I will recall Weber's analysis of the deformalization of law and work out some of his implicit assumptions concerning moral theory; they prove to be incompatible with his declared value-skeptical position. In the second part, I will examine three positions within the recent German debates concerning formal changes in law; my aim there is to marshal reasons for a more appropriate concept of the rationality of law. Finally, I will develop, at least in rough outline, the thesis that legality can derive its legitimacy only from a procedural rationality with a moral impact. The key to this is an interlocking of two types of procedures: processes of moral argumentation get institutionalized by means of legal procedures. My reflections have a normative character. However, as the second lecture should make clear, I am developing them not from the perspective of legal doctrine but, rather, from the perspective of social theory.

I. MAX WEBER'S CONCEPT OF LEGAL RATIONALITY

1

What Weber described as the "materialization" of civil law, is today recognized as the wave of legal regulation associated with the welfare state. It has to do not only with the quantitative growth, with the increasing density and depth, of regulation in the legal provisions of a complex society.[3] Given the interventionist requirements of an avowedly active government that both steers and compensates, the functions and internal structures of the legal system are altered as well. Law as a generalized medium is not only more widely utilized; the form of law also changes according to the imperatives of a *new kind* of requirement.

---

[2] F. Kübler, ed., *Verrechtlichung von Wirtschaft, Arbeit und sozialer Solidarität* (Baden-Baden, 1984); A. Görlitz and R. Voigt, *Rechtspolitologie* (Hamburg, 1985).

[3] R. Voigt, ed., *Abschied vom Recht?* (Frankfurt, 1983).

Weber already had in view the regulatory law of the welfare state. This law is instrumentalized for the policies of a legislature that wants to meet demands for social justice with compensatory redistribution, stabilizing controls, and transforming interventions: "With the emergence of modern class problems, there have arisen substantive demands upon the law from a part of those whose interests are involved (namely labor), on the one hand, and from the legal ideologists, on the other. They . . . call for a social law on the basis of such emotionally colored ethical postulates as 'justice' or 'human dignity'. But this renders the formalism of law fundamentally questionable." [4] At this point the conceptual pair "formal-substantive" (or "formal-material") comes into play. With these concepts Weber shaped the relevant discussion up to the present day — and, in my opinion, steered it in the wrong direction. In his view, the demands for "substantive" justice invade the medium of law and destroy its "formal rationality." He supports his thesis primarily with examples from private law, which, from the liberal point of view, was once supposed to secure the liberty and property of contracting legal persons through public, abstract, and general laws. In fact, new special domains of private law have developed out of this corpus; tendencies toward deformalization are obvious — for example, in welfare and labor law, and in antitrust and corporate law.[5]

These tendencies can be described as "materialization" if one starts from the formalistic understanding of law that became dominant in Germany with Pandectist science and conceptual jurisprudence. In general, Max Weber explains the formal properties of law that were rigorously elaborated in this tradition by referring to the doctrinal work of lawyers. Legal experts foster the so-called "formalism of law" above all in three respects. First,

---

[4] Weber, *Wirtschaft und Gesellschaft*, p. 648.

[5] G. Teubner, "Verrechtlichung — Begriffe, Merkmale, Grenzen, Auswege," in Kübler, *Verrechtlichung von Wirtschaft*, pp. 289ff.; G. Teubner, ed., *Dilemmas of Law in the Welfare State* (Berlin, 1986).

the systematic perfection of a body of clearly analyzed legal provisions brings established norms into a clear and verifiable order.
Second, the abstract and general form of the law, neither tailored
to particular contexts nor addressed to specific persons, gives the
legal system a uniform structure. And third, a judiciary and an
administration bound by law guarantee due process and a reliable
implementation of laws. Deviations from this liberal model can
then be understood as encroachments upon the formal properties
of the law. The wave of regulatory law associated with the welfare state does in fact destroy the classical image of the system of
civil law, for example, the clear separation of private and public
law as well as the hierarchy of basic norms and statutes. The same
holds for the presumption of a well-ordered and unified body of
law. The unity of a more or less coherent legal corpus is not as
such objectified in the legal text. An anticipated unity is open to
constructive interpretation from case to case. Further, purposive
programs displace rule-oriented forms of law to the extent that
the enactment of law becomes dependent upon political intervention into social spheres, where the consequences are less and less
predictable. Just as concrete facts and abstract goals find their
way into the language of the law, characteristics that previously
were external to the law now more and more invade legal provisions.[6] Finally, this "rise of purpose within law" (Jhering) loosens
the legal ties of the judiciary and the administration, which formerly appeared to be unproblematic. Judges have to deal with
blanket clauses and, at the same time, have to do justice to a
greater variety of contexts and a greater interdependence of legal
provisions, which are no longer placed in a coherent and clear-cut
hierarchy. The same goes for "context-sensitive" administrative
action.

The formal properties of law were, then, characterized by a
systematization of the legal corpus, by the form of abstract and
general rules, and by strict procedures limiting the discretion of

6 Teubner, "Verrechtlichung," pp. 300ff.

judges and administrators. That view already involved certain idealizations; but even this liberal ideology broke down in the face of the legal changes in the welfare state. In this respect one might well speak of a "materialization" of law. But Weber could give this expression a critical sense only by establishing two further assumptions: (a) he considered the rationality of law to be grounded in its formal properties; and (b) the materialization of law for him meant its moralization, that is, the penetration of substantive justice into positive law. From this followed his critical thesis that the rationality intrinsic to the medium of law *as such* is destroyed to the degree that an internal connection is established between law and morality.

2

However, this train of thought is valid only if the formal properties of law, as Max Weber derived them from the formalistic understanding of law, can be interpreted in a narrow, morally neutral sense of "rational." Let me recall three aspects of the sense in which Weber used the term "rational" in this context.[7]

Weber *first* proceeds from a broad conception of technique (in the sense of techniques of prayer, painting, education, and the like) in order to make clear that the aspect of regularity in general is important for the *rationality of rule-governed behavior*. Patterned behavior that can be reliably reproduced provides the advantage of predictability. When it becomes a matter of technical rules for controlling nature and material objects, this rule-rationality takes on the more specific meaning of instrumental rationality. This has no application to legal norms. When, however, it is no longer a matter of the efficient employment of means, but of the preferential selection of goals from among pre-given values, Weber speaks, *secondly*, of *purposive rationality*. Under this aspect, an action can be rational to the extent that it is guided

---

[7] J. Habermas, *Theorie des Kommunikativen Handelns* (Frankfurt, 1981), vol. 1, pp. 239ff.

by explicit value orientations and is not controlled by blind effects or quasi-natural traditions. Weber regards value orientations as substantive preferences incapable of further justification and subject to choice by persons acting in a purposive-rational manner; an example would be the individual interests that private legal subjects pursue in economic exchange. *Finally*, Weber also calls rational the results of the intellectual work of experts who analytically master transmitted symbolic systems such as, for example, religious worldviews or moral and legal conceptions. These doctrinal achievements are guided by *scientific method* in a broad sense. They increase the complexity and the specificity of a type of knowledge embodied in teachings.

At first glance, it is easy to see how the formal properties of law mentioned above can be described as "rational," in a narrow, morally neutral sense, under the three aspects of the rationality of patterned behavior, the rationality of choice, and scientific rationality. The systematic elaboration of the legal corpus depends on the scientific rationality of experts. Public, abstract, and general rules secure spheres of private autonomy for the purposive-rational pursuit of individual interests. Finally, procedures for the strict application and implementation of laws make possible a noncontingent and thus a predictable connection between actions, statutory definitions, and legal consequences — above all in commercial transactions under private law. To this extent, the rationality of bourgeois formal law would be guaranteed precisely by its three formal properties. But is it in fact these aspects of rationality that provide legitimating force to the legality of the exercise of political power?

As a glance at the European workers' movement and the class struggles of the nineteenth century shows, the political systems that have so far come closest to Max Weber's model of legal domination were by no means experienced as legitimate *per se*. At most, this was true for the social classes that benefited most and for their liberal ideologists. If we accept the liberal model for purposes of an immanent critique, we can show that the legitimacy of bourgeois formal law results not from its declared "rational" characteristics but, at best, from certain moral implications that can be derived from those properties with the help of additional empirical assumptions regarding the structure and function of the underlying economic system.

3

If we run through the above-mentioned specifications of rationality in reverse order, this applies first to the legal protection or certainty of law, which is established on the basis of abstract and general laws through strict judicial and administrative procedures. Let us assume that the empirical conditions for equal protection are universally fulfilled. We have to keep in mind that legal protection — in the sense of the predictability of infringements on liberty and property — is a "value" that sometimes competes with other values — for example, with the equal distribution of opportunities and social rewards. Hobbes already had a maximization of legal protection in view when he required the sovereign to channel his commands through the medium of civil law. But the privileged place this value enjoys in bourgeois formal law is certainly not sufficiently justified by the fact that the predictability of the legal consequences of action is functional for a market society. For example, whether welfare-state policies that can only be realized with the help of blanket clauses and open legal concepts should be bought at the expense of predictable judicial decisions is a question that involves the moral assessment of different principles. Such normative conflicts must then be decided from the moral point of view of which of the competing interests lends itself to universalization.

This already touches, secondly, on the semantic form of legal norms. The classical form of abstract and general laws does not legitimate political power exercised in that form merely because it fulfills certain functional requirements for the privately autonomous and purposively rational pursuit of individual interests. It has been shown time and time again, from Marx to MacPherson,[8] that this would hold true only if everyone enjoyed equal access to the opportunity structures of a market society — and even then only under the premise that there is no preferable alternative to forms of life shaped by monetary and bureaucratic mechanisms. It is true, however, that in contrast to goal-oriented legal programs, rule-oriented programs do have the advantage, owing to their semantic generality, of more readily conforming to the principle of equality before the law. As a result of their abstractness, this type of law even corresponds to the further principle of treating equals equally and unequals unequally, at least when the regulated facts are actually general and not affected in their essential content by changing contexts. Thus, in contrast to Max Weber's functionalist argument, it turns out that the semantic form of abstract and general laws can be justified as rational only in the light of morally susbtantive principles. (Of course, this does not entail that *only* a legal order in the form of public, abstract, and general rules is able to satisfy the two principles of equal protection and substantive equality of the law.)

The third formal property, the scientific construction of a systematic body of law, also cannot by itself account for the legitimating effect of legality. Despite all the authority that the sciences have been able to muster in modern societies, legal norms still cannot achieve legitimacy merely by the fact that their language is made precise, their concepts explicated, their consistency tested, and their principles unified. Doctrinal work can contribute to legitimation only if and insofar as it helps to satisfy the specific demand for justification which arises to the degree that law as a whole becomes positive law. That is, from the perspective of legal subjects and lawyers alike, the contingency of positive law — the fact that law can be changed at will — can be reconciled with its

---

[8] C. B. MacPherson, *Die politische Theorie des Besitzindividualismus* (Frankfurt, 1967).

claim to legitimacy under one tacit presupposition: context-dependent legal changes and developments should be justifiable in the light of acceptable principles. Precisely the doctrinal achievements of legal experts have made us aware of the post-traditional mode of validity of modern law. In positive law all norms have, at least in principle, lost their sheer customary validity. Therefore, individual legal provisions must be justified as elements of a legal system which, as a whole, is viewed as reasonable in the light of principles. These principles can come into conflict with one another and be exposed to discursive testing. However, the rationality that is brought to bear at this level of normative discussion is more closely related to Kant's practical reason than to pure scientific reason. In any case, it is not morally neutral.

In sum, we can conclude that the formal properties of law studied by Weber could have granted the legitimacy of legality only under specific social conditions and only insofar as they were "rational" in a moral-practical sense. Weber did not recognize this moral core of civil law because he qualified moral insights as subjective value orientations. Values counted as contents incapable of further justification and seemingly incompatible with the formal character of law. He did not distinguish the preference for values which, within the limits of specific cultural life forms and traditions, *commend* themselves, so to speak, as superior to other values, on the one hand, from the moral oughtness of norms that *obligate* equally all whom they address, on the other. He did not separate the value judgments spread across the whole range of competing value contents from the formal aspect of the binding force or validity of norms, a validity that does not vary with the contents of the norms. In a word, he did not take ethical formalism seriously.

4

This is evident in his interpretation of social contract theories. Weber contrasts modern natural law — *Vernunftrecht* — with positive formal law. He holds "that there can be no purely formal natural law": " 'Nature' and 'reason' are the substantive criteria for what is legitimate from the standpoint of natural law." [9] It must be conceded that social contract theory from Hobbes to Rousseau and Kant still retains certain metaphysical connotations. But with their model of an original contract in which free and equal legal associates, after assessing their interests, lay down the rules for their common life, they already satisfy the requirement for a procedural justification of law. In this modern tradition expressions such as "nature" and "reason" no longer refer to metaphysical ideas. Rather, they serve to explain the presuppositions under which an agreement must be able to come about if it is to have legitimating force. The procedural conditions for rational will formation can be inferred from the contractual model. Once again, Weber does not sufficiently distinguish between structural and substantive — or formal and material — aspects. Only for this reason is he able to mistake "nature" and "reason" for value contents from which formal law was the first to free itself. He falsely identifies the procedural properties of a post-traditional level of justification with substantive values. Therefore, he does not see that the model of the social contract (in a way similar to the categorical imperative) can be understood as proposing a procedure whose rationality is supposed to guarantee the correctness of whatever decisions come about in a procedural manner.

These reminders are meant to explain why law and morality cannot be distinguished from one another by means of the concepts "formal" and "substantive." Our considerations so far lead rather to the conclusion that the legitimacy of legality cannot be explained in terms of some independent rationality which, as it were, inhabits the form of law in a morally neutral manner. It must, rather, be traced back to an internal relationship between law and morality. This is also the case for the model of bourgeois formal law that crystallized around the semantic form of abstract and general

---

[9] Weber, *Wirtschaft und Gesellschaft*, p. 638.

rules. The formal properties of this legal type would at best offer grounds for legitimation only in view of particular moral principles. Now it is of course correct that the change in the form of law that Max Weber describes by the word "materialization" precisely withdraws the basis for these grounds. But this observation does not prove yet that the materialization of law must destroy every sort of formal property from which, in an analogous way, grounds for legitimation could be derived. This change in the form of law merely requires a radicalization of Weber's question about the kind of rationality inherent in law. Formal and de-formalized law are from the very beginning only different variants of positive law. The legal formalism that is common to both of these legal types must lie at a more abstract level. We may not identify particular features of bourgeois formal law — as represented by legal formalism — with the most formal properties of modern law in general.

For the purposes of this wider analysis, the concept must be broadly conceived and not connected from the outset to a specific form of law. H. L. A. Hart and others have shown that modern legal systems include not only legal precepts, permissions, prohibitions, and penal norms but also secondary norms, rules of empowerment and rules of organization that serve to institutionalize processes of legislation, adjudication, and administration.[10] In this way the production of legal norms is itself regulated by legal norms. Legally binding decisions in due time are made possible by procedurally defined but otherwise indeterminate processes. Furthermore, it must be borne in mind that these processes connect decisions with obligations to justify or burdens of proof. What is institutionalized in this manner are legal discourses that operate not only under the external constraints of legal procedure but also under the internal constraints of a logic of argumentation for producing good reasons.[11] The basic rules of argumentation

[10] H. L. A. Hart, *Der Begriff des Rechts* (Frankfurt, 1968).

[11] R. Alexy, *Theorie der juristischen Argumentation* (Frankfurt, 1978).

do not leave the construction and appraisal of reasons to the whims of participants. And they can in turn be altered only through argumentation. Finally, it is worthy of note that legal discourses, however bound to existing law, cannot operate within a closed universe of unambiguously fixed legal rules. This already follows from the stratification of modern law into rules and principles.[12] Many of these principles are both legal and moral, as can easily be made clear in the case of constitutional law. The moral principles of natural law have become positive law in modern constitutional states. From the viewpoint of a logic of argumentation, the modes of justification institutionalized in legal processes and proceedings remain open to moral discourses.

Now, if the formal properties of law — below the level of a differentiation into more or less materialized legal types — are to be found in the dimension of legally institutionalized processes, and if these procedures regulate legal discourses that remain permeable to moral arguments, we can make the following conjecture: legitimacy is possible on the basis of legality insofar as the procedures for the production and application of legal norms are also conducted reasonably, in the moral-practical sense of procedural rationality. The legitimacy of legality is due to the interlocking of two types of procedures, namely, of legal processes with processes of moral argumentation that obey a procedural rationality of their own.

II. THE DEFORMALIZATION OF LAW: THREE INTERPRETATIONS

1

Max Weber was still oriented toward a formalistic interpretation of law that has in the meantime been called into question by subsequent historical research. The liberal model had little to do with the reality of the law, either in late-nineteenth-century Ger-

---

[12] R. Dworkin, *Taking Rights Seriously* (Cambridge, Mass., 1977), ch. 2, 3.

many or elsewhere. The judiciary's being strictly bound to the law, for example, has always been a fiction.[13] However, the enduring impact of Weber's diagnosis is no accident. For as a *comparative* statement about a trend in the self-understanding and practice of legal experts, the thesis on the deformalization of law has a certain plausibility. More recent phenomena, unavailable to Weber, confirm his diagnosis.

Reflexive law. Weber had in mind the transformation of formal law into policy-oriented legal programs. As the example of collective bargaining law shows, soon another type of deformalized law emerged. I mean the delegation of negotiating competence to the conflicting parties and the institutionalization of quasi-political bargaining processes.[14] With this type of regulation, the legislator no longer directly seeks to achieve concrete goals. Rather, the procedural norms are supposed to regulate processes of will formation and to enable the participants to settle their affairs themselves. This reflexive, or two-level, mode of deformalization gains the advantage of greater flexibility by making legal parties autonomous. This type of reflexive law has expanded in the wake of corporatist developments.

Marginalization. Research on implementation over the past decades has confirmed the "gaps" that exist between the wording and the social effects of legal programs. In many social areas the law has anything but a strictly binding character. Awareness of marginality is partially due to research, that is, to facts not known before. But there are other phenomena: the increasingly experimental character of a goal-oriented regulation of events that are difficult to predict; the growing sensitivity on the part of legislators to problems of acceptability; and the assimilation of penal law to informal types of social control. Above all, substitution of

---

[13] R. Ogorek, "Widersprüchlichkeit und Einheit der Justiztheorie im 19. Jh." (1986).

[14] G. Teubner, "Substantive and Reflexive Elements in Modern Law," *Law and Society Rev.* 17 (1983): 239ff.

private agreements for criminal prosecution by the state, nego-
tiable settlements between offender and victim, and the like,
accelerate the "erosion of norms" and strengthen the trend toward
a questionable "consensus orientation." [15] To a certain degree
all these trends rid contemporary law of its classical coercive
character.

Functional imperatives. As the concept of "regulatory law"
already suggests, we interpret the wave of legal regulation associated with the welfare state as the instrumentalization of law for
policies of the legislature. But this description attributes to actors'
intentions what they often only do more or less unconsciously —
as agents of an increasingly complex state apparatus or under the
pressure of systemic imperatives of an economy that, though
autonomous, still requires stabilization. We can also see in the
administration of justice how normative viewpoints are being
subordinated to the imperatives of self-maintaining bureaucracies
or to the functional pressures of self-regulating markets. In the
conflict between rights on the one hand, and collective goods on
the other, functional requirements of subsystems regulated by
money and power prevail. These media-regulated subsystems are
themselves no longer integrated via norms and values.

Morality versus the Positivity of Law. With the increasing
mobilization of law, the question of the conditions of the legitimacy of legality gets intensified. With the growing rate of change,
positive law undermines its own basis of validity. With every
change of government, new interests gain a majority, interests
which, for example, affect laws dealing with housing, family, or
taxation. Paradoxically, this gets connected with the counter-
vailing tendency to appeal to "correct" law in the name of a
moralized law — for example, in the form of civil disobedience,
or in connection with issues of abortion, divorce, protection of the

---

[15] W. Naucke, *Die Wechselwirkung zwischen Strafziel und Verbrechensbegriff*
(Stuttgart, 1985), and *Versuch über den aktuellen Stil des Rechts, Schriften der
H. Ehler Akademie* (Kiel, 1986).

environment, and so on. There are also systematic reasons for this. Today moral principles originating in natural law are part of positive law. The interpretation of the constitution is therefore increasingly shaped by legal philosophy; in this regard W. Naucke ironically speaks of a "judicial administration of natural law." [16]

All these tendencies fall under the phrase "deformalization" of law. At the same time, under the rubric of "legal regulation" (or juridification: *Verrechtlichung*), they become the object of legal critique. From this perspective as well, the present debates are linked with Max Weber's analysis. His question concerning the rationality of the form of law aimed at criteria for law that could be accepted as both right and functional. To that extent, this discussion throws light on our question, how legitimacy is possible on the basis of legality. In what follows, I want to describe three positions that have arisen in the context of German discussions; I shall not enter into the corresponding American discussions. These positions share the participant's perspective, in which the legal system is analyzed from within.[17] The German discussion is tacitly shaped by conflicting views on the deformation of law during the Nazi period. One interpretation places a greater trust in the judiciary and the administration, the other in the parliamentary legislature. This polarization has the advantage of stimulating us to consider all three governmental powers rather than looking for the conditions of the legitimacy of legal domination only from within the judiciary.

2

Historical experiences during the Nazi period left especially clear traces in a controversy conducted in the fifties between Ernst Forsthoff and Wolfgang Abendroth concerning liberal versus

---

[16] Naucke, *Versuch über den aktuellen Stildes Rechts*, p. 21.

[17] I will deal only briefly with systems theory in my second lecture and cannot go into the law-and-economy approach at all.

welfare-state issues.[18] It resumes debates that were carried out
between Carl Schmitt and Hermann Heller — among others — during the Weimar Republic and after.[19] What matters in our context is that Forsthoff continues by doctrinal means Max Weber's
criticism of the deformalization of law. He believes that tendencies toward deformalization can be arrested if typical welfare-
state interventions are channeled into the liberal forms of the
classical constitutional state. In this view, the principle of the
welfare state as it is laid down in the Basic Law of the Federal
Republic (*Grundgesetz*) should not be given equal status with
the liberal principles of the constitutional state. The liberal logic
of the constitutional state is again spelled out in terms of the form
of public, abstract, and general norms. As long as the political
legislator pursues only those goals that can be realized in such
rule-oriented programs, independent court and administrative
decisions remain predictable. An active state, intervening in the
social status quo through a planning and service-oriented administration, would distort the liberal state. That the legitimacy of
legal domination will stand or fall with the semantic form of legal
norms is a premise that Lon Fuller has analyzed in detail as the
"internal morality of the law." [20]

The weakness of this position lies in its purely defensive character. Forsthoff knows that there once was "a structural corre-
spondence" between the liberal state and the liberal economic
order. Given the structural changes that have taken place in the
meantime, he must make the unrealistic assumption that the frame
of the liberal state has become independent of its social origins
and has independently established itself as a "technical," that is,
context-neutral game of constitutional rules. Forsthoff cannot
explain how the wave of legal regulation associated with the

18 E. Forsthoff, ed., *Rechtsstaatlichkeit und Sozialstaatlichkeit* (Darmstadt,
1968).

19 I. Maus, *Bürgerliche Rechtstheorie und Faschismus* (Munich, 1980).

20 R. L. Sumners, *Lon. L. Fuller* (Stanford, 1984), pp. 33ff.

welfare state could be kept within the limits of a legal type of law that has meanwhile become dated, without renouncing the welfare-state compromise that in substance can no longer be annulled.[21]

The democratic legal positivism of his opponent, Wolfgang Abendroth, seems to fit this reality better. According to the premises of Weber's and Forsthoff's legal formalism, the regulatory law of the welfare state must remain a foreign element. Compromises in formula do not help either.[22] By contrast, Abendroth wants to bring the principle of the welfare state and the liberal guarantees of the constitutional state together under the roof of democratic self-determination. For him the social order is at the disposal of the democratic will formation of the people as a whole. The democratic state is the center of a society that organizes and transforms itself. The legal form serves only to implement reformist policies through binding decisions. Law does not possess a structure of its own which might then be deformed. The legal form is represented, rather, as a malleable shell subject to the various tasks and accomplishments of planning administrations. In a positivistic manner, all internal determinations of rationality are removed from the concept of law. The ethical minimum is transferred from the semantic form of the legal norm to the democratic procedure of legislation. Abendroth trusts the rule of law to the Rousseauean hope that a democratic legislature remaining consistent with itself will not enact any resolutions that would not be capable of general agreement. With this idea of legislative activism, Abendroth still remains, however, blind to the specific phenomena of juridification associated with the welfare state, and blind as well to the systematic pressures arising from the market economy and the bureaucratic state.

[21] C. Offe, *Contradictions of the Welfare State* (London, 1984).

[22] E. R. Huber, "Rechtsstaat und Sozialstaat in der modernen Industriegesellschaft," in Forsthoff, *Rechtsstaatlichkeit*, p. 589.

3

In the meantime, however, a metacritique of the criticism of legal regulation or juridification stemming from Abendroth has emerged. At the center of this critique lies the thought that replacing strictly formal law by weak, deformalized regulations opens the way for the courts and the administration to get around the supremacy of the legislature and thus to steer around parliamentary legislation, which now has only a legitimating function. Ingeborg Maus argues, for instance, that materialized and specific types of reflexive law destroy the classical separation and balance of powers, since the legal tie of the judiciary and the administration to democratic law is dissolved by the promotion of blanket clauses and indeterminate goals, on the one side, and by the delegation of decision-making competence on the other.[23] The judiciary fills in this expanded scope for discretion with its own legal programs and value orientations. The administration operates between the implementation and the shaping of legal programs and pursues policies of its own. The legislative window dressing provides only the thinnest of legitimations for the judiciary's own value judgments and for the administration's corporatist ties and arrangements with the most powerful interests at any given time. The adaptation of the legal system to such "situation-sensitive" administrative action is supported only by a judiciary that weighs values and is oriented to the peculiar features of each individual case.

To be sure, this critique moves in the same direction as the legal formalism of liberals. But the two positions are distinguished from one another by their normative premises. Although Maus shares the liberal concern for well-defined legal propositions that narrowly circumscribe the scope of discretion for courts and administrations, she no longer sees the rationality of the Rule of Law as residing in the semantic form of the abstract and general

---

[23] I. Maus, "Verrechtlichung, Entrechtlichung und der Funktionswandel von Institutionen," in G. Göhler, ed., *Grundlagen einer Theorie der politischen Institutionen* (Cologne, 1986).

norm. Legitimating force is exclusively attributed to the democratic process of legislation. If it were only the change from conditional to goal-oriented legal programs that allowed the judiciary and the administration to circumvent legislative control, this line of argument would lose its point and ultimately coincide with the liberal one. On the other hand, it is also not sufficient to treat the supremacy of the legislature over the other two governmental functions merely sociologically, as a question of power. Behind Abendroth's approach there was still a trust in class analysis and a hope for a class compromise that could be shifted to the advantage of labor parties within the framework of the democratic welfare state. Today our confidence in the background assumptions of Marxist, as well as other, philosophies of history has largely disappeared. In its place there is the need for a straightforward normative justification of why parliaments deserve primacy. Abendroth's legal positivism is not sufficient for this. If the normative gap left by a positivist concept of democratically enacted laws can no longer be filled with a privileged class-interest, then the conditions of legitimacy for democratic law must be sought in the rationality of the legislative process itself.

Thus, from our discussion there emerges the interesting desideratum of investigating whether the grounds for the legitimacy of legality can be found in the procedural rationality built into the democratic legislative process. In the event that this desideratum can be met, there is, of course, at least one further problem. As soon as abstract and general norms that rule out all indeterminacies no longer serve as the prototypical form of regulation in the welfare state, we are left without a mechanism for transmitting any stipulated rationality of legislative procedures to the procedures of adjudication and administration. Without the automatic operation of a strict legal tie, as is assumed only in the liberal model, it remains an open question how the procedural rationality established for the former could be translated into the procedural rationality of the latter.

4

This question, focused on the rationality of judicial decision making, provides the starting point for a third line of argument. This position is less sharply formulated than the liberal or the democratic criticism of soft, deformalized law. There are at least two sorts of answers to the question of how the judiciary deals with deformalized law — a natural law version and a contextualist version. First, however, we must describe the pertinent phenomena.

The judicial review of the supreme court offers itself as an object of analysis. Of course, family, labor, and social law also confront the courts with material that cannot be treated according to the classical model of civil law procedures for subsuming individual cases under well-defined general laws.[24] But the tendencies toward a type of interpretation and decision making that not only fills gaps in the law but constructively develops it are most obvious in the interpretation of constitutional law.

Here it is especially clear that the liberal model of a contrast between state and society has broken down. The barrier between the governmental sphere of "the common weal" and the social sphere of the "private pursuit of individual interests" has become pervious. The constitution is represented as a dynamic whole wherein conflicts between individual welfare and the common weal must be settled at any given time in an ad hoc manner, in the light of a holistic interpretation of the constitution and guided by overarching principles.[25] The clear hierarchy between basic norms and statutory laws has dissolved, as has the character of basic rights as clear-cut rules.[26] There is scarcely any right that could not be limited by the consideration of principles. For this reason, the Federal Constitutional Court of West Germany estab-

---

[24] Salgo, "Soll die Zuständigkeit des Familiengerichts erweitert werden?" *Zeitschrift für das gesamte Familienrecht* 31 (1984): 221ff.

[25] E. Denninger, "Verfassungsrechtliche Schlüsselbegriffe," in FS. Für R. Wassermann (Baden-Baden, 1985), pp. 279ff.

[26] R. Alexy, *Theorie der Grundrechte* (Baden-Baden, 1985).

lished a "principle of interdependence": every individual element of the legal system can be interpreted *differently,* according to the context, given an understanding of the constitutional "value system" (*grundgesetzliche Wertordnung*) as a whole. With this anticipation of a reconstructed meaning of the whole, a two-tiered relationship is established between the legal order and the principles of legitimation — not, to be sure, at the level of the literal meaning of the legal text but in terms of the interpretive method. This gives rise to considerable legal indeterminacy. In this context, E. Denninger speaks of the replacement of legal domination — domination on the basis of the legality of laws and measures — by a "domination on the basis of judicially sanctioned legitimacy.[27]

But this makes even more precarious the critical question of whether the judiciary can still claim to use their unavoidably widened scope for discretion rationally — that is, with intersubjectively testable arguments. The affirmative answers characteristic of our third position are generally motivated by a mistrust of a parliamentary legislature that can be demagogically seduced. In this respect it presents a mirror image of the line of argument of the democratic position. Once again, a particular assessment of the totalitarian regime of the National Socialists filters through. From this point of view, a judiciary able to direct itself to suprapositive principles is supposed to constitute a counterweight to "a decisionistic and power-ridden positivism," "to a thoughtless, legally blind, intimidated or violated majority." [28] Since the legitimating power of the democratic sovereign has been undermined by legal positivism, the legislature must be subordinated to the control of a judiciary that is bound by law but also by "the highest laws of substantive justice." [29] Whether this is derived from

[27] Denninger, "Verfassungsrechtliche Schlüsselbegriffe," p. 284.

[28] F. Wieacker, *Privatrechtsgeschichte der Neuzeit* (Göttingen, 1967), p. 560.

[29] Ibid., p. 604.

Christian natural law or from value ethics, or whether one calls, in neo-Aristotelian tones, upon the customary ethos of a place, it is all the same: the appeal to a concrete value order that is beyond disposal and discussion confirms in fact Max Weber's fear, namely, that the deformalization of law would open the gates for the influx of substantive, and thus controversial, value orientations that are at root irrational.[30]

It is characteristic of those who advocate such a value-based administration of justice — whether the basics be determined by natural law or in a contextualist fashion—that they share Weber's premises, but with a change of sign. They place procedures, abstract principles, and concrete values all on the same level. Since moral principles are always already immersed in concrete-historical contexts of action, there can be no justification or assessment of norms according to a universal procedure that ensures impartiality. Neo-Aristotelians are especially inclined to an ethic of institutions that renounces the gulf between norm and reality, or principle and rule, annuls Kant's distinction between questions of justification and questions of application, and reduces moral deliberations to the level of prudential considerations.[31] At the level of a merely pragmatic judgment, normative and purely functional considerations are then indistinguishably intermingled.

In this view, the Federal Constitutional Court, in its assessment of values, has no criteria by which it could distinguish the place of normative principles (such as equal treatment or human dignity) or important methodological principles (such as proportionality or appropriateness) from functional imperatives (such as economic peace, the efficiency of the military, or, in general, the so-called feasibility proviso). When individual rights and collective goods are aggregated as values in which each is as particular as the next, deontological, teleological, and systems-

---

[30] U. K. Preuss, *Legalität und Pluralismus* (Frankfurt, 1973).

[31] H. Schnädelbach, "Was ist Neoaristotelismus?" in W. Kuhlmann, ed., *Moralität und Sittlichkeit* (Frankfurt, 1986), pp. 38ff.

theoretical considerations indistinguishably flow into one another. And the suspicion is only too justified that in the clash of value preferences incapable of further rationalization, the strongest interest will happen to be the one actually implemented. This explains, moreover, why the outcome of judicial proceedings can be so well predicted in terms of interests and power constellations. This third line of argument is only of relevance insofar as it draws attention to an unresolved problem. The example of the judiciary's dealings with deformalized law shows that the moralization of law now so manifest cannot be denied or annulled; it is internally connected to the wave of legal regulation triggered by the welfare state. However, both natural law — whether in the form of Christian ethics or value ethics — and neo-Aristotelianism remain helpless in the face of this, because they are unsuited to working out the rational core of legal procedures. Ethics oriented to conceptions of the good or to specific value hierarchies single out particular *normative contents*. Their premises are too strong to serve as the foundation for universally binding decisions in a modern society characterized by the pluralism of gods and demons. Only theories of morality and justice developed in the Kantian tradition hold out the promise of an *impartial* procedure for the justification and assessment of principles.

III. THE RATIONALITY OF LEGALLY INSTITUTIONALIZED PROCEDURES: PRELIMINARY QUESTIONS

1

If, in societies of our type, legitimacy is supposed to be possible on the basis of legality, then the belief in legitimacy, deprived of an unquestioned religious or metaphysical backing, must somehow be based on the rational properties of law. But Weber's assumption that an independent, morally neutral rationality intrinsic to law counts for the legitimating force of legality has not stood up. Political power exercised in the form of a positive law that is in need of justification owes its legitimacy instead — at least in part — to the implicit moral content of the formal properties of law. These formal properties should not be too concretely fixed to specific semantic features. Rather, what has legitimating force are the procedures that distribute burdens of proof, define the requirements of justification, and set the path of argumentative vindication. Further, the source of legitimation should not be looked for on one side only, either in the political legislature or in the administration of justice. Under conditions of welfare-state policies, even the most careful legislator cannot bind the judiciary and the administration solely through the semantic form of a certain legal type; he cannot do without regulatory law. We can find the rational core — in a moral-practical sense — of legal procedures only by analyzing how the idea of impartiality in the justified choice and application of binding rules can establish a constructive connection between the existing body of law, legislation, and adjudication. This idea of impartiality forms the core of practical reason. If we leave aside for now the problem of an impartial application of norms and consider the idea of impartiality under the aspect of justifying norms, it was developed in theories of morality and justice that laid down procedures for how someone could decide practical questions from the moral point of view. The rationality of any such pure procedure, prior to all institutionalization, is measured by whether the moral point of view is adequately explicated in it.

At present I see *three serious candidates* for such a procedural theory of justice. All of them come out of the Kantian tradition, but they differ from one another in the models by which they interpret the procedure of impartial will formation.[32] John Rawls adheres to the model of a contractual agreement and builds into the description of the original position those normatively substantive constraints under which the rational egoism of free and equal

32 J. Habermas, "Gerechtigkeit und Solidarität," in W. Edelstein, G. Nunner, eds., *Zur Bestimmung der Moral* (Frankfurt, 1986).

parties must lead to the choice of correct principles. The fairness of the result is guaranteed by the procedure through which it comes about.[33] Lawrence Kohlberg, by contrast, makes use of George Herbert Mead's model of a universal reciprocity in perspective taking. Ideal role taking replaces the idealized original position. It requires the morally judging person to put herself in the position of all who would be affected by putting into effect the norm in question.[34] From my point of view both models have the disadvantage of not doing complete justice to the cognitive claim of moral judgments. In the model of the contractual agreement, moral judgments are *assimilated* to rational-choice decisions; in the model of role taking, they are assimilated to empathetic acts of understanding. Karl-Otto Apel and I have therefore proposed that we look at moral argumentation itself as the adequate procedure of rational will formation. The argumentative testing of hypothetical validity claims represents such a procedure because no one who wants to argue seriously can avoid the idealizing presuppositions of this exacting form of communication. Every participant in an argumentative practice must pragmatically presuppose that in principle all those possibly affected could participate, freely and equally, in a cooperative search for truth in which only the force of the better argument appears.[35]

I cannot go into this here. In the present context, it has to suffice to indicate that there *are* serious candidates for a proceduralist theory of justice. Only then does my thesis not just hang suspended in the air — the thesis, namely, that proceduralized law and the moral justification of principles mutually implicate one another. Legality can produce legitimacy only to the extent that the legal order reflexively responds to the need for justification that originates from the positivization of law and responds in

---

[33] J. Rawls, *Theorie der Gerechtigkeit* (Frankfurt, 1976).

[34] L. Kohlberg, *The Philosophy of Moral Development* (San Francisco, 1981).

[35] J. Habermas, *Moralbewusstsein und kommunikatives Handeln* (Frankfurt, 1983).

such a manner that legal discourses are institutionalized in ways made pervious to moral argumentation.

2

On the other hand, the boundaries between law and morality ought not to be blurred. The procedures offered by theories of justice to explain how one can make judgments from a moral point of view share with legal processes only the feature that the rationality of the procedure is supposed to guarantee the "validity" of the procedurally achieved results. But legal procedures approximate the requirements of complete procedural rationality because they obey institutional and, indeed, independent criteria by which it can be determined, from the perspective of a nonparticipant, whether or not a decision has come about according to the rules. The procedure of moral argumentation, which is not yet legally regulated, does not meet this condition. Here procedural rationality remains incomplete. Whether something is judged from a moral point of view cannot be decided apart from a participant's perspective, since at this point there are no external or preceding criteria. None of the procedures proposed within moral theory can do without idealizations, even when — as in the case of the pragmatic presuppositions of argumentation — these idealizations can be shown to be unavoidable, or without any alternative, in the sense of a weak transcendental necessity.

It is, however, precisely the weaknesses of this kind of *incomplete* procedural rationality that makes intelligible why specific matters do require *legal* regulation and cannot be left to moral norms of such a post-traditional type. Whatever the procedure by which we want to test whether a norm could find the uncoerced, that is, rationally motivated, consent of all who may possibly be affected, it guarantees neither the infallibility nor the unambiguity of the outcome, nor a result in due time.

An autonomous morality provides only fallibilistic procedures for the justification of norms and actions. The high degree of cognitive uncertainty is heightened by the contingencies connected with the context-sensitive application of highly abstract rules to complex situations that are to be described as appropriately and completely, in all relevant aspects, as possible.[36] Furthermore, there is a motivational weakness corresponding to this cognitive one. Every post-traditional morality demands a distantiation from the unproblematical background of established and taken-for-granted forms of life. Moral judgments, decoupled from concrete ethical life (*Sittlichkeit*), no longer immediately carry the motivational power that converts judgments into actions. The more that morality is internalized and made autonomous, the more it retreats into the private sphere.

In all spheres of action where conflicts and pressures for regulation call for unambiguous, timely, and binding decisions, legal norms must absorb the contingencies that would emerge if matters were left to strictly moral guidance. The complementing of morality by coercive law can itself be morally justified. In this connection K. O. Apel speaks of the problem of the warranted expectation of an exacting universalistic morality.[37] That is, even morally well-justified norms may be warrantedly expected only of those who can expect that all others will also behave in the same way. For only under the condition of a general observance of norms do reasons that can be adduced for their justification count. Now, if a practically effective bindingness cannot be generally expected from moral insights, adherence to corresponding norms is reasonable, from the perspective of an ethic of responsibility, only if they are enforced, that is, if they acquire legally binding force.

Important characteristics of positive law become intelligible if we conceive of law from this angle of compensating for the weak-

[36] K. Günther, Anwendüngsdiskürse, Dissertation iur. University of Frankfurt, 1986.

[37] K. O. Apel, "Kann der postkantische Standpunkt der Moralität noch einmal in substantielle Sittlichkeit aufgehoben werden?" in Kuhlmann, *Moralität und Sittlichkeit*, p. 232ff.

nesses of an autonomous morality. Legal norms borrow their
binding force from the government's potential for sanctions. They
apply to what Kant calls the external aspect of action, not to
motives and convictions, which cannot be controlled. Moreover,
the professional administration of written, public, and systematically elaborated law relieves *legal* subjects of the effort that is
demanded from *moral* persons when they have to resolve their
conflicts on their own. And finally, positive law owes its conventional features to the fact that it can be enacted and altered at will
by the decisions of a political legislature.

This dependence on politics also explains the instrumental
aspect of law. Whereas moral norms are always ends in themselves, legal norms are also means for realizing political goals.
That is, they serve not only the impartial settlement of conflicts of
action but also the realization of political programs. Collective
goal-attainment and the implementation of policies owe their
binding force to the form of law. In this respect, law stands
between politics and morality. This is why, as Dworkin has shown,
in judicial discourse, arguments about the application and interpretation of law are intrinsically connected with policy arguments as
well as with moral arguments. That will be our topic in the second
lecture.

3

The question about the legitimacy of legality has so far moved
the theme of law and morality into the foreground. We have
clarified how conventionally externalized law and internalized
morality complement one another. We have to keep in mind the
differences as we turn to the more interesting question of the
interpenetration of law and morality. This interlocking is illumi-
nated by the fact that in constitutional systems the means of positive law are also reflexively utilized in order to distribute burdens
of proof and to institutionalize modes of justification open to
moral argumentation. Morality no longer lies suspended above
the law as a layer of suprapositive norms — as is suggested in

natural-rights theories. Moral argumentation penetrates into the core of positive law, which does not mean that morality completely merges with law. Morality that is not only complementary to but at the same time ingrained in law is of a procedural nature; it has rid itself of all specific normative contents and has been sublimated into a procedure for the justification of possible normative contents. Thus a procedural law and a proceduralized morality can mutually check one another. In legal discourses, the argumentative treatment of moral-practical questions is, so to speak, domesticated by legal constraints. Moral discourse is limited methodically by ties to the law of the land, substantively by the selection of themes and by the distribution of burdens of proof, socially by regulations for participation and role taking, and in the temporal dimension by time constraints imposed on proceedings. But, conversely, moral argumentation is also institutionalized as an open process that obeys a logic of its own and thus controls its own rationality. The legal frame does not intervene in the clockwork of argumentation in such a way that the latter comes to a standstill at the boundary of positive law. Law itself licenses and triggers a dynamic of justification that may transcend the letter of existing law in ways unforeseen by it.

This concept is certainly in need of further differentiation with regard to the varied discourses of legal scholars, judges, or lawyers, as well as in view of the varied subject matter, ranging from morally charged to merely technical issues. If these different points of reference have been clarified, it should also be possible critically to reconstruct the practices of different courts from the viewpoint of how far legal procedures make room for the logic of argumentation, or how far they systematically distort arguments through implicitly introduced external constraints. Of course, such effects are to be found not only in the rules regulating legal proceedings but also in the way in which they are in fact practiced. Sometimes a specific class of arguments offers itself for this sort of consideration. I am thinking, for example, of justifications of

court decisions that exclude normative considerations in favor of
presumed functional demands. Precisely in such cases it can be
seen that the judiciary and the legal system cannot operate in
vacuo but have to react to social demands. Whether they must
submit to systemic imperatives — either from the economy or
from the state apparatus itself — even when they violate or dis-
turb well-established principles does not depend on the courts
themselves nor on the tendencies prevailing in the legal public
sphere but — in the last analysis — on the political struggles at
the frontier between system and lifeworld.

The legitimating force of the rationality of legal procedures is
not to be found only in court proceedings, however, but also —
and to a greater degree — in the process of democratic legislation.
At first glance, it is not very plausible that parliamentary activities
could have a rational core in a moral, practical sense. Here it
seems to be a matter of the acquisition of political power and of
the power-steered competition between conflicting interests, in
such a way that parliamentary proceedings would be amenable to
straight empirical analysis but not to critical reconstruction according to standards of fair bargaining or even of discursive will
formation. At this point I can offer no satisfactory model myself;
I can only point to the long series of process-oriented theories of
constitutional law that pursue a critical-reconstructive approach.[38]
In these, majority rule, parliamentary business procedures, elec-
toral laws, and the like are analyzed from the perspective of how
far they can promote types of deliberation and decision making
that take equally into consideration all relevant aspects of the issue
and all interests involved. I see the weakness of these theories not
in their process-oriented approach but, rather, in the fact that they
do not develop their normative viewpoints out of a logic of moral
argumentation and do not apply them to the communicative presuppositions for an unconstrained dynamic of justification. Fur-

[38] J. Choper, *Judicial Review and National Political Process* (1980); J. Ely,
Democracy and Distrust (1980).

thermore, intraparliamentary will formation is only a small segment of public life.[39] The rational quality of political legislation does not depend only on how elected majorities and protected minorities work within the parliaments. It depends also on the levels of participation and education, on the degrees of information and articulation of issues in the broader public. The quality of public life is in general shaped by the opportunity structures that the media and the institutions of the public sphere actually open up.

However, all these approaches must face the question of whether their mode of questioning is not hopelessly naive in view of the rapidly increasing complexity of our society. If we consider the critique developed by legal realism and further radicalized today by the Critical Legal Studies Movement, every normative investigation that observes the Rule of Law from an internal perspective and, so to speak, takes it at its word, seems to fall into an impotent idealism. For this reason, in the next lecture, I will alter my perspective and switch over from normative theory to social theory.

LECTURE TWO: ON THE IDEA
OF THE RULE OF LAW

In taking up Max Weber's question, how is legitimacy possible on the basis of legality, I have tacitly accepted an approach that describes legal development from the perspective of the rationalization of law. This approach requires an otherwise uncommon combination of descriptive and normative research strategies. In the history of science we see a similar division of labor — for example, between the external, or historical, explanation of a paradigm shift and the internal, or philosophical, reconstruction of those unsolved problems that finally led to the degeneration

---

[39] R. D. Parker, "The Past of Constitutional Theory — and Its Future," *Ohio State Law Journal* 42 (1981): 223ff.

of a research program. The passage from traditional to modern
political systems — to what Weber called legal domination — is
a complex phenomenon which, in connection with other processes
of modernization, calls first for an empirical explanation. On the
other hand, adopting the internal perspective of legal development, Max Weber interpreted the formal qualities of law as the
result of a process of rationalization. So far we have followed
Weber along this path of an internal reconstruction, though not
without reservations. We saw, *first*, that even if we conceive
modern law under the premises of legal formalism, the form of
modern law cannot be described as "rational" in a morally neutral
sense. *Second*, we showed that the change in the form of law
occurring with the welfare state need not destroy its formal properties — if we take "formal" in a more general sense. The formal
properties can be more abstractly grasped with a view to the complementary relationship between positive law and a procedural
theory of justice. But, *third*, this result left us with the problem
that the standards for an extremely demanding procedural rationality have migrated into the medium of law. As soon as the
implicit question about law's being both right and functional is
made explicit in this way — a question that has provided the basis
for almost all legal criticism since Max Weber — the realist
counterquestion is raised: whether the legal system in an increasingly complex society can at all withstand a heightened tension of
this sort between normative demands and functional requirements.
The suspicion arises that a law which must function in such an
environment wears the idealistic self-understanding of justification through moral principles only as an ornament.

Many regard this question as nothing more than a rhetorical
retreat and turn at once to the third-person perspective of the
sociology or economics of law. For the social-scientific observer,
what is normatively binding for participants is represented as
something that participants only hold to be so. From this point
of view, belief in legality loses its internal connection to good

reasons. In any case, the structures of rationality deployed for purposes of reconstruction lose all meaning. But with this conventional change of perspective, the normative problematic is merely neutralized by fiat. It can return at any time. For this reason, a functionalist reinterpretation of the normative problematic is more promising. On this approach, the normative is not left out of consideration from the start but, rather, disappears along the way to an explanation.

To begin with I want to take up Luhmann's systems theory of law and draw attention to phenomena that his explanatory strategy has failed to grasp. Starting from the conclusion that the autonomy of the legal system cannot be satisfactorily grasped within the categories of systems theory, I will then investigate the sense in which modern law differentiated itself from the traditional complex of politics, law, and morality by means of social contract theories. Finally, I will take up the question of whether, out of the collapse of rational natural law, an idea of the rule of law can emerge that does not remain an impotent "ought" in a society of high complexity and accelerated structural change but, rather, puts down roots in it.

I. Systemic Autonomy of Law?
Luhmann's Sociology of Law

1

Luhmann conceives of law as an autopotetic system and on this basis develops an exacting theory that can also be used for legal criticism.[40] What appears from the internal perspective of legal doctrine as a normatively regulated practice of discourse and adjudication, Luhmann explains in a functionalist manner as the result of processes of self-maintenance of a social subsystem. The systems theory of law can be briefly described in terms of three

---

[40] N. Luhmann, *Rechtssoziologie* (Opladen, 1983) and *Ausdifferenzierung des Rechts* (Frankfurt am Main, 1981).

conceptual decisions. First, the deontological quality of binding rules is redefined so that it is amenable to a purely functional analysis. Then the positivist interpretation of law is translated into the functionalist model of a legal system that has differentiated itself from other social subsystems and become completely autonomous. Finally, the legitimacy of legality is explained as a kind of sophisticated self-deception required by the paradoxical nature of the legal code and achieved by the very means of the legal system itself.

First, Luhmann strips normatively generalized behavioral expectations of their deontological, that is, obligatory, force.[41] The illocutionary meaning of commands, prohibitions, and permissions disappears and with it the specifically binding force of these speech acts. From the perspective of learning theory, Luhmann reinterprets normative expectations of behavior as a variant of purely cognitive expectations based upon predictions rather than in terms of rights and duties. In his version, norms can stabilize expectations, which are maintained even in cases of disappointment, only at the cost of a cognitive deficit. Within this empiricist perspective, normative expectations appear as dogmatically frozen cognitive expectations, held with an unwillingness to learn. But since a refusal to learn and to adapt is risky, normative expectations have to be backed by a special authority. Among other things, they must be guaranteed by political institutionalization and enforced by the threat of sanction, or in other words, they must be transformed into law.

However, the more complex societies become, the more the legal system, too, comes under pressure for change. It must quickly adapt itself to altered environments. In a further step, Luhmann describes positive law as an intelligent combination of the unwillingness to learn — in the general sense of normativity redescribed in empiristic terms — and the capacity to learn. Law acquires this capacity through differentiation to the extent that it severs

41 Luhmann, *Ausdifferenzierung des Rechts*, pp. 73ff.

itself from moral norms grounded in rational natural law or foreign to law altogether, on the one hand, and simultaneously makes itself independent of politics and thus from the legislature and administration, on the other. That is, it establishes itself *alongside* other social subsystems as a functionally specialized self-referential and self-reproducing subsystem that processes information inputs only according to its own code. The legal system pays for this kind of systemic autonomy with a paradox also inherent in Hart's rule of recognition: the legal code that is viewed externally as a social fact, an emergent property, or a customary practice — in any case, as something that occurs contingently — is yet supposed to be capable of being accepted internally as a convincing criterion of validity. This reflects the paradox built into the mode of validity of positive law: if the function of law consists in stabilizing normatively generalized behavioral expectations, how can this function still be fulfilled by a law that can be arbitrarily changed and whose validity is due solely to the decision of a political legislator? Luhmann, too, must provide an answer to the question, how is legitimacy possible on the basis of legality?

Finally, a differentiated legal system cannot, by appealing to legitimating grounds external to law, break through the circularity that emerges with an autonomous legal code — namely, law is what is correctly enacted as law. If law is supposed to be accepted as valid, despite the fact that as positive law it holds only until further notice, at least the fiction of the law's being "right" must be maintained for the legal addressees obligated to obedience as well as for the experts who noncynically administer the law.

At this point Luhmann gives an interesting interpretation to the idea of legitimation through procedure.[42] With regard to the addressees, institutionalized legal processes serve to check the readiness for conflict of defeated clients in that they absorb disappointments. In the course of a procedure, positions are specified in relation to open outcomes of this sort. Conflict themes are

---

[42] N. Luhmann, *Legitimation durch Verfahren* (Neuwied, 1969).

stripped of their everyday relevance and are painstakingly reduced to merely subjective claims to such an extent "that the opponent is isolated as an individual and depoliticized." Thus, it is not a matter of producing consensus but, rather, only of promoting the mere appearance of general acceptance, or the likelihood of its being assumed. Viewed from the perspective of social psychology, participation in legal processes has a disarming effect because it promotes the impression that those disappointed at any given time "are not allowed to appeal to institutionalized consensus but, rather, must learn." [43]

Of course, this explanation is adequate only for the uninitiated and not for the judicial experts who administer the law as judges, lawyers, and prosecutors. Lawyers who deal with legal cases and are increasingly oriented to consequences recognize their scope for discretion and know that predictions are uncertain and principles ambiguous. If this official use of law is not to destroy the belief in its legitimacy, the initiated must interpret legal procedures differently from the way clients do — namely, as an institutionalization of obligations to bear the burden of proof and to provide good reasons for any decisions. Arguments exist so that lawyers can indulge in the illusion of not making decisions according to whim: "Every argument diminishes the surprise value of further arguments and finally the surprise value of decisions." [44] Certainly, from a functionalist perspective argumentation may be described in this way; but Luhmann considers this the whole truth, since he attributes no rationally motivating power to reasons at all. In his interpretation, there are no good arguments for why bad arguments are bad; fortunately, however, through argumentation the appearance is created "as if reasons justify the decisions, rather than (the necessity to come to) decisions justifying the reasons." [45]

---

[43] Luhmann, *Rechtssoziologie*, p. 264.

[44] N. Luhmann, *Die soziologische Beobachtung des Rechts* (Frankfurt am Main, 1986), p. 35.

[45] Ibid., p. 33.

2

Under these three premises, the change in the internal structure of law (diagnosed since Max Weber) can easily be interpreted as the consequence of a successful differentiation of the legal system. The adaptations that an increasingly complex society demands of a legal system forces the transition to a cognitive style, that is, to decision making which is context sensitive, flexible, and prepared to learn. This shifting of weight from the specific tasks of normatively guaranteeing generalized expectations of behavior to the task of system steering[46] may not go to such an extreme that the identity of law itself would be endangered. This limiting case would occur, for example, if a legal system, all too willing to learn, replaced its doctrinal self-understanding from within with a systems analysis undertaken from without. For example, internalizing an objectivist description á la Luhmann would have to have as a consequence the cynical dissolution of any normative consciousness among lawyers and would endanger the independence of the legal code.

The concept of the systemic autonomy of law also has a critical value. Luhmann sees in the tendencies toward deformalization a danger of law's being mediated by politics; in his framework, "overpoliticization" appears as the danger that de-differentiation would take place if the formalism of law were weakened and finally absorbed by calculations of power and utility. The autonomy of the legal system depends upon its capacity to steer itself reflexively and to delimit itself from politics as well as from morality. In this way, Luhmann is led back to Weber's question regarding the rationality of law, which he supposed he had left behind. In order to define the autonomy of the legal system at least analytically, he has to identify the constitutive principle that specifically distinguishes law from, say, power or money. Luhmann needs an equivalent for the rationality intrinsic to the struc-

---

[46] Luhmann, *Ausdifferenzierung des Rechts*, pp. 388ff.

ture of law. Initially, with Weber and Forsthoff, he regarded the semantic form of abstract and general rules — that is, conditional legal programs — as constitutive for law in general. In the meantime, however, Luhmann can no longer play down susbtantive and reflexive law as mere deviations. Therefore, he now sharply distinguishes between the legal code and legal programs, so that the autonomy of the legal system need only depend upon the maintenance of a differentiated legal code. About this code, however, he has nothing to say but that it permits the binary distinction between justice and injustice. From this tautological formula, no further specifications of the internal structure of law can be gained. It is no accident that Luhmann fills in with a question mark the place where the unity of the code should be explained.[47] I see in this something more than the desideratum of a conceptual explication that is lacking for the moment.

If Luhmann will concede to legal discourse only the value of a self-illusion shielded by doctrinal efforts, he can no longer conceive the formal properties of legal processes as a guarantee for the rationality of law. Instead, it is even a necessary condition for the autonomy of the legal system that legal discourses remain context bound, related to individual cases and particular arguments; they are not to become independent, self-propelling philosophical discussions dealing with the paradoxical validity basis of positive law. Legal arguments remain functional only so long as they suppress this paradox from the awareness of the "official use of law." Foundational reflections may not be stirred up by them. The code may not be analyzed simultaneously from within and from without. It must remain unproblematic. But in fact we observe just the opposite. The debate over juridification shows that the deformalization of law has provoked critical considerations and caused law to be made problematic across its whole spectrum.

[47] N. Luhmann, *Ökologische Kommunikation* (Opladen, 1986), pp. 124ff.

3

In the United States as well, with the Critical Legal Studies Movement, a discussion has broken out in which legal formalism is closely scrutinized and mercilessly dismantled.[48] The criticism is supported by case studies and summed up in a thesis about indeterminacy. This does not mean that the results of judicial proceedings are completely indeterminate. Every experienced practitioner will be able to make predictions with a high probability of accuracy. The outcome of court procedures is indeterminate only in the sense that it cannot be predicted on the basis of legal evidence. It is not the law and the legal circumstances that sufficiently determine the decision. Rather, extralegal considerations and would-be arguments fill in the scope of judicial discretion. By way of unreflected background assumptions and social prejudices condensed into professional ideologies, unacknowledged interests carry the day more often than good reasons.

As can be learned from the harsh reactions to it, CLS-criticism is in fact perceived as an attack upon the normative code of the profession. We must insist, however, against Luhmann's systems analysis and also against the self-understanding of the Critical Legal Studies Movement, that this sort of "dysfunctional" self-reflection of the legal system can be developed from within the practice of lawyers only because legal discourse works with tacit assumptions about rationality which can be taken at their word and critically turned against established practices. Along with the procedural distribution of burdens of proof, a self-critical impulse also becomes institutionalized — one that can pierce through the self-illusion Luhmann falsely raises to the level of a systemic necessity.

[48] R. W. Gorden, "Critical Legal Histories," *Stanford Law Review* (Jan. 1984): 57ff. R. M. Unger, *Critical Legal Studies Movement* (Cambridge, Mass., 1986).

Certainly, the wide literature concerning the indeterminacy of the decisions of the courts[49] contradicts the conventional wisdom, which, for example, M. Kriele brings against Luhmann's functionalistic reading of the role of argumentation in legal proceedings: "Luhmann apparently fails to recognize the decisive reason for the legitimating function of procedures: . . . they increase the chance that all relevant viewpoints will be acknowledged and that the temporal and material ordering of priorities will be talked out as well as can be; and therefore they increase the chance that the decision will be rationally justified. The persisting institutionalization of procedures increases the chance that official decisions were also justified in the past and will be justified in the future." [50] But this wisdom is also conventional in another sense; it expresses tacit assumptions about rationality that are practically effective as counterfactual presuppositions as long as they function as standards to which the criticism and self-criticism of the participants may appeal. These presuppositions of rationality, deeply built into the practice of legal discourse, could lose their operative impact only at the moment of their withdrawal as critical standards. But with that all criticism of law would lose its point and its basis.[51]

It is not only the sheer existence of the type of criticism practiced ever since the emergence of the legal-realist school that speaks against Luhmann's theory. Its substantive results also show that the systemic autonomy of law, which Luhmann assumes, does not go very far. The autonomy of the legal system is not already guaranteed simply because all arguments of extralegal origin are translated into the language of positive law and connected with legal texts. Luhmann is satisfied with just this condition: "The

49 A. Altman, "Legal Realism, Critical Legal Studies, and Dworkin," *Philos. and Publ. Affairs* 15 (1986): 205ff.

50 M. Kriele, *Einführung in die Staatslehre* (Opladen, 1981), pp. 38f.

51 F. F. Michelman, "Justification (and Justifiability) of Law in a Contradictory World."

legal system achieves its operative closedness through the fact that it is codified by the difference between what is just and unjust and [that] no other system works according to this code. The two-valued coding of the legal system generates certainty that one is in the right and not in the wrong when one is in the right." [52] It already follows from the immanent critique of legal positivism, as it has been advanced from Fuller to Dworkin, against Austin, Kelsen, and Hart, that adjudication and the application of rules can less and less get by without declared and explicit recourse to policy arguments and to the assessment of principles. But this means, in Luhmann's terms, that the legal code in fact cannot work independently of the codes of political power and of morality, and that the legal system is to that extent by no means "closed." Moreover, the semantic self-referentiality of the legal system, secured by the legal code, also does not exclude the possible intrusion of latent power structures, be it via the legal programs of the political legislator or via the pretense of would-be arguments through which extralegal interests find their way into the administration of justice.

It is evident that the concept of systemic autonomy, even if it were to have empirical reference, does not conform to the normative intuition we connect with the "autonomy of law." We consider legal proceedings independent only to the extent that, first, the legal programs do not violate the moral core of modern law; and only to the extent that, second, the political and moral considerations unavoidably entering into the administration of justice take effect through their rational substance and not through the mere rationalization of legally irrelevant interests. Max Weber was right: only regard for the intrinsic rationality of law can guarantee the independence of the legal system. But since law is internally related to politics, on the one side, and to morality, on the other, the rationality of law is not only a matter of law.

[52] Luhmann, *Die soziologische Beobachtung*, p. 26.

II. REASON AND POSITIVITY: ON THE INTERPENETRATION
OF LAW, POLITICS, AND MORALITY

1

If we want to make clear why the differentiation of law never dissolves its internal relation to politics and morality, a glance back at the rise of positive law is in order. In Europe this process extended from the end of the Middle Ages to the great codifications of the eighteenth century. Even in the common-law countries, common law was overlaid by Roman Law under the influence of academically trained jurists. It was thereby accommodated step by step to the conditions of a rising capitalist economy and to the bureaucracy of the emerging territorial states. It is difficult to gain an overview of this entangled and multiform process; I shall consider it here only in view of our philosophical topic. The philosophical significance of the transformation of traditional into positive law is better explained against the background of the tripartite structure of the decaying medieval legal system.

From a certain distance, we can detect in our native traditions correspondences to those three elements that (according to the comparative sociology of law) were typical of the legal cultures of ancient empires in general.[53] The legal system was overarched by a sacred law interpreted and administered by theological and legal exegetes. Bureaucratic law, enacted in accord with sacred traditions by the king or emperor, who was also the supreme judicial authority, constituted its core. Both types of law overlay a customary law that was usually unwritten and, in the final analysis, went back to the preliterate sources of tribal law. In the European Middle Ages, the situation was different; the canon law of the Catholic church continued without interruption the high technical and conceptual level of *classical* Roman Law, while the royal law of imperial decrees and edicts was connected to at least the idea of the Imperium Romanum even before the rediscovery of

[53] R. Unger, *Law and Society* (New York, 1976).

the Corpus Justinianum. Even customary law was indebted to the mixed Roman-Germanic legal culture of the Western provinces; and from the twelfth century onward it was handed down in writing. Nevertheless, in its essential features the structure familiar in all civilizations was repeated — the branching into sacred and secular law, whereby, within the horizon of one of the few great world religions, sacred law was closely tied to the order of the cosmos and to sacred history. This divine, or natural, law was *not at the disposal* of the political ruler; in this sense, it was *indisponible (unverfügbar)*. Rather, the canopy of sacred law provided the legitimating context within which the ruler exercised his secular power through the functions of adjudication and bureaucratic legislation. It is in this connection that Weber spoke of the "two-fold realm of traditional domination" *(Doppelreich der traditionalen Herrschaft)*.[54]

During the Middle Ages this traditional character of law was maintained. All law derived its validity from its divine origin in Christian natural law. New law could be created only in the name of reforming or restoring the good old law. This tie to the traditional understanding of law inconspicuously reveals an interesting tension that existed between two elements within the royal law. As supreme judicial authority, the sovereign stood *under* sacred law. Only in this manner could the legitimacy of the latter carry over into his worldly power. A legitimation premium for the exercise of political power accrued to the ruler from his pious and reverent protection of a supposedly inviolable legal order. At the same time, however, standing at the head of an administration organized into official positions, the sovereign could also make use of law as a medium that lent his commands — for example, in the form of edicts and decrees — binding force. As a means for the bureaucratic exercise of domination, law could fulfill ordering functions only as long as it retained, in the form of sacred legal traditions, the noninstrumental, indisponible character that the

[54] Also see W. Schluchter, *Okzidentaler Rationalismus* (Tübingen, 1980).

sovereign had to respect in his role as the supreme judge. There existed an unresolved tension between these two moments of the indisponibility of law presupposed in the courts and the instrumentality of law used for political domination. But it could be kept in balance as long as the sacred foundation of law remained unchallenged and the base of customary law, backed by tradition, was firmly anchored in everyday practices.[55]

2

If one starts from the observation that in modern societies precisely these two conditions could less and less be fulfilled, the positivization of law can, from an internal point of view, partly be explained as a reaction to such changes.[56] To the extent that religious worldviews gave way to a pluralism of privatized gods and demons, and common-law traditions were more and more penetrated, via the *usus modernus*, by scholarly law, the tripartite structure of the legal system had to collapse. Law shrank to just one of the three dimensions; it hence occupied only the place that bureaucratic royal law had previously filled. The political power of the ruler was emancipated from its tie to sacred law and became independent. It was, accordingly, burdened with the task of filling the gap that the theologically administered natural law had left behind and of achieving this on its own, through political legislation. In the end all law was supposed to flow from the sovereign will of the political legislator. Making, executing, and applying laws became three moments within a single, politically controlled feedback process. It remained so even after the institutional differentiation into three balanced powers of the state.

In this way, the relationship between the two moments of law's indisponibility and instrumentality changed. Today, with a

---

[55] H. Schlosser, *Grundzüge der Neueren Privatrechtsgeschichte* (Heidelberg, 1982).

[56] The functionalist interpretation of the shift to positivized law neglects this internal aspect. Cf. Luhmann, *Rechtssoziologie.*

sufficient differentiation of roles, which is the significance of the separation of powers, legal programs are still prior to the administration of justice. But can obligating authority still arise from an arbitrarily changeable political law as it had previously from sacred law? Does positive law in general still retain an obligatory character when it can no longer derive its validity from a prior and superordinate law, as had bureaucratic royal law in the traditional legal system? Legal positivism has always given affirmative answers to these questions.[57] In one variant, law is totally stripped of its normative character, and the only instrumentally defined legal norms are conceived as commands of a sovereign (Austin). In this way, the moment of indisponibility is pushed aside as a metaphysical relic. The other variant of legal positivism still holds to the premise that law can fulfill its core function of regulating conflict only as long as some sort of noninstrumentality is retained in the very code of the legal system. However, this moment is now supposed to be attached only to the form of positive law, no longer to the contents of natural law (Kelsen). From this perspective the legal system, sharply separated from politics and morality, together with the courts as its institutional core, survives as the only place where law can, on its own, preserve its form and thus its autonomy. (We have already become acquainted with this thesis in Luhmann's version.) In both cases the consequence is that the metasocial guarantee of the validity of law on the basis of sacred law can be dropped without any functional equivalent replacing it.

The historical origins of modern as well as traditional law speak against this thesis. As we learn from anthropology, law as such precedes the rise of the state and of political power in the strict sense, whereas politically sanctioned law and legally organized political power arise simultaneously.[58] It seems that the

---

[57] N. Hörster, *Recht und Moral* (Göttingen, 1972).

[58] U. Wesel, *Frühformen des Rechts* (Frankfurt am Main, 1984).

archaic development of law in tribal societies first made possible the emergence of a political rule in which political power and compulsory law mutually constituted one another. It is not very likely, then, that in modern times law could ever be either completely absorbed by politics or wholly split off from it. There is some evidence that specific structures of moral consciousness have played an important role in the emergence of the symbiosis between compulsory law and political power. Moral consciousness played a similar role in the passage from traditional law to a secular and positive law backed by the power of the state and handed over to the disposition of the political legislator. The moment of indisponibility, which, even in modern law, still constitutes an irrevocable counterweight to the political instrumentalization of law as medium, is indebted to the interpenetration of politics and law with morality.

3

This constellation arises for the first time with the symbiosis between compulsory law and political power. In neolithic tribal societies, three mechanisms are typically in force for dealing with internal conflicts: practices of self-defense (feuds and vendettas), the ritual invocation of magical powers (oracles, duels), and the arbitrator's mediation as a peaceful equivalent of dispute settlement for force and sorcery.[59] Such mediators lack the authority for binding decisions and for enforcing their judgments against the resistance of kinship loyalties. Along with the feature of enforceability, courts of justice and judicial procedures are also lacking. Law is, moreover, so intimately connected with moral and religious notions that genuinely legal phenomena are difficult to distinguish from other phenomena. The concept of justice lying at the basis of all forms of conflict resolution is intermingled with mythical interpretations of the world. Vengeance, retaliation, and retribution work to restore a disturbed order. This order,

[59] Ibid., pp. 329ff.

constructed of symmetries and oppositions, extends equally to individual persons and kin groups as well as to nature and society as a whole. The severity of the crime is measured by the consequences of the act, not by the intentions of the perpetrator. A sanction has the sense of a compensation for resulting damages, not the punishment of someone guilty of violating a norm.

This concretistic representation of justice does not yet permit a clear separation between legal questions and questions of fact. It seems that in those archaic legal processes, normative judgments, the prudent weighing of interests, and statements of fact are intertwined. Concepts such as accountability and guilt are lacking; intention and negligence are not distinguished. What counts is the objectively produced harm. There is no separation between civil and criminal law; all violations of the law are equally offenses that demand retribution. Such distinctions first become possible when a completely new concept emerges and revolutionizes the world of legal notions. I mean the concept of context-independent legal norms, set above the conflicting parties as well as the impartial arbitrator, and thus generally recognized as binding in advance. Around the core of such norms crystallizes what L. Kohlberg calls a "conventional" moral consciousness. Without such a concept of legal norms, the arbitrating judge could only persuade and induce the conflicting parties to reach compromises. His personal reputation, due to his status, his wealth, or his age, might have been influential toward that end, but he was lacking political power; he could not yet appeal to the impersonal, obligating authority of law and to the moral insight of the participants.[60]

Allow me to propose the following thought experiment. Suppose that even before something like political authority arises, conventional legal and moral notions emerge from more elaborated mythical worldviews. Then, for example, a conflict-mediating tribal chief could already rely upon the morally binding force of

[60] L. Pospicil, *Anthropologie des Rechts* (Munich, 1982).

intersubjectively recognized legal norms. But he could not yet join to it the coercive character of a threat of sanction backed by state authority. And yet the role of the chieftain, whose leadership until then rested only on his de facto influence and prestige, must significantly change once the concept of a morally binding norm is applied to arbitration. Three steps are important in this scenario. First, such a chieftain, as the protector of intersubjectively recognized norms, would share in the aura of the law he administers. So the normative authority of the law could be carried over from the authority of the judge to the personal power of the leader generally. The de facto power of an influential person is thereby inconspicuously converted into the normatively authorized power of a commander who can make collectively binding decisions rather than merely exercise influence. Second, as a result, the quality of the judicial decision itself can change. Behind the morally obligating legal norms now no longer stands only the tribe's pressure to conform or the de facto influence of a prominent person but the threat of sanctions from the authority of a legitimate ruler. In this way there arises the ambivalent mode of validity of compulsory law, which fuses recognition and force. Third, with this the political ruler would in turn acquire the medium of political power with which he could create an organization of offices and hence exercise his domination through bureaucracy. As an organizational means, law also takes on an instrumental aspect alongside the aspect of the indisponibility of traditional law. For this scenario, morality functions as a catalyst in the fusion of compulsory law and political power.

Although these considerations also have an empirical component, I am primarily concerned with the clarification of conceptual relationships.[61] Let me repeat: only in increasingly complex worldviews does moral consciousness develop toward a con-

---

[61] K. Eder, *Die Entstehung staatlich organisierter Gesellschaften* (Frankfurt am Main, 1976); J. Habermas, *Zur Rekonstruktion des Historischen Materialismus* (Frankfurt am Main, 1976).

ventional level; only the concept of traditionally anchored and morally obligating norms changes the administration of justice and makes possible the transformation of actual influence into the normative power of political authority; only control over legitimate power permits the political enforcement of legal norms; only compulsory law can be used for the administrative organization of state authority. If one analyzes in detail this interpenetration of religiously embedded morality, of domination legitimated by law, and of legally organized political administration, it becomes evident that the two positivist concepts of law mentioned above are untenable.

4

The reduction of legal norms to the commands of a political sovereign would mean that law, in the course of modernity, had been dissolved into politics. But the very concept of the political would thereby be undermined. Under this premise political power could no longer be understood as legal authority, since a law which has become completely at the disposal of politics would lose its legitimating force. As soon as legitimation is presented as the exclusive achievement of politics, we have to abandon *our* concepts of law and politics. A similar consequence results from the second interpretation, that positive law can maintain its autonomy on its own through the doctrinal accomplishments of a faithful judiciary, which operates, however, independently of politics and morality. If the normative validity of law were to lose all moral relation to aspects of justice that reach beyond the contingent decisions of the political legislator, the identity of law itself would become diffuse. In this case, legitimating criteria would be lacking under which the legal system could be tied to the preservation of a specific internal structure of law.

Assuming that modern societies are not able totally to renounce law (or to produce a functionally equivalent but completely different kind of practice under the continued pseudonym of "law"), the positivization of law creates a problem — if only for conceptual reasons. An equivalent must be found for a disenchanted sacred law — and for a hallowed customary law — which could preserve a moment of indisponibility for positive law. At first, such an equivalent was in fact developed in the form of modern natural law theories, which had an immediate impact not only on the philosophy of law but also on legal doctrines and on the great codifications of the eighteenth and nineteenth centuries.[62]

In our context I would like to draw attention to two points: (a) In modern natural law theories, a new, post-traditional level of moral consciousness was articulated, which made modern law dependent on principles and standards of procedural rationality. (b) Depending upon whether the positivization of law as such or the resulting need for justification was pushed to the foreground (as the phenomenon in need of explanation), social contract theories were developed in opposing directions. However, in either variant they were unable to establish a plausible relation between the moments of the indisponibility and the instrumentality of the law.

(a) Modern natural law theories reacted to the disintegration of traditional, religiously and metaphysically grounded, natural law and to the demoralization of politics, which was more and more conceived in naturalistic terms as a mode of sheer self-maintenance. Since the bureaucratic state, in the modern role of the sole and sovereign legislator, secured an exclusive hold on law, law was in danger of becoming assimilated to a mere means of organization, of losing all connection with justice and thus its genuine normative character. With the positivity of law the problem of justification did not disappear, it only shifted to the narrower basis of a post-traditional, secular ethic, decoupled from metaphysical and religious worldviews.

One constitutive element of civil law is the contract. The autonomy to conclude contracts authorizes private legal subjects to create subjective rights. In the idea of the social contract this

---

[62] Wieacker, *Privatrechtsgeschichte der Neuzeit* (Göttingen, 1969), pp. 249ff.

model is used in an interesting way morally to justify political power exercised in the forms of positive law, that is, legal domination. A contract that each autonomous individual concludes with all other autonomous individuals can contain only what all can rationally will in view of their own interests. In this manner, only those regulations can come about that have the uncoerced agreement of all. This procedural idea reveals that the reason of modern natural law is, in its essence, practical reason — the reason of an autonomous post-traditional morality. This requires that we distinguish between norms, justifying principles, and procedures according to which we test whether norms could count on universal agreement in view of valid principles. Inasmuch as the idea of the social contract is used for the legitimation of legal domination, positive law is internally linked to moral principles. This suggests the hypothesis that in the passage to modernity, the transition to a postconventional moral consciousness again served as the pacemaker for legal development.

(b) Social contract theories have appeared in different versions. Authors like Hobbes are more deeply fascinated by the phenomenon of the sheer positivity of law and its contingencies, authors like Kant by the deficits in its moral base. As is well known, Hobbes develops his theory from premises that do away with all moral connotations for positive law as well as for political power. Law enacted by the sovereign is supposed to be able to make do without a rational equivalent for the disenchanted sacred law. Of course, as his theory offers its addressees just such a rational equivalent, Hobbes becomes entangled in a performative contradiction. The manifest content of the theory, which explains the functioning of a completely positivized and thereby morally neutralized law, comes into conflict with its own pragmatic role, for it is designed to explain to its readers why they, as free and equal citizens, can well have good reasons to choose an unconditional subordination to the commands of an absolutist state. Later, Kant makes explicit the normative assumptions tacitly presupposed by Hobbes and develops his theory of law from the start within the frame of moral theory. He derives the universal principle of right, which objectively lies at the basis of all legislation, from the categorical imperative. From this highest principle of legislation follows the original subjective right of each to obligate every other legal subject to respect his freedom as long as it agrees with the like freedom of all according to universal rules. Whereas for Hobbes positive law is ultimately an organizational means for the exercise of political power, for Kant it retains an essentially moral character. But even in these mature versions, social contract theories have difficulties with the task of clarifying the conditions of the legitimacy of legal domination. Hobbes sacrifices the non-instrumental character of law for its positivity; with Kant, natural, or moral, law, derived a priori from practical reason, achieves the upper hand to such an extent that law threatens to merge with morality — legality is reduced to a deficient mode of morality.

Kant builds the moment of indisponibility into the moral foundation of law in such a way that positive law is almost totally subordinated to rational law. In a legal system prejudiced by rational law, no room remains for the instrumental aspect of a law the legislator can use in the pursuit of his policies. After the canopy of Christian natural law has collapsed, the pillars of a politics disenchanted by naturalism, on the one side, and of a law converted into political decision, on the other, remain standing as ruins. Kant reconstructs the disintegrating edifice by simple substitution: autonomously grounded rational law is supposed to occupy the vacant seat of natural law. What thereby changes, in comparison with the tripartite legal system of traditional societies, is the mediating function of the administration of justice that had carried sacred legitimation over to the sovereign and his bureaucratic rule. Jurisdiction now recedes behind the political legislature and treats legal programs as an input from politics. The institutionally separated governmental powers now all fall into the shadow of a *res publica noumenon*, justified by a reason, that is supposed to find its truest possible counterimage in the *res publica phenomenon*. Kant conceives the positivization of law as the realization of the basic principles of rational natural law — a process which still stands under the imperatives of practical reason.

To the extent that politics and law are pushed into the subordinate position of organs for realizing the laws of practical reason, politics loses its scope for legislative discretion and law its positivity. Kant must therefore reach back to the metaphysical premises of his two-world doctrine so as to distinguish legality from morality in a way that remains full of contradictions.[63]

III. The Idea of the Rule of Law as a Substitute for Rational Natural Law

It is not only for philosophical reasons that modern natural law theories have since been abandoned. To put it simply — the social reality which rational natural law was supposed to interpret became too much for it. It soon became clear that the dynamics of a society integrated through the market could less and less be captured in terms of legal theories and could even less be brought to a standstill within the framework of a legal system sketched out in an a priori fashion. Every attempt to derive the foundations of private and public law, once and for all, from highest principles must run aground on the complexity of society and the mobility of history. Contract theories — and by no means only the idealistic versions among them — had been designed too abstractly. Their designers had not been aware of the social preconditions for their favored possessive individualism. Nor had they acknowledged that the fundamental institutions of civil law, property and contract, as well as the human rights shielding the individual persons against the bureaucratic state, would promote social justice only under the conditions of a fictitious, small-scale market economy.

---

[63] W. Kersting, *Wohlgeordnete Freiheit* (Berlin, 1984), pp. 16ff.

At the same time, these contract theories — and by no means only those proceeding in an a priori fashion — were designed too concretely. The acceleration of social change was not taken into account and the pressures for adaptation that emanated from capitalistic growth and from modernization in general were underestimated.

In Germany, the moral content of Kant's rational law was split up and continued on the parallel paths of the doctrine of private law and of the idea of the Rule of Law. But in the course of the nineteenth century, it became positivistically dried up along both paths. From the perspective of Pandectist science, law essentially merged with the civil-law code administered by lawyers and legal theorists. The moral content of law was to be secured here, within the system of private law itself, rather than from the side of a democratic legislature.[64] F. C. von Savigny, who construed all of private law as an edifice of subjective rights, held the view, with reference to Kant, that the semantic form of subjective right is in itself moral. Universal subjective rights define private autonomous spheres of control and guarantee individual freedom by way of subjective entitlements. The moral core of civil law consists in the fact that "a domain is assigned to the individual will in which it reigns independently of every foreign will." [65] However, it quickly became clear from the actual development of law that subjective rights are something secondary in comparison with objective law and thus could by no means offer the conceptual foundation for the system of civil law as a whole. Consequently, the concept of subjective right has been reinterpreted in a positivistic fashion and purified of all moral connotations. In B. Windscheid's definition, subjective rights merely convert the commands of the objective legal order into the entitlements of individual legal subjects.

---

[64] H. Coing, "Das Verhältnis der positiven Rechtswissenschaft zur Ethik im 19. Jh.," in J. Blühdorn, J. Ritter, eds., *Recht und Ethik* (Frankfurt am Main, 1970), pp. 11ff.

[65] F. C. von Savigny, *System des heutigen Römischen Rechts I* (1840), p. 333.

A parallel development can be traced in the idea of the rule of law, which Kant had, in any case, introduced only with hypothetical restrictions. The German theoreticians of the nineteenth century were primarily interested in the constitutional domestication of the administrative power of the monarch. In the period prior to the 1848 Revolution, Mohl and Welcker still relied on general and abstract norms that would prove to be a suitable medium for an equal promotion of all citizens "in the most comprehensive and reasonable development of all their spiritual and physical powers." [66] After the establishment of the Reich, Gerber and Laband already put forward the doctrine that legal norms represent the commands of a sovereign legislature set free from any substantive restrictions. It is this positivistic concept of law that was finally claimed for the parliamentary legislature by progressive constitutional law theorists of the Weimar period, such as Hermann Heller: "Within the *Rechtsstaat*, laws are only those, and all those, legal norms enacted by the legislative body of the people." [67]

I recall here the — certainly atypical — German development only because it is there that the erosion of the moral impact of the Kantian conception of law can be studied from both perspectives — that of the doctrinalist of private law, on the one side, and that of an increasingly parliamentarized legislature, on the other. In the Anglo-Saxon countries, where from the beginning the idea of the Rule of Law unfolded in unison with democratic developments, "fair trial" and "due process" were presented as a coherent model for legislation and jurisdiction at once. In Germany the positivistic destruction of rational law was carried out along different lines. Certainly, Kant's construction, according to which politics and law are subordinated to the moral imperatives

---

[66] Quoted from I. Maus, "Entwicklung und Funktionswandel des bürgerlichen Rechtsstaates," in M. Tohidipur, ed., *Der bürgerliche Rechtsstaat I* (Frankfurt am Main, pp. 13ff.

[67] H. Heller, *Ges. Schriften II* (Leiden, 1971), p. 226.

of rational law, is denied by both the Pandectist science and the theory of the *Rechtsstaat* — however, in one case, from the perspective of the judiciary, and in the other, from the perspective of the political legislature. This is why for those who, after the collapse of all kinds of natural law theories, were even less convinced by the alternative of sheer legal positivism the *same* problem presented itself on both sides, in respectively different forms.

The problem can be stated as follows: On the one hand, the moral foundations of positive law can no longer be provided by a superordinate rational law with a moral impact. On the other hand, it also cannot be dissolved without any equivalent — otherwise law would lose all of its noninstrumental aspects. In view of this dilemma, it must be shown how the moral point of view of impartial judgment can be stabilized from within positive law itself. This requirement is not yet satisfied by the fact that specific moral principles of rational natural law have been incorporated into positive constitutional law, for the contingency of *any* part of positive law is precisely the problem to be coped with. Rather, the morality implanted into the heart of positive law must retain the transcending force of a self-regulating procedure that checks its own rationality. Under the pressure of this problem, some of Savigny's successors, who did not want to rest content with the positivistic reinterpretation of subjective rights, expanded the so-called scientific law of legal experts into a source of legitimation. In his doctrine of the sources of law (*Lehre von den Rechtsquellen*) Savigny had still assigned to the judiciary and the law schools the modest and only derivative function of "making conscious and representing in scientific ways" the positive law which arises both from custom and legislation.[68] Toward the end of the century, G. F. Puchta gave this view an interesting shift: the production of law should not be left to the political legislature alone, since otherwise the state could not be grounded in law and

---

[68] F. C. von Savigny, *Allgemeine Natur der Rechtsquellen* (1840), quoted from W. Maihofer, ed., *Begriff und Wesen des Rechts* (Darmstadt, 1973), p. 44.

justice, that is, could not act essentially as a "Rechtsstaat." Rather, in addition to the application of the law of the land, the judiciary should assume the productive task of a constructive interpretation, development, and completion of existing law in the light of principles.[69] This "law of the judges" (*Richterrecht*) was supposed to derive an independent authority from the scientific method of justification, that is, from the arguments of a scientifically proceeding jurisprudence. With this proposal, Puchta already offered the starting point for a theory that, from the perspective of the administration of justice, traces the legitimating force of legality back to the procedural rationality built into legal discourses.

Quite a parallel interpretation is suggested from the perspective of legislation, even though parliamentary debates differ in style and purpose from judicial discourses — they are designed for negotiating compromises and not for the doctrinal justification of judgments. From this side as well, those who could not reconcile themselves to positivism raised the question as to the grounds upon which parliamentary majority decisions might claim legitimacy. Following upon Rousseau's concept of autonomy, Kant had already taken a first step toward working out the moral viewpoint of impartiality in terms of the very procedure of democratic legislation. As a touchstone for the lawfulness of legal norms, he offered the criterion of universality — whether a law could have arisen from the united will of an entire people.[70] Unfortunately, Kant himself contributed to the confusion that soon overtook two completely different meanings of the "universality" of law: the *semantic* universality of abstract and general laws appeared in the place of the *procedural* universality characteristic of democratically generated laws as the expression of the "united will of the people."

[69] G. F. Puchta, *Vom Recht* (1841), quoted from Maihofer, *Begriff und Wesen des Rechts*, pp. 52ff.

[70] I. Kant, *Grundlegung der Metaphysik der Sitten*, sec. 46.

In Germany, where the discussion of democratic theory was first revived again only in the 1920s, this confusion had misleading consequences. One could maintain illusions about the very nature of a procedural theory of democracy and about the tedious burdens of proof to be discharged. First, it has to be shown by a theory of argumentation how in parliamentary deliberations policy arguments intermesh with legal and moral arguments. Second, it must be made clear how an argumentatively achieved agreement can be distinguished from compromise and how the moral point of view is also implemented in those fairness conditions that bargaining processes have to meet. But third, and above all, we have to reconstruct the way in which the impartiality of legislative decision making is supposed to be institutionalized by legal procedures, starting with majority rule, through parliamentary business procedures to election laws and the structures of public opinion — that is, the selection and distribution of issues and contributions within the public sphere. This analysis should be guided by a model that analytically represents the whole complex of the necessary pragmatic presuppositions of discursive will formation and fair bargaining. Only against such a foil could the normative meaning and the actual practice of such procedures be critically analyzed.[71]

Further, however, that confusion of procedural universality with the semantic generality of democratically enacted statutes had the consequence that one could ignore the independent problematic of the application of law. Even if the demands for a procedural rationality of law making were somehow satisfied, legal norms never had, and never will have, a semantic form or a well-defined content that would leave to the judge only an algorithmic application. This is so whether we are dealing with the regulatory law of the welfare state or not. As philosophical hermeneutics

---

[71] U. Neumann, *Juristische Argumentation* (Darmstadt, 1986), pp. 70ff.; A. Kaufmann, "Über die Wissenschaftlichkeit der Rechtswissenschaft," *Archiv für Rechts — und Sozialphilosophie* 72 (1986): 425ff.

shows,[72] the application of existing law is always indissolubly interwoven with constructive interpretation in Dworkin's sense. Therefore, the problem of procedural rationality is posed for judges and legal scholars in new and differing ways.

In legislative procedures, a morality that has migrated into positive law manifests itself to the extent that policy-oriented discourses operate under the constraints of the principle of the universalization of all interests involved — and thus of the moral viewpoint we must observe in the process of *justifying* norms. By contrast, in the context-sensitive *application* of norms, the conditions for impartial judgment are not satisfied by asking ourselves what all could will but by whether we have appropriately taken into consideration all relevant aspects of a given situation. Before we can decide what norms apply in a given case — norms that may well clash with one another and must then be rank ordered — it must be made clear whether the description of the situation is appropriate and complete with respect to all concerned interests. As Klaus Günther has shown,[73] in contexts of justifying norms, practical reason comes into play through testing the *universalizability* of interests, in contexts of applying norms, through an *adequate* and sufficiently *complete* comprehension of relevant contexts in the light of competing rules. The legal procedures through which the impartiality of the administration of justice is supposed to be institutionalized must accord with this regulative idea.

With these considerations, I have sketched in rough outline the idea of a state with a separation of powers and ruled by law which draws its legitimacy from a rationality of legislative and judicial procedures guaranteeing impartiality. By this nothing more is gained than a critical standard for analyzing how the con-

---

[72] J. Esser, *Vorverständnis und Methodenwahl in der Rechtsprechung* (Frankfurt am Main, 1972).

[73] K. Günther, Anwendüngsdiskürse, Dissertation iur. University of Frankfurt, 1986.

stitution in fact works. That idea does not simply confront abstractly — with an impotent "ought" — a reality to which it so little corresponds. Rather, procedural rationality, which has already partially penetrated positive law, designates the only remaining dimension — after the collapse of natural law — in which a moment of indisponibility and a structure removed from the grips of contingency can be secured for positive law.

The irritating ambivalence of the validity claims with which positive law appears can be explained through the interlocking of legal procedures with the logic of argumentations that check their own rationality in the light of the principles of universalization and appropriateness. In the first place, legal validity, guaranteed by the authority of legislative bodies, must be distinguished from the social validity of actually accepted or implemented law. But within the complex meaning of legal validity itself, there is an ambivalence due to modern law's own twofold validity basis — it rests both on the principle of enactment and on the principle of justification.[74] In the validity claim of moral norms, which — according to Rawl's constructivism — are at the same time constructed as well as *discovered*, the truthlike meaning of moral *judgments* prevails. In the validity claim of positive law, the contingency of enactment adds to this rightness claim the facticity of the threat of force.[75] However, the positivity of procedurally produced and compulsory legal norms remains accompanied and overlaid by a claim to legitimacy. The legal mode of validity refers both to the political expectation that citizens are willing to comply with enforceable commands and to the moral expectation of a rationally motivated recognition of a normative validity claim that can be vindicated only through argumentation. The limiting cases of legitimate resistance and civil disobedience show that such argumentations can also burst open the very legal form in which they themselves are institutionalized.

[74] Habermas, *Theorie des Kommunikativen Handelns*, vol. 1, pp. 346ff.
[75] R. Dreier, *Rechtsbegriff und Rechtsidee* (Frankfurt am Main, 1986).

That the demanding idea of the Rule of Law which I have reformulated is not excessive but, rather, springs from the soil of legal reality is indicated by the fact that what we call the autonomy of the legal system can be measured only against this idea. I am referring to the dimension in which the legally institutionalized mode of justification remains pervious to moral argumentation. If this dimension were closed off, we would no longer know what autonomy of the law could even mean. A legal system does not acquire autonomy on its own. It is autonomous only to the extent that the legal procedures institutionalized for legislation and for the administration of justice guarantee impartial judgment and provide the channels through which practical reason gains entrance into law and politics. There can be no autonomous law without the realization of democracy.

Medicine as a Profession and a Business

ARNOLD S. RELMAN, M.D.

THE TANNER LECTURES ON HUMAN VALUES

Delivered at
University of Utah

April 28 and 29, 1986

Dr. Arnold S. Relman, editor of the prestigious *New England Journal of Medicine*, has had a long and distinguished medical career. He has been professor of medicine at the Harvard Medical School and a physician at the Brigham and Women's Hospital in Boston since 1977. From 1968 to 1977 he was Frank Wister Thomas Professor of Medicine and chairman of the Department of Medicine at the University of Pennsylvania School of Medicine and served as director of medical services at the Hospital of the University of Pennsylvania. He has been the Conrad Wesselhoeft Professor of Medicine at the Boston City Hospital. He has been a visiting scientist at the University of Oxford and has held numerous visiting professorships and honorary lectureships throughout the world.

Lecture 1

The general subject of these lectures is the revolution in the medical care system that is sweeping this country, transforming the way we organize and finance the system, the way doctors work within it, and the way we think about health care. In particular I propose to discuss how the ethical values and assumptions upon which our medical system has long been based are now being challenged by new social, economic, and political realities.

In the first lecture, I will describe the health care revolution in broad terms, attempting to explain its origins and present direction. In the second lecture, I will focus on the changes occurring in the medical profession — a profession more troubled and less sure of itself than at any time in my memory. At the end, I hope to consider some of the public policy issues posed by these developments and speculate about the future options for the medical profession and for health care planners.

Underlying all of my discussion will be some basic questions. Is medical care a consumer good like any other, a commercial service provided by skilled vendors for consumers willing to pay the market price, or is there something fundamentally different about the relation between doctor and patient? Will American society be served best by treating medical care like commerce, by relying mainly on the market to solve the problems of allocation, access, cost control, and quality assurance, or should we regard medical care as a form of social service which our nation owes its citizens and which therefore ought to be provided in a more planned and regulated context? The tension between these two views of medicine — the economic and the social — is the leitmotif of these lectures, the theme around which I develop my interpretation of what is now happening to medical care in this country.

Let me begin by explaining what led up to the present economic troubles of our health care system. In essence two basic developments, one technological, the other political, worked synergistically to create an uncontrollable inflation. In the first place, there was a postwar scientific and technological explosion without parallel in history. Biomedical science was poised to expand just before World War II, and the resources poured into health care during and immediately after the war provided the impetus for a major national commitment to medical research and education, which led to a period of rapid growth. The establishment of the National Institutes of Health in Bethesda, Maryland, was followed by generous federal funding of research and training programs in the medical schools. Federal, state, and private philanthropic support for the construction of new or expanded medical schools and research institutions also played a role in fostering a vast postwar expansion of biomedical resources. New discoveries in basic and applied medical science, and new technology in almost every field, led to advances in diagnostic and therapeutic techniques, which produced new medical subspecialties. Meanwhile, the expanding medical schools were turning out new doctors in ever greater numbers, and about 70 percent of them became specialists rather than the primary-care practitioners who had up to then constituted the great majority of physicians.

The other seminal development was the expression of a liberal political consensus that more had to be done to increase the availability of medical services to all who needed them. The perception in the immediate postwar decades was that not only did we need more medical research, more medical schools, and more doctors but that we also needed to provide our citizens with more and better access to medical care. Construction of new hospitals was fostered through a federal program of grants and loans. State and local taxation as well as private philanthropy and bond issues also contributed to the expansion of hospital capacity. Many new programs extended medical services into the communities, but the limiting factor in achieving access for all people was the relatively high cost of hospital care, which few could afford to pay for out-of-pocket. Most affluent citizens, as well as the self-employed middle class, had begun to depend on privately purchased hospital insurance plans to pay their major medical expenses. By the decade of the 1960s, hospital insurance had become a virtually universal component of the fringe benefit package offered by large employers to their workers. The cost of the premiums was a business expense which reduced corporate tax liability, but the value of the benefits to employees was not taxable as income, so work-related medical insurance became a tax-free bonus in the form of a nearly unlimited hospital credit card, paid for by the company and, of course, ultimately subsidized by the company's customers.

Widespread as these arrangements were, major gaps in coverage still remained and were not filled until 1966 with the advent of Medicare and Medicaid. This legislation extended limited hospital insurance protection to most of the elderly and many, but by no means all, of the poor.

The prevailing view during those days was that medical care was a right of all citizens, regardless of their insurance coverage or their ability to pay. There was general agreement that everyone was entitled not to every medical service they wanted but to whatever care they really needed, and this care ought to be in the mainstream, that is to say, through private physicians of one's own choice and in semiprivate hospital accommodations. Medicare and Medicaid patients were not to be treated any differently, although, of course, anyone was free to pay for extra private amenities if they wished to do so. Indeed, the federal government was very insistent that, since it was paying customary charges, the services to Medicare and Medicaid patients were to be the same as those provided to any other semiprivate patient.

With the passage of this legislation, our country took a large step toward equality in health care, but we were still far from that

goal. Most people sixty-five years of age or older qualified for
Medicare coverage, regardless of financial need, but Medicare
benefits in hospitals and nursing homes were limited. Medicaid
benefits were more extensive, but to qualify, patients had to be
virtually destitute. Even then, assistance was not assured, because
state participation in the Medicaid program, which was intended
to take care of the very poor and the disabled, was in fact highly
variable. Many citizens unable to afford hospital or nursing-home
services did not qualify for Medicaid benefits, with the result that
even after the passage of the Medicare and Medicaid bills, some
10 to 12 percent of the population were without insurance and
therefore largely excluded from mainstream health services.

For those without any insurance or other means to pay for
their care, society's obligation to provide at least the necessary
short-term hospital care was met in part by free services in the
public tax-supported hospitals or in the voluntary, private not-for-
profit hospitals. The public tax-supported hospitals devoted a
much larger share of their income to free care than did the voluntary hospitals, but since there are many more of the voluntaries,
the latter provided in aggregate nearly two-thirds of all the charity
care in the country.

Of course, no medical care is free (except possibly to those
who receive it). The marginal cost of charity services in the public
hospitals was borne largely by local tax funds and in part by whatever surpluses could be generated from the income recovered from
third-party payers. In the voluntary hospitals, some of the cost
was paid by philanthropy, but most came from the surpluses generated from private paying patients and third-party payers. In
other words, most voluntary hospitals paid for the poor with the
profits they earned from their other sources of payment. In those
days, Medicare and Medicaid, Blue Cross, and all the other third-
party payers were quite willing to pay the customary hospital
charges, even when these included the costs of taking care of the
poor. Some critics quietly observed that, in effect, shifting costs in

this way was a hidden tax on those who paid for health care, levied without express legal authority. However, except for a few economic purists, no one publicly complained about this cross-subsidy. The private insurers seemed content to pay the bills as long as they could add the costs to their premiums, businesses accepted the rising premium costs for their employees as long as they could be passed along to customers and were tax deductible, and the federal government was willing to absorb its rising cost into the Medicare and Medicaid budgets because that was what the political climate allowed.

As for physicians, they had long been accustomed to providing discounted or free services to the poor as part of their professional obligation to a society which had subsidized their education, granted them a licensed monopoly, and vested them with unique power and authority. The Johnson administration's proposal for Medicare and Medicaid, which was intended to pay doctors as well as hospitals for taking care of the poor and elderly, was at first vigorously opposed by organized medicine's leaders because they feared government intrusion into the practice of medicine. But medical leaders were mollified when the government agreed to pay physicians and hospitals their customary and reasonable fees for Medicare and Medicaid patients and promised to leave the medical decisions entirely in the hands of the doctors. After the law passed, physicians began to be paid for providing services to the poor, which they had previously felt obligated to provide gratis as a condition for obtaining appointments to local hospital staffs. Revenues of doctors as well as hospitals rose rapidly, even as the poor and elderly benefited from new services.

I do not want to be misunderstood. My enthusiasm for the patchwork system we had achieved with the passage of Medicare and Medicaid is easily restrained. Although access of the poor and elderly to mainstream medical care was substantially improved, most of those with insurance still had only limited coverage which paid mostly for technical procedures and relatively

short hospital stays but rarely covered prolonged or chronic illnesses and offered little or no coverage of ambulatory care. Long-
term nursing-home coverage was available only to those who
qualified for Medicaid. With all its limitations, however, I believe
the system was better than what appears to be replacing it now.
But this is getting ahead of my story. Further discussion of this
point should be deferred until I explain how the economy of the
system began to destroy itself.

The seeds of a disastrous inflation were all there: a rapidly
expanding technological base; a growing and increasingly specialized corps of medical professionals trained to practice high-
technology medicine and reimbursed on a piecework basis; an
insurance system based on payment of customary charges, which
still excluded many patients and certain types of services but was
virtually open-ended in its funding of those it did cover; and more
than two decades of essentially unregulated proliferation of hospital facilities.

The inevitable result of this highly inflationary mixture was a
runaway growth in national expenditures for personal health care,
which ultimately became intolerable. In 1966, the year that Medicare and Medicaid were passed, we spent about $40 billion for
personal health care; in 1984 the figure was $342 billion. Slightly
more than three-quarters of this growth was due to general inflation of prices and the growth and aging of the population, but
even after making these corrections the average rate of real growth
during those eighteen years was about 6 percent per year. Perhaps
the most meaningful way to look at growth in health care expenditures is to follow it as a percentage of the gross national product
(GNP), which largely corrects for price inflation and reflects the
fraction of the national economy devoted to health care. Expressed
this way, expenditures for health care rose fairly steadily from
6 percent of the GNP in 1966 to nearly 11 percent in 1984.

Health care has now become the second largest sector of our
national economy. If it were the automobile industry or the com-

puter industry or any other domestic market, such rapid growth would have been hailed as an economic triumph. The jobs and general prosperity generated by this expansion would have been a source of great general rejoicing and numerous lyrical articles in the *Wall Street Journal* and *Business Week*. Why, then, has the growth of the health care sector been so widely regarded as a national disaster? The primary answer to that question, I think, is that those who are paying for most of the costs (i.e., the federal government and large businesses) are not the direct consumers and do not receive the health care benefits. They say they cannot afford to subsidize the system any longer.

Businesses devote an increasing fraction of their overhead to health benefits for their workers and retirees. In the automobile industry, for example, the major companies spend more on health benefits than on steel. The costs are passed along to consumers, of course, but in pushing automobile prices higher, they make American cars less competitive in world markets and threaten the industry's future. It is not surprising, therefore, that the large manufacturers are now firmly determined to reduce their health care expenditures.

The federal government spent over $100 billion in 1984 on Medicare and Medicaid alone and contributed about 29 percent of all the resources devoted to health care. State and local government funds contributed another 12 percent, making a total of 41 percent from government. Public financing of health care in this country has increased greatly since 1966, and the present contribution of government may seem large. However, in relative terms the United States lags far behind all other Western democracies in its governmental support of health care. Most of these countries pay for more than 60 percent of their total health care costs with public funds. Furthermore, during the past seven or eight years, the percentage of the public contribution to health care in this country has been slowly declining as all levels of government attempt to restrain such budgetary commitments. The federal government has a particularly difficult task in this regard, inasmuch as it seeks to reduce its deficit while also cutting taxes and increasing its military expenditures. Medicare and Medicaid outlays have been major targets for cost cutting because they are so large, because they have recently been rising at a rate of 10–15 percent per year, and because a political backlash against cuts in health care programs has not yet become a major force. The Reagan administration has therefore been doggedly whittling away at its Medicare and Medicaid obligations. As one of the two major payers of health care, it is determined to reduce the federal contribution either by cutting or shifting costs. Together with large corporate employers, the federal government has become the major force in a developing revolt of third-party payers against the old system of hospital reimbursement.

What needs to be emphasized here is that the current cutback in Medicare and Medicaid programs does not reflect an explicit change in public opinion about access to health care. Most Americans still believe that it is government's responsibility to subsidize necessary medical services for those who are not insured and cannot afford to pay for themselves. However, the prevailing view is that Medicare and Medicaid, like many other government programs, are inefficient and too expensive and that adequate medical services for the poor, the disabled, and the elderly could be provided at substantially lower costs. In any case, economic pressure, rather than public rejection of the right to health care, seems to be the primary force behind the present retrenchment in government support of health care.

At this point, before any further discussion of the recent changes in health care financing, one other crucial element in our story must be introduced. I refer to the rise of investor-owned hospital businesses and the growth of the commercial ethic in health care.

Small, privately owned proprietary hospitals were common during most of the first half of this century, but they functioned mainly as workshops for the private practices of their physician owners. Large, investor-owned hospital chains are a new and quite different phenomenon that first appeared in the mid-sixties, about the time of the introduction of Medicare and Medicaid. After the majority of people began to have health insurance that would pay hospital charges, groups of businessmen around the country soon began to recognize the attractive entrepreneurial opportunities afforded by the ownership of a chain of hospitals. To ensure a profit, all one had to do was to buy or build hospitals in relatively prosperous locations where the population was expanding and most people had insurance. The keys to financial success were: (a) a medical staff of busy, procedure-oriented specialists; (b) large price mark-ups on all supplies and technical services; (c) an efficient billing and collecting system; and (d) the meticulous avoidance of uninsured patients and those with "low-profit" illnesses, that is, patients with chronic problems requiring a heavy investment of human resources and few procedures or tests. Combining this winning formula with an aggressive acquisition policy, several large hospital chains have developed and prospered during the past fifteen years or so. Today about 15 percent of all non-federal hospitals in this country are owned, leased, or managed by for-profit businesses. Their geographic distribution is not uniform. In some states, especially those in the Southeast, the Southwest, and California, investor-owned hospitals now have a large share of the market (e.g., over 40 percent in Florida and California), but in many other states they are virtually nonexistent.

The great majority of these hospitals, nearly eight hundred, are controlled by the five largest multihospital systems: Hospital Corporation of America, American Medical International, National Medical Enterprises, Humana, and the Republic Health Care Corporation. These firms have become large, diversified health care corporations, with revenues in the billions of dollars and business interests not only in acute-care hospitals but in a wide variety of other health facilities, services, and products. In addition to the giant hospital chains, there are scores — perhaps by now even hundreds — of other large and small investor-owned companies, which operate psychiatric hospitals, nursing homes, diagnostic laboratories, free-standing radiologic centers, walk-in clinics, ambulatory surgery centers, home health care services, and health maintenance organizations (HMOs) all over the country. The majority of the private psychiatric hospitals and nursing homes in this country are now under for-profit ownership. A growing fraction, between a third and a half, of all HMOs are operated for profit, as are a majority of the new kinds of ambulatory-care facilities that appear to be springing up in almost every shopping mall. There are no accurate data, but I estimate that at least a quarter of all expenditures on personal health care is now going to for-profit business, and this new health care industry continues to grow at an annual compound rate of about 10 to 15 percent per year. The most recent development is the entrance of the giant hospital chains into the health insurance business. Together with their control of HMOs, this new move enables these corporations to direct patients to their own hospital facilities and further increase their market share.

As a growing sector of our medical care system comes under investor ownership, the public will want to know much more about the effect of this trend on the cost, quality, and availability of medical care. They will also want to look very carefully at the impact of investor-owned hospitals on the public and private institutions with which they will increasingly be competing. Does investor ownership offer any advantages to offset the loss of public or local community control of facilities that ought to be serving local community needs? This question was examined in a report recently issued by the Institute of Medicine of the National Academy of Sciences.[1] The authors of the study found that, before the recent change in hospital payment, for-profit hospitals charged

---

[1] B. H. Gray, ed., *For-Profit Enterprise in Health Care*, Report of the Committee on Implications of For-Profit Enterprise in Health Care, Institute of Medicine, National Academy of Sciences (Washington, D.C.: National Academy Press, 1986).

about 10 to 20 percent more than not-for-profit hospitals, had similar or slightly greater expenses, gave less free care, and did very little teaching or research. Quality of care could not be adequately assessed, but there were no obvious differences. The majority of the authors did not feel that present evidence warranted any major change of public policy toward investor-owned hospitals, but they said that the questions of quality and access will be particularly important if the health care system becomes increasingly competitive and investor ownership grows.

In any event, the whole system of paying for hospital care has now been turned upside-down by what one might call "the revolt of the payers." Instead of continuing their passive role and simply paying the bills, the federal and state governments and the large corporate employers have begun to impose their own financial arrangements on the system in an effort to contain costs.

Prospective or fixed-price payment has begun to replace reimbursement of charges as the financial basis of the system. Beginning in 1983, payment for the hospital care of Medicare patients has been gradually converted to the so-called diagnosis-related group (DRG) system, in which all diagnoses are grouped into a few hundred categories, each of which is assigned a fixed price. Hospitals are paid the price assigned to each patient's diagnostic group, regardless of the actual costs incurred. If the latter are greater than the DRG price, the hospital sustains a loss in taking care of the patient; if they are less, the hospital keeps the profit. If the price for each DRG category is set properly, the law of large numbers will ensure efficient hospitals an acceptable overall operating margin of profit. The system so far involves only Part A of Medicare, that is, the hospital services. To date, there has been no major change in Part B, the payments for physicians' services, but there is currently much discussion of this subject and it seems likely that some type of federal action will be taken before long, either to revise fee schedules or to begin folding some physician payments into the DRG system.

Another major new trend being pushed by the payers is a shift
to HMOs, which combine an insurance function with the direct
provision of health services. For a fixed price, per capita or per
family, HMOs undertake to provide all needed medical care —
ambulatory and in-hospital — except for certain specified services.
HMOs either own hospitals, or more commonly, contract with
community hospitals to provide the necessary in-patient care for
their patients. They employ individual physicians on a salaried
basis (the "staff-model" HMO) or they contract with a group of
physicians (the "group-model" HMO) to provide professional
services in the HMO's offices and in the hospital; or else they
contract with individual private practitioners to provide services
in the practitioners' own offices (the "IPA-model" HMO). HMOs
are growing rapidly in numbers and in total enrollment. Today
there are a few hundred HMOs, nearly 40 percent of which operate for profit. Total subscribers have reached almost 20 million,
an increase of nearly 20 percent in the last year alone.

In addition to DRGs and HMOs, many other kinds of contracted arrangements with hospitals and doctors are being developed by governmental and private payers. States like California,
for example, are contracting with hospitals to provide care for
patients on Medicaid and other programs at discounted rates.
Major employers, acting as their own health insurers, and private
health insurance firms are striking deals with hospitals or doctors,
which give the providers preferred access to large groups of insured patients in exchange for discounted charges or some type of
capitation payment. Sometimes hospitals themselves are acting as
insurers and offering such contracts to their own medical staffs.
Hospitals or doctor groups that make such arrangements to provide care at special rates are known as PPOs (preferred provider
organizations).

The net effect of all this has been to turn hospital economic
incentives around by a full 180 degrees. Under the old system, the
more services hospitals provided to each patient, the more they

would get paid and, if they were so inclined, the greater their opportunity for profit. Since insurance usually reimbursed only for hospital-based procedures, it was a system that encouraged hospitalization and the use of expensive technological tests and procedures.

Under the new system, ambulatory rather than hospital care is encouraged. Hospitals can prosper only by increasing their admissions and by reducing the average number of procedures per patient and the average length of stay. They have had to become much more cost conscious because they must compete with other hospitals in their community for contracts with insurers who are shopping for hospital services for their clients at the lowest possible price. The growth of hospital capacity over the past few decades has created a surplus of beds in many communities, which adds to the competitive economic pressures on hospital managers to keep their costs down and their beds filled. Suddenly, hospitals have become overpriced, underutilized businesses struggling to attract paying customers in a price-sensitive competitive market.

Among the first casualties in this cost-control crunch are the unreimbursed services hitherto provided by the not-for-profit community hospitals. In the new, competitive, price-sensitive hospital market, insurers are not interested in subsidizing the costs of services to patients other than their own beneficiaries. Thus, it becomes increasingly difficult for not-for-profit hospitals to cross-subsidize the care of the poor and uninsured or to support expensive teaching programs or to offer standby services and community programs that are costly and unprofitable.

The change in the health care climate in this country has been astonishing in its speed and scope. The growth of the for-profit sector has joined with the revolution in the financing of medical care to create a degree of commercialization quite unprecedented in my lifetime in medicine. Health care is now widely considered to be an economic product, and its delivery a business. Both for-profit and not-for-profit hospitals are encouraged to think of themselves as businesses, and their management is increasingly in the hands of MBAs whose concerns are primarily economic. Pick up any issue of the magazines hospital managers read these days and you read nothing but business talk. You read about "customers," "market share," "advertising and marketing," "joint ventures," "corporate restructuring," "cash flow problems," and "bottom line" results. You read much more about "products" than services, more about "competition" than collaboration, and more about identifying and satisfying consumer demands than meeting community health care needs. According to a recent survey, U.S. hospitals spent more than a billion dollars on marketing and advertising in 1985 and more than half again as much last year.

There is nothing wrong, and much that is sensible, about being concerned with economic efficiency. Our health care expenditures did get out of control, there is considerable slack and waste in the system, and much can be gained by more businesslike management of our hospitals. But that is quite different from turning control of hospitals over to investor-owned corporations and making the delivery of health care into a competitive commercial market, where services are provided according to ability to pay and profits become the prime consideration.

Spokesmen for the new health care industry often try to blur this distinction by arguing that profits are simply the cost of capital and that all economic enterprises must generate a profit to remain viable and accumulate the resources necessary for plant maintenance and renewal. According to this argument, even so-called not-for-profit hospitals — unless they can count on philanthropy or public funding — must operate at a profit (i.e., with a surplus of revenues over expenses) if they are to survive. Some go so far as to argue that the only significant distinction between not-for-profit and for-profit hospitals is that the latter pay taxes and have little access to tax-exempt financing. This point is given emphasis by the increasingly entrepreneurial behavior of not-for-profit hospitals in the new competitive climate of prospective payment.

Despite all this, I believe it denies the obvious to ignore the basic difference between the goals of the investor-owned for-profit hospital corporation and those of a not-*only*-for-profit community hospital. The latter tries to generate an operating surplus while meeting what it considers to be the health care needs of the community it serves. The investor-owned hospital is owned usually by a large corporation which seeks above all else to increase its revenues and market share so that it can generate dividends and capital gains for its investors.

An even more significant difference is to be found in the general philosophy of the leaders of the two kinds of institutions. Those who speak for the investor-owned health care corporations, as well as many economists and policymakers who advocate the new competitive marketplace, believe that health care is not basically different from other necessities like food, clothing, or shelter. All of the latter commodities are sold in a commercial market and defenders of the health care market profess to see no reason why medical care should not also be distributed that way. Indeed, many have argued that medicine is a business and that fee for-service physicians are private businessmen, interested in maximizing their income like others engaged in trade. Those who defend the voluntary sector usually look askance at this philosophy. While not denying that economic considerations have always played a role in private medical care, they would argue that there is something unique about medical care that places it apart from commerce and makes physicians basically different from skilled tradesmen.

I share the latter view. Medical care differs from most other essential commodities not only because it is often necessary for the protection of life and the quality of existence but because it can properly be provided only through the professional services of a trained and committed physician who must be trusted to choose the care that is needed. The patient or a surrogate gives consent but is rarely in a position to know what is needed. It is impossible to think of any commercial service or commodity that is as intimately related to the well-being and integrity of the individual consumer and as dependent upon the skill and commitment of another person. Consumers of medical care are often totally dependent upon the physician: the sicker and more worried they are, the more they must rely upon the advice and ministrations of the doctor. This is not the relation between consumers and vendors in a commercial market. In trade, consumers are supposed to make their own choices among different but more or less standardized products or services, and in deciding what they want to buy and what they are willing to pay, consumers accept the principle of caveat emptor, buyer beware.

Medical care is different. Patients may choose their doctors, their hospitals, or the kind of insurance coverage they want, but when they need medical care, the physician acts as their agent in deciding what is needed. Of course this is usually done with the consent and cooperation of the patient, but it is the physician who bears the responsibility for the decision, and it is the patient who must trust the physician to do the right thing. I will have more to say about this in the next lecture.

This trust, which physicians are sworn to honor, is the essence of the relationship between doctor and patient. Their professional ethical code requires that physicians place their obligation to serve the patient's interest above any personal economic interests. Businessmen are expected to deal honorably with their customers and to offer good products, but beyond that, they have no obligation to determine what is really best for their customers or to put the customers' welfare ahead of their own economic interests. Maximization of profits within the bounds of the law is the accepted rule, and in pursuit of maximal gain commercial vendors usually try to persuade potential buyers to choose their goods or services. Indeed, it is generally assumed that when informed buyer and competitive-but-honest seller each seek their own economic interests, the free market will operate to their mutual advantage. Such assumptions are clearly inapplicable and inappropriate to medical care.

If market principles do not properly apply to the relation between doctor and patient, what happens when medical care becomes a business and when doctors are encouraged to act like entrepreneurs? In the next lecture, I will discuss how the medical profession has been affected by the new economic climate and will attempt to forecast where current trends are likely to lead.

Lecture 2

In the first lecture, I explained how the rising cost of medical care has led to a revolt of the third-party payers and a radical reorientation of the economics of the health care system. A new kind of commercialized competitive market has developed, emphasizing contractual prepaid group arrangements for patients, discounted prospective payment for hospitals, and ambulatory care as a substitute for in-patient care. Investor ownership, previously confined largely to hospitals and nursing homes, has now expanded into HMOs and other forms of out-patient care. Giant vertically integrated health care corporations have emerged, which not only own a wide variety of facilities but sell the insurance that will pay for their use. Both for-profit and not-for-profit hospitals arc now competing for patients to fill their nearly half-empty beds, and in many parts of the country, they are reducing the number of beds or even closing their doors. The current wisdom seems to be that health care should be regarded as a business and that cost control can best be achieved through business competition, which will eliminate inefficient providers. Since there can be no business competition without profits and losses, investor ownership has been encouraged not only to stimulate the competitive process but to provide the venture capital to replace disappearing public funds. Health care, once considered largely a public and community responsibility, is now becoming privatized along with many other sectors of American society previously in the public domain.

In this lecture I propose to discuss the impact of this revolution on the medical profession. At the conclusion of that discussion I will consider some of the public policy issues posed by these developments and will speculate about future options for health policy in this country.

Any discussion of the current problems of the medical profession in the new economic climate should begin with a clear understanding of the central role of physicians in our health care system. At its core, the system revolves around the relations between doctors and their patients. The decisions and recommendations made by doctors largely determine the consumption of medical care resources. Doctors are paid only about nineteen or twenty cents of the medical care dollar, but their decisions and recommendations determine how most of the rest will be spent. In a very real sense, doctors are the purchasing agents for their patients. Therefore, no major change in the economics of the health care system is likely to occur without a change in the behavior of physicians. Expenditures for health care are not going to be reduced significantly unless, through one means or another, doctors modify their behavior or unless access to, or demand for, care decreases.

Medical care is much more than an economic transaction, however, and doctors are far more than purchasing agents for their patients. Doctors are entrusted with responsibility for the medical welfare of their patients, whose interests they are required by their professional oath to protect. Lawyers have somewhat similar responsibilities as trustees for their clients, but a patient's dependence on his physician, as I have argued in my first lecture, is relatively unique. It is a rare client whose very life depends on his lawyer's skill, but sick or injured patients often must rely on their physicians for the preservation of their life and the protection of the quality of their existence. To get the help they need, they expose their bodies to their physician and disclose intimate details of their personal life which they might not share with anyone else. Their dependence is further intensified by the vulnerability and helplessness often accompanying serious illness or injury, which can undermine the sense of personhood and limit the capacity for independent thought and action.

This is not to say that adult patients when they need medical care must simply be passive, trusting children. Much of the medical consumerism movement is quite properly directed against this notion, advocating instead that patients take more responsibility for decisions about their own health care. But despite the rhetoric, there really is no basic conflict between this view and the concept of professional responsibility. Paternalism is an element in, but certainly not the essence of, the doctor-patient relation. Patients should be as fully informed and involved in their own care as they wish and are able to be. Doctors clearly have an obligation to encourage their patients' autonomy by explaining as much as patients want to know about their illness and the available options for diagnosis and treatment. Except in emergencies, doctors also have a duty to obtain their patients' informed consent before taking any course of action. However, given what Kenneth Arrow has termed "the informational inequality" between doctor and patient,[2] and given the limitations imposed by the patient's anxiety and physical incapacity, fully informed consent is more an ideal than an attainable goal. The reality is that the physician usually bears the major responsibility for most medical care decisions and has to be trusted to counsel or act in the patient's best interest.

Although the relation between doctor and patient is not in essence a marketplace transaction, it certainly can be influenced by economic considerations and by the financial and organizational arrangements through which medical care is provided. Until recently, the dominant arrangement was fee-for-service solo or small partnership private practice. Let us briefly consider how the economics of this system affected the doctor's professional responsibility to his or her patient.

[2] K. Arrow, "Uncertainty and the Welfare Economics of Medical Care," *American Economic Review* 53 (December 1963), pp. 941–69.

Fee-for-service private practice is based on the assumption that patients should be free to choose their physician and, except in emergencies, physicians should similarly be free to choose whom they wish to serve. However, after accepting professional responsibility for a patient, the physician is obligated to serve the interests of that patient to the best of his or her ability as long as there is a medical need. The relation can be terminated at the patient's request at any time; the physician can also withdraw — provided the patient's welfare is protected and adequate alternative arrangements are made.

Financial reward is not supposed to be the prime consideration in this arrangement (or in any other type of medical practice), but in fee-for-service practice, physicians expect to be fairly paid for each identifiable service they provide, and it is assumed that the patient (or the insurer) will be prepared to do so. Before the advent of insurance, it was also assumed that patients would pay to the extent they could afford. This necessitated that fees be reasonable and commensurate with the patient's ability to pay. When patients could not afford to pay anything, it was expected that physicians would provide their services gratis, usually at the local community hospital, where they rendered free care to ward and clinic patients in exchange for the privilege of a staff appointment.

Fee-for-service medical care, of course, has an inherent conflict of interest. In economic terms, fee-for-service physicians are suppliers who are able to determine the demand for their own services. They make the decision to use the medical services which they provide and for which they will be paid on a piecework basis. It is an arrangement with a built-in potential for abuse. Until the past few decades, however, this traditional system of delivering medical care was generally supported by the public and held to be reasonably satisfactory. There were some abuses, of course, but on the whole the medical profession was deemed to be acting as it should, putting patients ahead of economic self-interest.

The reasons for the success of fee-for-service medical care during the first four or five decades of this century are easy to understand. First of all, there was the restraining influence of a well-established and generally accepted ethical code of organized medicine, which clearly said that medical practice must be based on the doctor's commitment to the patient's interest. The code also said that doctors should do only those things they believed would support that commitment. Of course, the chance of a physician's doing anything unnecessary was not very great when there were not many things for a physician to do beyond examining, counseling, and comforting. Except for the relatively few surgical specialists, most doctors until nearly the middle of this century had mainly their time and advice to offer. Up to that time the great majority of physicians were primary-care givers, who had only a modest and inexpensive array of procedures and remedies. When specialists were used, or surgery contemplated, the referrals usually came from the primary-care physician, so self-referral by specialists was not a problem as it is now. The major ethical concern was fee-splitting between referring physician and specialist. But there were not that many specialists or primary practitioners who would risk the professional ostracism associated with "kickback" practices of that kind. Most fees were relatively modest because relatively few patients were insured. Primary-care physicians usually knew the patients for whom they acted as advisers. They knew the financial as well as medical impact of illness on their patients, and they therefore were restrained in their recommendation of special procedures, as they were in the setting of fees.

Furthermore, one of the most important protections against exploitation in conflict-of-interest situations is disclosure, and disclosure is built into the solo practice, fee-for-service arrangement. Patients understand that if they choose to follow their doctor's advice to have some test or procedures done, the doctor expects to receive a fee for that service. Patients who do not trust the integrity and judgment of their doctor can consult someone else, but there can be no deception about the nature of the arrangement because the doctor's financial interest in the transaction is perfectly clear.

There is one final and very important reason why the fee-for-service system was not much abused. Until recently, most doctors had more patients than they could comfortably handle. They had no incentive to do more than was necessary for any patient because there were plenty of patients and much work to do. As long as physicians were in relatively short supply, there was no pressure on them to offer their patients more than the essential services.

However, all of these factors restraining the potential abuse of the solo practice, fee-for-service system began to disappear with the growth of technology and the extension of insurance coverage. The conversion of the medical profession from mainly low-technology generalists and primary-care practitioners to predominately high-technology specialists and the extension of open-ended, charge-reimbursing medical insurance to the majority of citizens raised physicians' incomes as well as their economic expectations. At the same time, the numbers of practicing physicians began to rise as a consequence of the government-supported expansion of medical schools which took place in the postwar decades. Between 1970 and 1986, the number of physicians per 100,000 population increased from 148 to 220, and the curve will continue to rise steeply unless there are sharp reductions in the size of medical school classes. More doctors per population means more competition for patients and more reason for professional behavior to be influenced by considerations of income and vulnerable to economic pressures.

With the advent of the cost-containment revolution in health care financing and the growing commercialization of health services, doctors suddenly find themselves in a drastically altered economic climate which is having a profound effect on their habits of practice. They are being pressured by HMOs, IPAs, PPOs, and many insurers to control expenditures. Inasmuch as a growing fraction of patients have contractual, prospective payment arrangements with these cost-conscious organizations, physicians have little choice but to accede. Hospitals are urging limitation of expenditures on hospitalized patients, and these strictures are reinforced with particular respect to Medicare patients by professional review organizations (PROs) and in general by peer pressure from the medical staff organizations. The threat to professional income, independence, and direct access to patients has been clearly perceived, and many physicians have reacted by seeking to extend the range of services in which they have a financial interest and over which they can exert some professional control. At the same time, the increasingly competitive health care corporations (both for-profit and not-for-profit) have been seeking arrangements with physicians that will increase the corporation's market share and protect its capacity to control costs. These arrangements include the employment of physicians, as well as contracts and joint ventures.

Some physicians, particularly those who have not yet established their own practices, are full-time employees of HMOs and other types of corporations providing medical care. Others, in private practice, have contracted with corporations to provide specified medical services for prearranged fees or under various profit-sharing arrangements. Still other kinds of contracts between corporations and practitioners reward the doctor for practicing in the corporation's facilities or using its services or products. Also becoming increasingly common are so-called joint ventures between doctors and hospitals or other health care corporations, by means of which doctors buy an equity interest as a limited partner in a health care facility, often one to which the doctors will refer their patients. A few adventurous practitioners, reluctant to tie themselves to health corporations not entirely within their control, are competing with the corporations in local markets by establishing their own businesses.

A decade or two ago, most private practitioners earned their practice-related income entirely from fees paid by insurers or patients for the professional services rendered by the practitioner. A small fraction of physicians worked for a salary in group practices that also collected fees for services rendered. Today, a physician's income may depend on a wide variety of business deals, many of them hardly imaginable before the advent of the new medical market. A few specific examples may give a better sense of what has been happening:

- To encourage cost control in the management of hospitalized Medicare patients, some hospitals are sharing profits earned from DRG payments with the private physicians involved in the care of these patients.

- To stimulate use of their operating rooms, a for-profit hospital chain shares profits from its surgical suites with the private surgeons who use the facilities.

- To induce physicians to practice there, some hospitals (for-profit and not-for-profit) offer them rent-free office space near the hospital, low-interest loans to help them start their practices, free office equipment, and so forth, all of which are contingent upon the physicians' continued use of the hospital's facilities.

- To keep their costs down, some HMOs pay their staff physicians bonuses based on profits earned in the management of patients.

- In a somewhat similar arrangement, some "managed care" plans allow the primary-care physician who controls expenditures to keep a percentage of the unspent premium.

- Many ambulatory care facilities, such as "same-day" surgery centers, diagnostic imaging centers, and clinical chemistry laboratories offer equity interest opportunities to physicians who use the facilities. Sometimes a group of physicians will start their own facility.

- Wholesale distributors of prescription drugs market prepackaged drugs to office-based physicians who prescribe the drugs and then sell them to their patients at a profit.

Many more examples could be cited, but this list should suffice to show the variety and ingenuity of these business arrangements. They clearly serve the economic interests of physicians and owners. Whether they also serve the best interests of patients is not so clear. Some of them verge on the illegal. Federal law prohibits the payment of any remuneration for the referral of Medicare or Medicaid patients or for the purchase of supplies for these patients. Many lawyers nevertheless believe that with appropriate precautions these arrangements can be structured to avoid violation of federal law, although in some jurisdictions state law may create other impediments. In any case, what these legal concerns imply is that government recognizes the potential risk to the public interest when physicians make deals with businesses. So far, however, there is no sign that government is seriously concerned about the propriety of business selling health care for profit.

Even if they do not violate the law, these new business arrangements take physicians into uncharted waters, where conflicts of interest abound and the separation between business and professional aims is obscured. No longer are physicians the trustee solely for their patients' interests; they become in addition agents for a corporate enterprise which regards patients as customers. Economic incentives to withhold services, to overuse them, or to choose particular medical products are inconsistent with the duty of the physician to act as unselfish trustee and agent for the patient. Even though physicians may believe they are doing what is best for the patient, there will still be the appearance of conflicting interests with a resulting erosion of public confidence in the physician's motivation, a confidence that has already been weakened by a growing public opinion that doctors are too interested in money and charge too much. Since trust is vital to good care, these public perceptions could lead to a deterioration in the quality of care as well as a change in attitude toward the medical profession by the public. Most damaging of all would be a change in the profession's view of itself, a change that could erode the sense of commitment which I have suggested is the essential core of medical practice.

What should the medical profession do, what can it do, to maintain its ethical standards in the new economic climate? I believe it must, first of all, be clear about its purposes and priorities. There should be more discussion of these matters in the forums of organized medicine and in the professional journals. Physicians have been too preoccupied with the incessant demands of practice to think much about the social role of their profession or its ethical foundations. But since these are public policy issues as well, and since many reforms will need public support or cannot legally be realized without government sanction, the discussion should be in public forums as well. The recent report entitled *For-Profit Enterprise in Health Care* released by the Institute of Medicine of the National Academy of Sciences has stimulated interest, but much more exposure is needed.

In the meantime, the profession could make an important start. It could demonstrate its priorities by dealing with the growing conflicts of interest between duty to patients and economic self-interest. This should begin with a resolve to limit practice income to fees or salaries earned from professional service personally provided or supervised. Medicine is a personal, caring profession, not a license to invest in health care businesses or sell medical goods. Physicians in private practice should avoid arrangements that reward them for using a particular facility, product, or service, or for withholding services from their patients. Furthermore, to protect their professional independence practitioners should avoid direct individual employment by a for-profit corporation. If they practice in any kind of for-profit setting they should either be self-employed or part of a self-managed and self-regulated medical group which contracts with the owners.

While endorsing the view that commitment to patients must be a physician's first priority, the American Medical Association currently rejects the guidelines suggested above as unnecessary and discriminatory. Thus, in a recent letter to the *New England Journal of Medicine*, Dr. James Todd (Senior Deputy Executive Vice-President of AMA) declared:

> There is no self-interest, economic or otherwise, that ethical physicians allow to supersede their duty to their patients. Changes in the medical marketplace will neither make ethical physicians more ethical nor deter the unethical. However, in a period of shrinking resources, reducing the options available to patients or advocating withdrawal from entrepreneurial activities by physicians would be contrary to the current and popular move toward competition as a method of restraining the increasing cost of health care. . . . Such a restrictive policy would impose unnecessary and unfair discrimination against members of a respected and respectable profession.[3]

I agree that an ethical canon against conflicts of interest would not of itself make ethical physicians more ethical or deter the unethical. It would, however, be a beacon to guide the many physicians who are confused and uncertain about this question, and it would have a powerful salutary effect on the public's confidence in the medical profession. As for the desirability or necessity of physician entrepreneurship, some have argued that participation by physicians in health care businesses is required to ensure the preservation of quality and the protection of patients' interests. But that claim cannot be taken seriously because independently practicing physicians can always exercise control over quality as long as they have responsibility for the important medical care decisions and for the choice of facilities and services used by their patients. It is only when they give up their independence by working as employees of for-profit corporations, or compromise their freedom by making business deals with the corporations, that physicians jeopardize their effectiveness as advocates for their patients.

[3] *New England Journal of Medicine* 314 (Jan. 23, 1986), p. 250.

Although the recent Institute of Medicine report avoided definite policy recommendations on the future of for-profit health care businesses, it was very firm about the importance of physicians remaining uninvolved. The study committee, representing a wide spectrum of health care interests, was unanimous in recommending that doctors "be as free of economic conflict of interest as possible." [4] The committee pointed out that as business ownership and profit considerations exert increasing influence over health care facilities and services, it becomes even more essential that doctors be able to act as independent advocates for their patients and as unencumbered monitors of the quality of care. Enlightened leaders of the new health care industry should want to endorse that view, since it cannot be in their interests, or in the public's, to risk the abuses and the deterioration of quality in medical care that would surely occur in a system in which the independence of physicians had been compromised.

Beyond the need to reaffirm its ethical foundations, the medical profession has other major tasks before it. Together with government, it will have to address the many problems that have led to the cost-containment crisis and the present turmoil in our health care system. It should begin to confront the manpower problem. We will shortly be facing a surplus of physicians. We also have disproportionately too few primary-care physicians and too many subspecialists in several fields. Closely related to this problem is the current system of customary fees, which rewards technical procedures excessively and underpays primary care. Present federal antitrust policy prevents organized medicine from unilaterally taking on these problems, but with legislative sanction, cooperation between the medical profession and government should be possible.

Other initiatives need to be taken to expand the assessment of medical technology. As mentioned earlier, new technology has been a powerful impetus to cost inflation in health care. Efficient

4 Gray, *For-Profit Enterprise in Health Care*, p. 164.

use of new tests and procedures requires detailed information about safety and effectiveness, which in most instances is inadequate or lacking. Only through greatly increased clinical studies will we acquire the necessary information, in the absence of which vast resources are apt to be wasted on useless, redundant, or unsafe procedures. The large funds needed for such studies should come from the third-party payers, who will benefit considerably from resulting savings. Organized medicine must push government and the insurance companies to provide the necessary support and should ensure that the new information is appropriately disseminated and employed in everyday practice.

Another way in which organized medicine can help improve the health care system is through the promotion of quality assurance and peer review. The quality and fitness of physicians need to be monitored, as well as the standards of everyday practice, in and out of the hospital. The mounting tide of medical malpractice claims reflects in part a diminishing public confidence in the medical profession. Physicians blame perverse incentives in the legal system, with, I believe, considerable justification, but other major causes of the chronic malpractice crisis we are suffering these days surely include a deterioration in the doctor-patient relation, and the profession's failure to monitor quality of physicians and services as rigorously as the public has a right to expect. Remedying these deficiencies would lower costs as well as improve the quality of medical services and would undoubtedly help protect the public against the abuses inherent in a market-driven health care system. Here again, although the medical profession must show the way, governmental sanction and support are essential. The Health Care Quality Improvement Act of 1986 is an excellent example of the way enlightened and timely federal legislation can help the profession meet its responsibilities for self-regulation and quality control. The tort reform bills recently enacted by many state legislatures in response to pressures from state medical societies are another manifestation of government response to professional initiatives which are generally recognized to be in the public interest.

But the most pressing problem in our health care system today is its inequity. In the first lecture, I pointed out that the revolution in health care financing has left little room for cross-subsidization of the poor. Voluntary hospitals formerly provided nearly two-thirds of the care for the indigent and funded it with charity or the surpluses earned from charge or cost-paying patients. Charity has not kept pace with the inflation of medical costs, and profitable patients are being replaced by patients under prospective payment and contractual arrangements that allow no overhead for unreimbursed care. Furthermore, in some parts of the country voluntary and public hospitals have been partially replaced by investor-owned hospitals, which generally provide even less charity care than the voluntary hospitals. Public hospitals are more over-burdened with indigent patients and less adequately funded than ever before, and federal and state support of health services of all kinds is being cut back. The number of uninsured or underinsured people is now estimated to be between 35 million and 40 million and still growing. Access to health care among the poor and elderly is decreasing, while evidence accumulates to suggest that their health is being adversely affected.

The market is an efficient mechanism for the distribution of economic goods and services according to ability to pay, but it has no interest in those who cannot pay. If we allow the market to be the major factor in the allocation of our health care services, which is the fashion these days, we can be sure that the poor will get far less than their proportional share and very probably less than they need. As a civilized and affluent society we cannot avoid responsibility for providing all our citizens with necessary care — and that means we must be prepared to pay for it.

Uniquely qualified to determine the need for care, as well as monitor its quality, effectiveness, and safety, the medical profession has a special public responsibility. Working with local, state, and federal government and with consumer groups, organized medicine should be in the vanguard of a national movement to ensure adequate, efficient care for all at a price our society can afford to pay. To be effective, the profession must be trusted as the advocate of the public interest. That, as I have tried to suggest in these lectures, requires physicians to think about their moral obligations. In the new market-dominated climate of health care, they will have to decide whether they wish to take their stand firmly by the side of their patients or whether they will join the new army of medical entrepreneurs.

THE TANNER LECTURERS

1976–77

OXFORD   Bernard Williams, Cambridge University

MICHIGAN   Joel Feinberg, University of Arizona
"Voluntary Euthanasia and the Inalienable Right to Life"

STANFORD   Joel Feinberg, University of Arizona
"Voluntary Euthanasia and the Inalienable Right to Life"

1977–78

OXFORD   John Rawls, Harvard University

MICHIGAN   Sir Karl Popper, University of London
"Three Worlds"

STANFORD   Thomas Nagel, Princeton University

1978–79

OXFORD   Thomas Nagel, Princeton University
"The Limits of Objectivity"

CAMBRIDGE   C. C. O'Brien, London

MICHIGAN   Edward O. Wilson, Harvard University
"Comparative Social Theory"

STANFORD   Amartya Sen, Oxford University
"Equality of What?"

UTAH   Lord Ashby, Cambridge University
"The Search for an Environmental Ethic"

UTAH STATE   R. M. Hare, Oxford University
"Moral Conflicts"

1979–80

OXFORD   Jonathan Bennett, Univ. of British Columbia
"Morality and Consequences"

CAMBRIDGE   Raymond Aron, Collège de France
"Arms Control and Peace Research"

HARVARD   George Stigler, University of Chicago
"Economics or Ethics?"

MICHIGAN   Robert Coles, Harvard University
              "Children as Moral Observers"

STANFORD   Michel Foucault, Collège de France
              *"Omnes et Singulatim: Towards a Criticism
                  of 'Political Reason' "*

UTAH   Wallace Stegner, Los Altos Hills, California
              *"The Twilight of Self-Reliance: Frontier Values
                  and Contemporary America"*

1980–81

OXFORD   Saul Bellow, University of Chicago
              "A Writer from Chicago"

CAMBRIDGE   John A. Passmore, Australian National University
              "The Representative Arts as a Source of Truth"

HARVARD   Brian M. Barry, University of Chicago
              *"Do Countries Have Moral Obligations? The Case
                  of World Poverty"*

MICHIGAN   John Rawls, Harvard University
              "The Basic Liberties and Their Priority"

STANFORD   Charles Fried, Harvard University
              "Is Liberty Possible?"

UTAH   Joan Robinson, Cambridge University
              "The Arms Race"

HEBREW UNIV. Solomon H. Snyder, Johns Hopkins University
              "Drugs and the Brain and Society"

1981–82

OXFORD   Freeman Dyson, Princeton University
              "Bombs and Poetry"

CAMBRIDGE   Kingman Brewster, President Emeritus, Yale University
              "The Voluntary Society"

HARVARD   Murray Gell-Mann, California Institute of Technology
              "The Head and the Heart in Policy Studies"

MICHIGAN   Thomas C. Schelling, Harvard University
              "Ethics, Law, and the Exercise of Self-Command"

STANFORD   Alan A. Stone, Harvard University
              "Psychiatry and Morality"

UTAH   R. C. Lewontin, Harvard University
"Biological Determinism"

AUSTRALIAN
NATL. UNIV.   Leszek Kolakowski, Oxford University
"The Death of Utopia Reconsidered"

1982–83

OXFORD   Kenneth J. Arrow, Stanford University
"The Welfare-Relevant Boundaries of the Individual"

CAMBRIDGE   H. C. Robbins Landon, University College, Cardiff
*"Haydn and Eighteenth-Century Patronage
in Austria and Hungary"*

HARVARD   Bernard Williams, Cambridge University
"Morality and Social Justice"

STANFORD   David Gauthier, University of Pittsburgh
"The Incompleat Egoist"

UTAH   Carlos Fuentes, Princeton University
"A Writer from Mexico"

JAWAHARLAL
NEHRU UNIV.   Ilya Prigogine, University of Brussels
"Only an Illusion"

1983–84

OXFORD   Donald D. Brown, Carnegie Institution of Washington,
Baltimore
"The Impact of Modern Genetics"

CAMBRIDGE   Stephen J. Gould, Harvard University
"Evolutionary Hopes and Realities"

MICHIGAN   Herbert A. Simon, Carnegie-Mellon University
*"Scientific Literacy as a Goal in a High-Technology
Society"*

STANFORD   Leonard B. Meyer, University of Pennsylvania
"Ideology and Music in the Nineteenth Century"

UTAH   Helmut Schmidt, former Chancellor, West Germany
"The Future of the Atlantic Alliance"

HELSINKI   Georg Henrik von Wright, Helsinki
"Of Human Freedom"

1984–85

OXFORD Barrington Moore, Jr., Harvard University
  "Authority and Inequality under Capitalism and Socialism"

CAMBRIDGE Amartya K. Sen, Oxford University
  "The Standard of Living"

HARVARD Quentin Skinner, Cambridge University
  "The Paradoxes of Political Liberty"

  Kenneth J. Arrow, Stanford University
  "The Unknown Other"

MICHIGAN Nadine Gordimer, South Africa
  "The Essential Gesture: Writers and Responsibility"

STANFORD Michael Slote, University of Maryland
  "Moderation, Rationality, and Virtue"

1985–86

OXFORD Thomas M. Scanlon, Harvard University
  "The Significance of Choice"

CAMBRIDGE Aldo Van Eyck, The Netherlands
  "Architecture and Human Values"

HARVARD Michael Walzer, Institute for Advanced Study
  "Interpretation and Social Criticism"

MICHIGAN Clifford Geertz, Institute for Advanced Study
  "The Uses of Diversity"

STANFORD Stanley Cavell, Harvard University
  "The Uncanniness of the Ordinary"

UTAH Arnold S. Relman, Editor, *New England Journal of Medicine*
  "Medicine as a Profession and a Business"

1986–87

OXFORD Jon Elster, Oslo University and the University of Chicago
  "Taming Chance: Randomization in Individual and Social Decisions"

CAMBRIDGE   Roger Bulger, University of Texas Health Sciences Center,
Houston
*"On Hippocrates, Thomas Jefferson and Max Weber:
the Bureaucratic, Technologic Imperatives and the
Future of the Healing Tradition in a Voluntary Society"*

HARVARD   Jürgen Habermas, University of Frankfurt
"Law and Morality"

MICHIGAN   Daniel Dennett, Tufts University
"The Moral First Aid Manual"

STANFORD   Gisela Striker, Columbia University
"Greek Ethics and Moral Theory"

UTAH   Laurence H. Tribe, Harvard University
"On Reading the Constitution"

1987–88

OXFORD   F. Van Zyl Slabbert, South Africa

CAMBRIDGE   Louis Blom-Cooper, Q.C.

HARVARD   Robert Dahl, Yale University

MICHIGAN   Albert Hirschman, Institute for Advanced Study

STANFORD   Ronald Dworkin, Oxford University

UTAH   Joseph Brodsky, Russian poet

MADRID   Javier Muguerza, Institute of Philosophy of the Superior
Council of Scientific Investigations, Madrid

INDEX TO VOLUME VIII, 1987

THE TANNER LECTURES ON HUMAN VALUES

THE TANNER LECTURES ON HUMAN VALUES
was composed in Intertype Garamond with Garamond Foundry display type
by Donald M. Henriksen, Scholarly Typography, Salt Lake City.